Chapter 20: Put Your Learning into Practice 163

HardiTraining®

A Comprehensive Approach to Mastering Stressful Circumstances

Khoshaba and Maddi

Copyright© 1999-2008, The Hardiness Institute, Inc.
ISBN#: 0-9759384-09000

Contributing Consultants
Keith Jensen, Director of Trio Support Services, Utah Valley State College and Certified Hardiness Trainer
The Marketing Partners, Irvine, California, Graphic Design

Note: The content of the nutrition and exercise components is solely informational and educational. It is not intended as medical advice and under no circumstance should it replace the expert advice and care of a qualified medical or nutritional professional.

The Hardiness Institute, Inc.
4199 Campus Road, Suite 550
Irvine, California 92612
Phone 949-252-0580 Fax 949-252-8087
E-mail: hardiness1@aol.com or dkhoshaba@hardinessinstitute.com
Web Site: www.hardinessinstitute.com

CHAPTER 1 — *Managing Change*

Life Changes

A positive or negative life change brought about by our or others doing can disrupt our daily living routines. When change occurs, at school, work, or home, we must process how it affects our lives, access or develop resources to effectively master it, and figure out how it fits into our overall life plan. Change is life's law, and if handled well, it can be an opportunity to develop ourselves.

A life change often brings with it new pressures that can consume our time and focus. Despite such pressures, others may expect us to continue to fulfill our family, social, church, and work responsibilities. Uncertainties as to a change's outcome can make us question whether all the effort is worth it.

Change alters our daily landscape in many ways. We may find ourselves in new roles, interacting with an increasingly diverse group of people, and having to adapt to changing norms, rules, and functioning procedures. This can greatly discomfort us.

Whether small or large, life's changes increase personal pressures, disrupt normal functioning, and call into play key physical, mental, and behavioral resources to manage them. If we are unprepared to effectively manage a life change, we may let its more daunting aspects prevent us from turning it around.

Stressful Changes Are A Sign Of The Times

Today, we cope with an unprecedented rate of change that will continue well into the twenty-first century. Many of the ongoing social, economic, and political changes taking place now are outside of our control. In the United States, for example, we rapidly moved from an industrial, to a service, to an information-based society. Worldwide business competition increasingly redistributes wealth, as the U.S. post World War II supremacy wanes. The collapse of the Soviet Union and other global civilization changes continue to impact us all.

What is our reaction to such trends? Businesses now favor smaller, more rapidly changing work units over larger sized corporations. And, downsizing and restructuring emphases make job security a thing of the past. Today, we can no longer expect to work for one employer alone. Workplace changes, and the stresses they bring, are the order of the day.

At one time, we were able to retreat to private life to avoid daily stresses, but it's more difficult to do this today. The family is less a safe haven than it once was because we tend to move around more and break ties with our families of origin. And, we increasingly raise our children in single-parent households, due to high divorce rates. When television, faxes, computers, and telephone solicitations constantly bombard us, how can we savor leisure and self-retreat? Excessive stimulation from these sources stresses us to the maximum. As daily stress rises, we tend to perform poorly, mentally burn out, get ill more frequently, and in the extreme, behave more aggressively.

What Can You Do About All These Stresses?

It is difficult to stem the tide of these megatrends; nor can you halt the parade of changes that take place at school, work, or home. The more you resist change, the more it feels like an assault. The best thing to do is develop attitudes and skills that help you to cope effectively with stressful changes.

This helps you to bring about a sound mind in a sound body, and to withstand the onslaught of stressful changes, by turning them to your advantage. You may even be able to turn potentially disruptive changes into opportunities, thereby actually improving your life rather than just surviving. There is no point in shrinking your life to the size of a postage stamp just to avoid stresses. For a life that small, there is little basis for fulfillment and effective performance.

The HardiTraining® program can give you the sound mind and body with which to improve your performance, morale, and health, even if the world falls apart around you.

How Did HardiTraining Come About?

Some twenty years ago, a graduate student of Dr. Salvatore Maddi's brought him an article she had found in *Family Circle* magazine. It emphasized the importance of avoiding stressful circumstances, lest they kill you. That was the message of the 1970s, when people still believed that you could easily arrange to avoid stress. Now we know better. Even then, Dr. Maddi simply could not believe that what he was reading was good advice. After all, one of the admonitions in the article was to avoid driving on the Los Angeles freeways if you were feeling stressed out. There's a small chance that you can do this, especially if your work commute necessitates freeway use.

Dr. Maddi had faith that the same human imagination which fashioned modern urban life in order to increase opportunity could somehow figure out how to cope effectively with rapid change. He and his graduate students embarked on a memorable study to discover people who thrived on change and to understand how they did it. In 1973, he approached his friend, Carl Horn, a Vice President at Illinois Bell Telephone (IBT), to get permission to study employees of that company. IBT welcomed Dr. Maddi with open arms, as they knew the feared AT&T deregulation and mandated divestiture was just around the corner, and they were looking for help.

Starting in 1975, Dr. Maddi and his students began following 450 male and female managers (upper, middle, and lower levels) at IBT. Each year, these subjects were tested extensively by questionnaires, interviews, projective tests, experiential sampling, and medical examinations. Six years into the longitudinal research design that began in 1981, the divestiture hit in what is still regarded as the largest upheaval in corporate history (maybe IBM came a little close to it recently). In one short year, IBT almost downsized by one half. One manager reported having ten bosses in twelve months, and that he and his coworkers had little idea what was going on. The study continued for another six years until 1987, when Dr. Maddi arrived at the University of California, Irvine.

This study has been hailed as a landmark in understanding the effects on people of rapid increases in stressful circumstances. A book and many papers have been published about this study and have won awards, been supported by government grants, and been covered extensively by the media.

One general finding of this study was that as the rate of stressful circumstances experienced by company managers rose precipitously from 1975 through 1986, their performance, morale, and company loyalty declined, while their illnesses and troubles at home increased. But this does not mean that everyone in the sample suffered.

Specifically, about two thirds of the sample was debilitated by the rising tide of stress. The remaining one third, however, not only survived, but actually thrived. They remained healthy and vigorous by seeing the workplace changes as opportunities rather than disaster. They performed better than their less hardy coworkers and found creative ways to professionally advance, despite ongoing workplace changes. Our Hardiness Model that follows shows what happened to them. The Hardiness Model provides you with a blueprint for the training sessions to come.

FIGURE 1. The Hardiness Model For
Performance, Health and Leadership

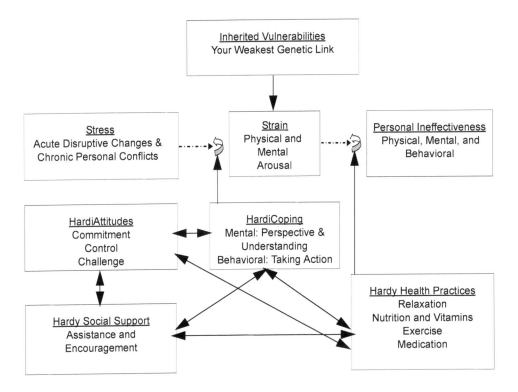

The upper portion of Figure 1 contains the bad news or what we call your **stress vulnerability factors** with regard to stress, performance, and health. It begins with **stress,** continues through **strain,** and ends with **performance ineffectiveness**.

Stress

Stress can be either acute or chronic. **Acute stress** is the disruptive, time-limited changes that happen in life. They are often unexpected and temporarily inconvenience us. Maybe, for example, you fail an important test or a romantic relationship ends, or it rains on your outdoor party. As you can see from these examples, acute stresses can be big or small. **Chronic stress** has less to do with changes than with a continuing mismatch between what you want and what you get, or how you see yourself and what you have to do. Maybe you see yourself as a capable person, but you're always treated as if you can't do anything, or you want to lavish love on someone, but you can't find an appropriate person. These two kinds of stresses accumulate: the more you have of one, the less it takes of the other to get you in trouble.

What's The Nature Of This Trouble That Stress Can Get You Into?

Acute and chronic stress registers in your mind as danger. Your mind registers these danger signals and sends them to your body. Your body responds the only way it knows how to meet the danger. Walter B. Cannon first identified this response as the body's fight-or-flight reaction to stress. In this reaction, adrenaline, fatty acids, and sugar dump into the bloodstream to energize you. Additionally, your digestive and immune systems temporarily suppress to support fight or flight excitatory functions, like heightened alertness and muscle activation.

Evolution intended for the fight-or-flight reaction to be decisive and swift. Our ancient ancestors coped with predators by either fighting them or running away. Once they confronted the threat, whether they ran away from, won, or lost the battle, it was over. In turn, their brain and body arousal decreased, and they returned to normal daily activities until the next threat came along.

Today, however, we are too civilized to fight or run away from threat. If you disagree with a teacher or boss, for example, and you want to maintain the relationship, you find civilized ways to manage the problem, rather than fight or run away from it. As civilized persons, we have responsibilities, rules, and decorum. Socialization pressures prolong the fight-or-flight reaction in us beyond its evolutionary design.

Strain

The stressful circumstances now fester in your mind, and fuel and extend bodily mobilization that shades over into what Hans Selye called exhaustion. We call this depletion of bodily resources **strain** (see Figure 1, page 4).

Obvious signs of strain include sweaty palms, muscle tightness, headaches, racing heart, rumbling or nauseated stomach, loss of appetite or cravings for food, irritability, anxiety, racing mind, difficulty concentrating, or difficulty falling or staying asleep. Less obvious signs of strain include a rise in blood pressure, blood triglycerides, and blood cholesterol, or a suppressed immune system. When a prolonged fight-or-flight response intensifies and deepens your strain, you risk ineffective performance, decreased morale, and impaired health.

At The Mental Level. Symptoms can include mental fatigue, poor memory and judgment, and narrow focus, amongst others.

At The Physical Level. Minor symptoms can include flu, allergies, headaches, vague aches and pains, and anxiety. And, if prolonged, these physical symptoms can activate degenerative diseases, like heart disease, cancer, diabetes, osteoporosis, and arthritis.

At The Behavioral Level. Symptoms show up in performance deficits that can range from missing deadlines, social apathy, and self-defeating actions, such as aggression, irresponsibility, and food and chemical substance abuses.

Inherited Vulnerabilities

The last bit of bad news is at the top of Figure 1 (see Figure 1 on Page 4). Prolonged physical, mental, and behavioral strain can take place along the lines of your **inherited vulnerabilities**. Our genetic inheritance defines our strengths as well as our weaknesses. If, for example, there is heart disease in your family, you risk cardiovascular symptoms in times of strain.

How Important Is Lifestyle In Performance Effectiveness?

Inadequate lifestyle behaviors insufficiently protect you against mounting stress and can undermine your performance, morale, conduct, and health. Poorly managed stress interferes with memory, attention, reasoning, imagination, and problem solving. For you, this can result in unsatisfying experiences and accidents.

Poorly managed stress also undermines your morale. It can increase anxiety, depression, and suspiciousness, all of which can increase in you self-defeating, harmful behaviors. It further can erode empathy, altruism, and social responsibility, all of which can make you socially indifferent, insensitive, and aggressive toward others. Indeed, we now know that poor lifestyle habits insufficiently neu-

tralize stress and that they play a big role in premature deaths. Among other things, this knowledge brought about a big change in the way that we explain illness and how we avoid it. For generations, the one-germ, one-disease, and one-treatment health formulation characterized the delivery of health care services.

At the turn of the century in the United States, poor industrial conditions increased bacterial disease in society. Medicine, thus, concerned itself with cures for bacterial diseases, which led to the germ theory of disease. By 1960, the primary causes of death in the United States were degenerative rather than infectious diseases. These degenerative illnesses are called the wear-and-tear disorders, like heart disease, cancer, and stroke.

U.S. Center for Disease Control Top Five Leading Causes Of Death

Today, the government and the health care industry focus on the role of lifestyle behavior in performance, health, and quality of life. Health-eroding lifestyle behaviors, such as ineffective coping strategies, destructive social interaction patterns, inadequate relaxation and nutrition, and sedentary activity patterns, threaten our health and longevity. The United States Center for Disease Control Mortality Report of 2004 cited the following five diseases as leading causes of death from 1950 through 2002.

TABLE Centers for Disease Control and Prevention, National Center for Health Statistics. Health, United States, 2004

Cause of Death	Total Deaths%	Major Originating Factors
Heart disease	30.3	diet, smoking, lack of exercise, stress, poor health education
Cancer	23	diet, smoking, environmental pollution, poor health education
Stroke	7	diet, smoking, stress, lack of exercise, poor health education
Unintentional injuries	4.1	alcohol, education, lack of governmental and business safety protection
Chronic lower respiratory conditions	5.2	smoking, lack of exercise, nutrition, air pollution

These data include all races, both sexes, and all ages (1 through 75 years of age). Importantly, lifestyle continues to be a major contributing factor to the onset, or exacerbation, of most of the illnesses.

Can Improvements In Lifestyle Increase Your Performance Effectiveness?

Fortunately, there is good news contained in the lower half portion of Figure 1 (Figure 1 on Page 4). **Stress resistance resources**, depicted by the semi-circles, interrupt the bad news sequence, and protect your performance, morale, conduct, and health, in their buffering effect.

The buffer shown to the right is **health practices**, which are ways in which you can decrease your body's strain reactions so as to avoid the exhaustion that increases the risk of performance ineffective-

ness. The major health practices are physical exercise, relaxation, sound nutrition, and prescription medication. In physical exercise, you are using the body and mind as they were intended to be used in the fight-or-flight reaction (without actually fighting or running away), and this drains off the mobilization before the depletion of bodily resources sets in. In relaxation, you are directly reversing the fight-or-flight mobilization, which can also ward off the exhaustion phase.

In the mobilization process, the body produces fat and sugar for quick energy, and increases blood pressure and cholesterol as well. You reduce the negative effects of this process by eating foods that do not make your body overwork. Medications prescribed for problems of strain mimic the effects of the health practices.

The other buffer (Figure 1 on Page 4) is **HardiCoping**. HardiCoping decreases the stressfulness of a situation by decreasing strain. You maintain performance, leadership, and health when you cope in this transformational way. At the mental level, HardiCoping broadens the way you think about a stressful circumstance (whether acute or chronic) and this, in turn, deepens your **understanding** of it.

By mentally restructuring the way you think about a circumstance, the stressfulness of the situation decreases. This frees you up to think about ways of transforming the problem into an opportunity for new learning and development. When you develop a plan of action and implement it, you complete the HardiCoping process. Now, the stressful circumstance is less of a curse. For some, it can seem like a blessing in disguise. These actions greatly reduce your strain.

Health practices and HardiCoping can be hard to do during stressful times. For many people, strain undermines their discipline and motivation, to say nothing of enthusiasm for exercising, relaxing, and eating healthily. In addition, stressed people oftentimes do not feel they have time to mull over what's troubling them, or to risk rocking the boat through decisive action.

That's where the other two boxes in the diagram come into play. **HardiAttitudes** and **Hardy Social Support** provide the motivation to carry on HardiCoping and health practices, even though the going is getting rough.

HardiAttitudes involves three beliefs that you maintain about yourself in interaction with the world, namely, Commitment, Control, and Challenge, or the three C's. People strong in **Commitment** believe that they can increase the interest, value, and importance of whatever they are doing by involving themselves deeply in it. They are not likely to pull back and avoid things. People strong

in **Control** believe that if they struggle and try, they may well be able to influence the direction and outcome of things going on around them. They are not likely to sink into passivity and powerlessness. People strong in **Challenge** believe that what makes their lives worthwhile is to continue to grow in knowledge and wisdom through what they learn from experience (whether positive or negative). They are not likely to feel entitled to easy comfort and security. Can you see how HardiAttitudes would motivate HardiCoping and health practices?

Hardy Social Support involves being able to give to and get from others assistance and encouragement in living well. **Encouragement** is a process of empathizing with others and helping them to believe in their ability to do whatever is at hand. **Assistance** also implies empathy, but emphasizes how to use one's own resources and capabilities to help the other in reaching what is wanted or needed. Those giving and getting Hardy Social Support must be able to discern and reject (in others and in themselves) overprotection or competition masquerading as something helpful. The trouble with overprotection is that it takes responsibility and initiative out of the other person's hands. And, subtle competition undermines rather than builds up the other person's motivation to take the initiative. It is assistance and encouragement from others that motivates our efforts at HardiCoping and health practices.

HardiAttitudes and Hardy Social Support influence HardiCoping and health practices. The opposite is also true. If you engage in HardiCoping or health practices, the feedback you get from doing that can help build up your HardiAttitudes and Hardy Social Support.

If, for example, a life skills program such as this one motivates you to cope with your problems, interact constructively with others, and relax, exercise, and eat well, the feedback you get from seeing yourself this way gives you more control over, commitment to, and challenge from your life. Your HardiAttitudes strengthen, which motivates you to cope and interact in this way again. There is a real reciprocity between HardiAttitudes and Hardy Social Support. Increases in one lead to increases in the other.

Why Do We Approach Lifestyle Training As We Do?

All the boxes in the lower half of the Hardiness Model (Figure 1 on Page 4) form an **interlocking lifestyle system.** That's why the arrows connecting those boxes go both ways in the diagram. Changes in one box synergistically influence changes in the other boxes. The more lifestyle components involved, the larger the overall hardiness-enhancing effect. And, in this case, the hardiness-enhancing effect decreases strain, which decreases the likelihood of performance, leadership, morale, conduct, and health ineffectiveness. The more stress-resistance resources you can marshal, the greater the hardiness-enhancing effect. This is why we recommend a comprehensive and interlocking lifestyle approach for maximum health, performance, and morale enhancement.

Five lifestyle components makeup HardiTraining, and together, these components strengthen your performance, leadership, morale, conduct, and health resistance. They additionally act powerfully to buffer you against stress, strain, and ineffective performance.

HardiCoping: In this component, you learn.

- How to identify acute and chronic stresses
- How to solve the problems they represent by achieving perspective and understanding, and then taking decisive action
- How to use the feedback from solving the problems to deepen your HardiAttitudes of commitment, control, and challenge.

Social Support: In this component, you learn.

- How to communicate constructively by improving your message-sending and message-receiving skills
- How to give and get socially supportive assistance and encouragement
- How to constructively resolve social conflict
- How to use the feedback from application of social support skills to deepen your HardiAttitudes of Commitment, Control, and Challenge

Relaxation: In this component, you learn.

- How to become aware of physiological signs of strain
- How to decrease physiological arousal and tension characteristic of the fight-or-flight reaction by abdominal breathing, muscle relaxation, imagery, and meditation exercises
- How to use the feedback from increased relaxation to deepen your HardiAttitudes of Commitment, Control, and Challenge

Nutrition: In this component, you learn.

- How to identify eating habits that decrease performance, fuel, and fat burning
- How to boost physical fitness and mood through a diet balanced in carbohydrates, protein, and fat

- How to use the feedback from eating healthily to deepen your HardiAttitudes of Commitment, Control, and Challenge

Exercise: In this component, you learn.

- How to identify your physical activity habits
- How to boost physical fitness through the frequency, duration, intensity, and specificity of physical activity, and enjoy it
- How to use the feedback from healthy physical activity to deepen your HardiAttitudes of Commitment, Control, and Challenge

The five training components are like the fingers of your hand, and the HardiAttitudes are like the palm of your hand. The fingers and the palm work together in an integrated way to support your overall health and performance. There is no other performance enhancement program as advanced as HardiTraining, and we hope you feel excited that you are on the threshold of entering into it. If you stick with it, it will make a decisive difference in your life and the lives of those around you.

The Specifics Of Going Through HardiTraining

We organized this book's format in ways that assist your learning. Classroom instruction clarifies HardiTraining concepts and procedures and guides you in the training process. This format also provides you with numerous opportunities to get support and feedback from hardiness professionals and fellow trainees about your ongoing development.

To maximize your learning, it's best to follow the workbook's chapter format. Read a chapter's ideas and concepts, and compete its exercises, before you proceed to the next chapter.

There are also workbook checkpoints to evaluate your learning. Once you complete a training component's final checkpoint, you are ready to begin a new HardiTraining section. Additionally, workbook exercises build upon one another, so that you get many opportunities to practice what you learned.

The more HardiTraining lifestyle components you incorporate into your everyday life, the greater health and performance you will enjoy. Once again, we welcome you to a healthier, happier, more effective life through HardiTraining.

HardiCoping

What Is HardiCoping?

HardiCoping is a problem-solving approach in which you fix stressful situations by thinking them through and taking needed actions to turn them around in a positive direction.

First Step: Perspective and Understanding. In thinking through a stressful situation, your aim is to put it in a broader perspective so it doesn't seem so terrible after all, and to find a deeper understanding of it so you have an idea of how to deal with it. The perspective and understanding you gain will already help you to feel better, even though you have not taken any actions.

Second Step: Developing an Action Plan. After the thinking through process, you develop an action plan that can actually change the situation around so that it is less stressful for you. What you have learned in the thinking through process helps you develop the action plan. The action plan will have a goal, steps you need to take to reach the goal, and a timeline for doing the steps.

Third Step: Taking Action. After developing the action plan, you do what it calls for. In other words, you take definite steps to reach your goal of changing the situation so that it is less stressful for you. As you take these steps and reach your goal, this will make you feel much more hardy about yourself. And, if you use HardiCoping whenever stressful situations happen, you will feel so much better about your life. Examples you will read later will show you what we mean.

Identifying Stressful Circumstances

Types Of Stresses

As you previously read, stressful situations place your body in a tense fight-or-flight mode. This physical arousal can increase in you tense, irritable, angry, anxious, and depressed feelings and interfere with sleep patterns. It can also increase your tendency to deny and avoid stresses, through regressive coping behaviors, like over eating or drinking.

One good way to prevent this downward behavioral cycle is to learn how to identify stressful situations, by how they make you feel and behave. There are, as you already know, two types of stress that can make us uncomfortable and disrupt our functioning.

Acute Stress

These are unexpected, disruptive, or painful daily changes in us or our routine. Things may be going along smoothly, and all of a sudden, something happens to throw you off. Acute stress can be big, like prematurely leaving college, job loss, or a serious illness in you or a family member. Or, it can be small, like a flat tire, argument with a family member or friend, or an academic or work project deadline. Whether big or small, however, the event is stressful if it makes you feel tense or in some way uncomfortable.

Chronic Stress

Rather than acute daily changes, chronic stress stems from continuing mismatches or conflicts between what you want and what you perceive you get. And, to change them, you may need to disrupt and rearrange significant aspects of your life. Chronic stresses can be big, like a lack of intimacy between you and your significant other, unfulfilling work, or dissatisfaction with your living residence. Whether a chronic stress is big or small depends upon how much it undermines your functioning. A stressful, ongoing chronic conflict can make you feel tense and unhappy. And, if poorly managed, it can make some people escape through behaviors, like over eating or spending, alcohol or drug abuse, or other self-destructive activities.

For many of us these days, stressful situations are the rule rather than the exception. As they increase in frequency, it may be difficult to identify and sort them out. We may have strain symptoms, like sleeplessness, heartburn, tension, irritability, or food and alcohol cravings without recognizing the stresses any longer. It's true that sometimes "the fish is the last to discover the water." To see them clearly, you must stand back from stresses. If you clearly know your stresses, you can solve them with the tools of HardiCoping.

HardiCoping Exercise 1: Identifying Acute And Chronic Stresses

Think about your current life experience. Try to identify stressful situations that trouble you now. Use as a guide situations in your life that make you feel tense, angry, anxious, depressed, unsatisfied, or uncomfortable, especially those that lead you to want to escape through self-destructive activities. Describe each stressful situation, then decide whether it's a minor or major or acute or chronic stress.

1. My stress is: Major or Minor; Acute or Chronic

   _____
   _____
   _____
   _____

2. My stress is: Major or Minor; Acute or Chronic

   _____
   _____
   _____
   _____

3. My stress is: Major or Minor; Acute or Chronic

   _____
   _____
   _____
   _____

4. My stress is: Major or Minor; Acute or Chronic

   _____
   _____
   _____
   _____

5. My stress is: Acute or Chronic; Major or Minor

   _____
   _____
   _____
   _____

If you are upset or anxious, you may not be able to think clearly enough to define the stresses you now face. If so, try this exercise again when you are more relaxed. If you did successfully identify them, use the HardiCoping techniques that follow to work on successfully managing these current stresses.

EXERCISE END

First HardiCoping Checkpoint

Please check in with your Hardiness trainer at this point to evaluate your learning thus far.

Summary Concepts And Terms

ACUTE STRESS

CHRONIC STRESS

DEVELOPING AN ACTION PLAN

HARDICOPING

INTERLOCKING LIFESTYLE SYSTEM

PERSPECTIVE AND UNDERSTANDING

TAKING ACTION

Test Your Knowledge

To test what you learned so far, see if you can correctly answer the following questions. Remember, the more information you have to think about what happens to you, the more building blocks you have to generate creative solutions to everyday living problems. This, in turn, strengthens your HardiAttitudes.

Commitment. The more information you seek to learn about yourself and the world, the more you demonstrate your belief that you are worthwhile and important enough to gather information that helps you.

Control. The more information you gather about yourself and your world, the greater your ability to influence the direction of your life.

Challenge. The effort you apply in learning the Hardiness skills shows that you regard the time spent in developing yourself as a normal challenge of life.

For the answer key,

1. The problem-solving approach in which you fix stressful situations by thinking them through and taking needed action is

    _____.

2. Hardy _____ involves three beliefs that you maintain about yourself in interaction with the world.

3. People who believe they can increase the interest value and importance of whatever they are involved in are high in the HardiAttitude called

    _____.

4. People who believe that what makes their lives worthwhile is to continue to grow in knowledge and wisdom through life experience are high in the HardiAttitude called _____.

5. People who believe that if they struggle and try, they may well be able to influence the direction and outcome of what goes on around them are

high in the HardiAttitude of

_____.

6. _____ and _____ are the first steps in HardiCoping.

7. Developing an _____ is the second HardiCoping step.

8. The third HardiCoping step is

    _____.

9. Unexpected, disruptive changes are called _____ stress.

10. A continuing mismatch or conflict between what you want in life and what you get is called _____ stress.

Learning Goals

*   Can you distinguish between acute and chronic stress?

*   Do you understand the relationship between stress, strain, and performance ineffectiveness?

*   Do you appreciate the ways that hardiness and health practices buffer people during stressful situations?

*   Do you appreciate how HardiAttitudes motivate people to solve problems through HardiCoping?

*   Do you understand how the three HardiCoping techniques work together to reduce strain?

CHAPTER 3

HardiCoping: Perspective and Understanding

The first step in HardiCoping involves thinking through a problem situation in a way that makes it less stressful for you. One way you do this is to set the situation in a broader perspective so that it doesn't seem so terrible after all. Another way is to think it through in a way that gives you a deeper understanding of what caused it and, hence, what to do about it.

You need to search for perspective and understanding about the stressful situations in your life that you have just identified. But before plunging into that, here are some helpful hints on perspective and understanding.

Five Useful Forms Of Perspective

People often use five different kinds of perspectives. These forms of perspective can help you adjust to a stressful situation through HardiCoping.

Commonplace Perspective

This is a fancy word but it just means that you are able to see the stressful situation you are working on as an example of the kinds of things that regularly happen in many people's lives. As you think through a stressful situation, you may find that you are not the only one cursed with this stress-provoking problem, nor is it the only time in your life it is likely to occur.

Manageability Perspective

Another form of perspective happens when you see your stressful situation as neither the best nor the worst thing that has happened or will happen. This can give you great relief. When people overreact, they treat their stressful problem as the end of the world. It almost never is. You should try to see your stress as not the best, but also not the worst that can happen. In other words, it's manageable.

Improvement Perspective

A major way of finding perspective is to view the stressful situation as something changeable. It is only a short step from this to the recognition that the situation can be improved. If you feel it can be improved, your discomfort will surely decrease.

Time Perspective

Another form of perspective that helps is to realize that the stressful situation is time limited. Any problem may seem much more tolerable if it will soon be over. So search for a time perspective as another way of adjusting to what has happened.

Unpredictability Perspective

Another form of perspective that helps is to realize that there are some situations that cannot be predicted. On the other hand, accepting the unpredictability of some circumstances may make them somewhat more tolerable.

Five Useful Forms Of Understanding

Keep in mind that acquiring perspective helps you adjust to and feel better about the problem, but does not necessarily point to solutions. Solutions require understanding. Whenever you are trying to use HardiCoping on a stressful situation, you may want to keep in mind the following five frequent ways of understanding problems to see which of them seems accurate.

Personal Limitation

Did the stressful problem involve some limitation of your own? Did you lack the ability, patience, or skills to accomplish your work or to relate successfully to those around you? Were you perhaps too timid or aggressive? Often, recognizing personal limitations involves realizing that we are complicating the present situation by bringing to it pent up feelings and attitudes from our past. What we all need to reflect on at times of stress is if and how our own attitudes and behavior might be part of the problem by creating conflict with others or difficulty in performing tasks.

Misunderstanding

Stressful conflict may often result when people just misunderstand each other. Your statements or actions may be taken by the other person(s) entirely differently than you intended. And, you may also be misunderstanding their statements or intentions. Perhaps you took your adviser's stern look as disapproval of you (when it really expressed his or her own worries), and your pulling back was, in turn, taken by the adviser as your lack of interest in school (when it really meant that you felt rejected).

If such a misunderstanding continues or worsens, you might be disciplined or decide to quit, just through a failure of clear communication.

Clash Of Wills

Destructive competition is a desire to win at any cost. Feeling competitive is a frequent cause of stressful situations. Strong disagreements, whether competitive or not, can lead our own and others' wills to clash. When coping with stressful circumstances, you need to consider whether you and others are trying to undermine each other. Are you angrier with them than you care to admit? Are they furious with you? Are you as set in your own ways as they are in theirs?

Victimization

Perhaps what is involved does not seem to you like mere misunderstanding, or even a clash of wills. The competitiveness, inflexibility, or judgmental behavior of others may be producing the problem with little or no contribution from you. If so, you are being victimized. But this is tricky. Be careful. The easiest, but by no means most accurate thing people do when burdened by stress is to see themselves as victims. Sometimes we are indeed victimized. But be careful to avoid falling into easy understandings, like I'm a victim that do little to develop your hardiness.

External Forces

Powerful outside forces may drive a stressful situation. This is an understanding to consider, as you attempt to understand your stressful problem. Health or economic pressures, constraints to behave in specific ways, laws or other social regulations, or even a natural catastrophe may affect your life.

Better to recognize these forces, if they are present, rather than rush to attribute such problems to other causes, like a personal limitation. Sometimes you can influence external forces and sometimes you cannot.

Now you are ready to hear about the technique we call **Situational Reconstruction**, which will help you search for perspective and understanding when trying to solve a stressful situation. If you can solve the stressful problem despite the outside forces, fine. But if you cannot, it is best to stop butting your head against the wall and find another way of accepting or decreasing the stress.

Situational Reconstruction: Thinking Through Alternatives

In the beginning of this technique, you describe the stressful situation on which you will work. Then, you imagine how the situation could be even worse and also how it could be better.

Having gone that far, you let your imagination go even more by thinking up stories about what would have to happen to actually bring about each of the better and worse versions you just identified. What would you, the others, the situation, the tasks, have to be like or change into for things to get worse or better?

How likely to happen (on a scale from 0 to 100%) are these two stories of how things could get worse or better?

Next, ask yourself what you could do specifically to help bring about the better and avoid the worse stories?

The steps thus far involve thinking through alternatives, or spading up the ground to see what you find, as you search for a solution to the problem posed by the stressful situation. If you can find different ways to look at what happened, then you may discover the solution.

When you have come this far, then you step back from what you have done and try to pull it all together into a broader perspective and a deepened understanding. We find that using your imagination to think through alternatives helps you achieve perspective and understanding. You also reflect on whether the Situational Reconstruction process has removed some of the stressfulness of the situation with which you are coping. Often, this happens. After this, the process is complete.

To make the process more vivid, please read about how Andy and Barbara went through Situational Reconstruction. Try to get a sense of the process of finding perspective and understanding from what you read.

Andy's Situational Reconstruction

"Alarmed by what's happening in school, I feel up to my a... in alligators. I can't seem to get things done on time. I'm actually afraid of failing out after doing so well in high school. I've done my best, but now it just doesn't seem good enough. What's going to happen if I have to leave school? My parents would hate it, and I'd lose my friends. I sort of tried to ask my adviser for help, but I just couldn't pull it off."

Think of a way in which the stressful situation could be even worse than it is.

For Andy, this step was extremely difficult; his circumstances, he said, were already very bad. But, reluctantly, he let his imagination go to work. "They could start throwing more work at me; I can't even handle what I'm doing now." Then, I'd be feeling even more overwhelmed. I could get sick; maybe, I'd get an ulcer? These days my stomach is always upset. I might get such poor grades that when I come up for yearly review...I might get suspended."

Think of a way in which the stressful situation could be better than it is.

Andy's preoccupation with his troubles made it hard for him to imagine how things could get much worse or much better. But he persisted. "Well, it's not likely that they will decrease the course work."

"So I have to say that life would be a lot better if, somehow, I didn't feel so overwhelmed all the time. I could work more efficiently if I didn't always feel under the gun."

Make up a story about how the worse version of the stressful circumstance you identified in Step 2 might actually take place. What would have to change in you, or the others involved, to worsen the situation? Once you have finished the story, estimate (from 0 to 100%) how likely it is to come true.

"To feel even more overwhelmed, I'd have to fall apart even more, give up on myself, and see myself as incompetent and a failure. I may be worried now, but I've never fallen apart in my life. I'm not a quitter. It's not likely that I could make myself less gutsy. Why would I? I guess if I didn't get much support at home or from my buddies--maybe then I could fall apart more. But my family and friends keep helping me to hang in there. They keep reminding me that I'm OK.

"To be put on suspension, I'd have to be performing even more poorly, or have unsupportive teachers. I'd have to stop trying, not care about the quality of my work, and break faith with the college. I'm not made that way. And, there are a few teachers at this college who know what I can do, what I did when I first got here."

"I don't think they'd want me suspended, even though the workload has gotten out of hand lately. They understand the problem. Sure, my new adviser is a question mark, but he'd have to care less about us than he seems to...Now, let's see...what are the chances of me becoming more overwhelmed and the college losing faith in me?...Maybe about twenty percent."

Note: Let's pause a moment and examine what Andy learns in these early efforts. Actually, he is already beginning to get a broader perspective on himself and his relationship to his work. His effort to construct a story that is even worse gives him considerable reassurance, even at this early stage of the exercise. The likelihood of matters getting worse seems small. He begins to appreciate that he managed to perform well in the past, no matter how severe the pressures. People at school and at home believe in him more than he sometimes does himself. He also takes a step toward deepened understanding when he realizes that by feeling so overwhelmed, he is actually sapping his self-confidence and esteem, which can make matters worse.

Make up a story about how the better version of the stressful circumstance you identified in Step 3 might actually take place. What would have to change in you, and the others involved, to better the

situation? Once you have finished the story, estimate (from 0 to 100%) how likely it is to come true.

"How could I feel less overwhelmed? I'd have to concentrate on being less of a worrier, and on blaming the workload less. And, I should pay more attention to the people at home and at school who believe in me."

"If I worried and blamed less, I could smell the roses more, count my blessings. Who knows? If I was less angry with my teachers, I might be able to find better ways to work more efficiently. Maybe I could arrange to see my friends only twice a week and my family once a week. That would give me more time for schoolwork, and I'd get more of it done. I think the likelihood of my feeling less overwhelmed is good, maybe thirty or forty percent."

Note: See how Andy's mood is changing as he considers ways to improve his circumstances? He is complaining less and taking charge more. He has made a most important discovery that constitutes deepened understanding. His constant overwhelmed feeling was even more due to internal pressures (a matter of poor self-esteem) than of external pressures (though there certainly was a lot of work to do). He saw himself as likely to fail more than others did. The facts, he begins to see, are that he did a creditable job in high school, and that his teachers, family, and friends believe in him. His attention is beginning to be focused on overcoming the insecurities he has been feeling about himself.

What specifically can you do to bring about the better version of your problem and prevent the worse version from happening?

"I should analyze the pressures on my time more and prioritize the tasks and group them to improve my efficiency. I must become less worried and angry, believe more in myself, and get more involved in my work. I need to share what I'm doing with my teachers more. That way, maybe I can get to know them better. And, maybe they can learn something from me about how to help students who struggle. I need to let the support from my family and friends sink in more, believe in myself, rather than just complaining."

On the basis of what you have learned so far, indicate a way or ways of putting the stressful situation in perspective.

"You know, things are unlikely to worsen, unless I panic. And, if don't panic, and remember that I am a good, hard worker with something to offer, things could actually get a lot better. After all, what's happening is just another sign of growing up. Lots of people have been there before and will still be here when it's over."

Note: On reflection, Andy is able to see the stressful situation from two fresh perspectives. First, the increased pressures on him are largely the result of having so much to do, not any failure on his part (this understanding involves External Forces).

And, this crisis is no different from the crises facing many other college students (this is the Commonplace Perspective). Further, his problem in dealing with those pressures can be solved, in this case by increasing his self-confidence through remembering his effectiveness over the long haul and acting on it to help solve this crisis (this is the Improvement Perspective). He is not doomed to feeling incompetent and overwhelmed, nor is he doomed to compulsive eating and drinking.

On the basis of what you have learned, indicate how you now understand what happened and the ways the stressful situation can be improved.

"`All I have to fear is fear itself,' as the saying goes. I need to keep my wits about me and do what needs to be done. Nobody is out to get me. Lots of students are under the same pressure. We need to handle it together. It's not me against them. It's what's happening in college as we grow up."

Note: Andy pinpointed his major source of stress, as letting increased work pressures lower his self-confidence. It became clear to him that his teachers are not his enemy (He rejects, here, the Victimization and Clash of Wills understanding). He settles instead on External Forces and Personal Limitation as bases for understanding. While he concludes that there's little he can do about External Forces, he knows he can work on bolstering his self-confidence. Improved self-confidence will help him to see ways that he can work more efficiently and organize his life better. This will help him to get his life back on track.

When all is said and done, do you feel any better? Is the stressfulness of the problem reduced? Is a resolution in sight?

Andy beamed as he answered this question: "I really see the light at the end of the tunnel, and it's not a train coming towards me. I know what I have to do to make things better, and I think I can do it. At the very least, I feel lots better. I don't feel stuck anymore. There are things I can do to work better and to organize my life more. That feels much better!" Having done so well with Situational Reconstruction, Andy is ready to develop and carry out an action plan.

Barbara's Situational Reconstruction

Barbara was a hard-working student, doing well in her last year of college. She tried Situational Reconstruction because she felt her personal life was in jeopardy. She had been dating a guy for two years, and they were really serious about their relationship. She hoped to marry, only to discover, as she got to know him better, just how disturbingly different he was from her.

His disorganized, devil-may-care approach to life clashed with her organized ways. She was simultaneously turned off at the thought of marrying such a man, and deeply pained at the thought of losing him because she still loved him. Needless to say, Barbara identified this stressful situation as chronic.

Describe the stressful situation in your own words.

"I'm really in conflict. I still love Bill a lot--we can still have good, romantic times. But I recoil at being in his apartment. It's dirty and disorganized. Whatever you want is either not there or impossible to find. And it's not only the apartment. His personal finances are a mess, even though he seems to somehow stay on top of things at school. I'm both angry and loving, disgusted and turned on. I can't live this way. I don't want to spend the rest of my life taking care of an overgrown baby--but I also don't want to be alone anymore."

Think of a way in which the stressful situation could be even worse than it is.

"I could have already promised to marry him, and the wedding could already be planned. Then it would be hard to turn back, even if he were insisting that he's right and I'm wrong. Then my disgust could have wiped out my love."

Note: Can you see in this statement some glimmering of how Barbara ended up pursuing a solution to the problem?

Think of a way in which the stressful situation could be better than it is.

"Bill could be the most organized and responsible person in the world--ha, ha. No chance of that! But I could be more flexible and tolerant, and less uptight, without withdrawing or getting angry. And, he could be more willing to change too. Then we could work on our relationship problem together, using our love to lead to compromises, so that we don't have to break up."

Note: What's your prediction as to where Barbara's quest for resolution of her stressful circumstance will take her?

Make up a story about how the worse version of the stressful circumstance you identified in Step 2 might actually take place. What would have to change in you, and the others involved, to worsen the situation? Once you have finished the story, estimate (from 0 to 100%) how likely it is to come true?

"To have already promised to marry him, I'd have to either be harder up than I am right now, or less careful about the person of whom who I plan to live. Sure, I want to get married. I've had two close relationships before, but this is the first where I really wanted to settle down. But I don't need to get married so much that I'd do it without first resolving this problem.

"For my dissatisfaction with his messy ways to have already wiped out my love, I guess I'd have to have started less in love with him. I have loved, and still do love, him so much. My heart aches just to think about it. For love to have ended, I'd have to be less committed to him, so I could just turn away. I wouldn't confront him--which is not my way. More likely I'd just detach, and pretty soon there would be no love left. I've done this several times before-- avoid confrontation at any cost, and end up not caring anymore.

"Speaking of likelihood, there's a good chance (maybe fifty percent) that I could walk away from this relationship like I've done in the past...But, you know, the more I think about it, the more I realize that I really value Bill's good heart and loving nature. He'd have to be a lot less flexible and willing to consider his shortcomings, for me to give up on the relationship, without trying to make it better. So, on balance, I think there's only about a twenty percent chance of my worst-case scenario coming true."

Note: Were you right in your prediction of where Barbara is going? Can you see her direction now? What is it?

Make up a story about how the better version of the stressful circumstance you identified in Step 3 might actually take place. What would have to change in you, and the others involved, to better the situation? Once you have finished the story, estimate (from 0 to 100%) how likely it is to come true?

"If only I could be more flexible. I want this guy, and I've lost out sometimes because of inflexibility. What I'd have to do is use my strong love for him as a building block to reconsidering my ways so as to be more flexible. But, just to avoid the confrontation, I'd have to stop withdrawing. I know withdrawing will just stop me from loving him.

"Bill loves me too, and that should motivate him to work on our differences along with me so that we can build a better relationship together."

"He is a real problem solver at school, and so am I. That proves we can do it, even though it's harder in private life. I can see us admitting the problem to each other and planning a strategy for how to work on it and taking steps. Maybe this has a sixty percent chance of working out."

Note: See how this caring woman is putting together the pieces of a solution to her stressful problem? You can do this too with your problems.

What specifically can you do to bring about the better version of your problem and prevent the worse version from happening?

"To avoid the worse version, I have to resist my natural tendency to just withdraw rather than confront. Instead, I'll have to help Bill not be defensive about his lifestyle. I'll have to raise my concerns, as preferences, rather than fundamental truths. And, voice my concerns about his messiness, as his way, rather than something fundamentally wrong with him. I most likely should find less attacking ways to refer to his living style, rather than messiness or irresponsibility.

"To bring about the better version, I'll have to present our differing ways as something to problem-solve about. We love each other very much, and we are very good problem solvers. With this start, we should be able to work together to find a win-win solution and build our future on that. He needs to realize how much I want us to work out. If he wants it too, then the rest is really just problem solving. I don't have to be so organized, and he doesn't have to be so messy--each gives up a little and helps the other in the process."

On the basis of what you have learned, find a way or ways of putting the stressful situation in perspective.

"Marriages are based on loving compromise. It's like I didn't know this before, or wasn't willing to try hard enough. My guess is that the marriages that really work out involve two people who know how to compromise and are willing to. If we accept this and really work on our problems, our relationship may really succeed."

Note: Barbara's perspective is two-fold. First, she is now seeing their relationship difficulty as natural enough when two adults with different lifestyles try to be together (this is the Commonplace Perspective). So, the commitment to compromise in her relationship is no different in her mind than what people have always and will always do to build sound marriages. Second, she now believes that she can improve the relationship that she and Bill can, and will, work on their differences (this is the Improvement Perspective).

On the basis of what you have learned, how do you now understand the stressful situation and the ways in which it can be improved?

" Bill and I are both set in our ways. He doesn't need order in his private life, and I do. We really disagree about this, but somehow we love each other very much too (this is a Clash of Wills understanding)."

"He's not trying to hurt me, and I'm not trying to hurt him. What we have to do is develop a spirit of compromise, and then work hard on helping each other not feel too threatened or put off."

Note: Barbara now understands the clash of wills that stands behind the stressful circumstance. Rec-

ognizing this is, of course, a necessary step in solving the problem through compromise.

When all is said and done, do you feel any better? Is the stressfulness of the problem reduced? Is there a resolution in sight?

"You bet I feel better. I'm actually enthusiastic about talking it over with Bill and finding a path to ending our problem. Thank you for this help."

Note: We hope you see how Situational Reconstruction can work for people. Certainly, Barbara came out of it at a gallop--more than ready to put together a decisive action plan and implement it.

OK, now it's time for you to try Situational Reconstruction. Pick one of your most stressful circumstances from Exercise 1 to work on. Then, begin to write down your responses to the various steps.

HardiCoping Exercise 2: Situational Reconstruction, Finding Alternatives

This is a problem-solving exercise that is always the starting point in our efforts to cope with stressful circumstances. The steps of the exercise speak for themselves. Just let your imagination go in steps 2 through 6. Then in steps 7 and 8, try to reflect on what you have done. See if you can get some relief through doing the mental part of HardiCoping in this exercise.

Step 1 Describe your stressful circumstance in your own words.

_____

_____

_____

_____

_____

Step 2 Think of a way in which the stressful circumstance could be even worse than it is right now.

_____

_____

_____

_____

Step 3 Think of a way in which the stressful circumstance could be better than it is right now.

_____

_____

_____

_____

Step 4 Make up a story about how the worse version of the stressful circumstance you identified in Step 2 might actually take place. What would have to change in you and the others involved to make things even worse? Once you have finished the story, estimate (from 0 to 100%) how likely it is to come true.

_____

_____

_____

_____

I estimate that this story is _____% likely to come true.

Step 5 Make up a story about how the better version of the stressful circumstance that you identified in Step 3 might actually take place. What would have to change in you and the others involved to make things better? Once you have finished the story, estimate (from 0 to 100%) how likely it is to come true.

_____

_____

_____

_____

I estimate that this story is _____% likely to come true.

Step 6 What specifically can you do to bring about the better version of your problem and stop the worse version from happening?

_____

_____

_____

_____

Step 7 On the basis of what you have learned, find a way or ways of putting the stressful circumstance in perspective.

_____

_____

_____

_____

Step 8 On the basis of what you have learned, how do you now understand the stressful situation and the ways in which it can be improved?

_____

_____

_____

_____

Step 9 When all is said and done, do you feel any better? Is the stressfulness of the problem reduced? Is there a resolution in sight?

_____

_____

_____

_____

How did this technique work for you? Take a moment and see whether you feel more as though you know what to do and think you can actually do it.

EXERCISE END

Second HardiCoping Checkpoint

Please check in with your Hardiness Trainer at this point to evaluate your learning thus far.

Moving On Or Getting Stuck

Now you have practiced Situational Reconstruction for the first time. Maybe it went really well, and you emerged with lots of perspective and understanding that has already begun to lower your stress level. This lowering of stress shows you that Situational Reconstruction is truly the mental part of HardiCoping. The stress is lower because you constructively changed the way you think about the stressful problem. But, you can only change the stressful situation around so far, with mental steps alone. To solve the stressful problem further, you need to take some action out there in the world, where the stressful circumstance exists. And, if you gained perspective and understanding, then you are really ready to move to devising and carrying out a decisive action plan.

Let's consider first however what to do if Situational Reconstruction did not go so well for you. Of course, that might be due to your having to practice the technique more. But even when you are skilled with Situational Reconstruction, you might still fail or get stuck. There are basically three ways of getting stuck. First, you might not be able to really think up better and worse alternatives, how they might come about, and what you could do to facilitate the better alternatives. Second, you might not be able to gain much perspective and understanding of the stressful circumstance. Finally, you might think you did well in the exercise, however, if you

really get no relief of stress, even though you should, you are also stuck. If you got stuck in one or more of these ways, then you are not ready to make or implement an action plan. After all, without clarity, what action plan would make sense?

Don't panic. If you got stuck, just admit it to yourself. It is not a sign of failure. Rather, it means that the stressful circumstance is such that you need to use the other HardiCoping techniques we have available.

Focusing

Exploring Emotional Reactions

One way you might get stuck doing Situational Reconstruction is that the stressful circumstance is arousing strong emotions in you that, for one reason or another, you are not admitting to yourself. Maybe you think the strong emotions would be too disruptive in your busy life or too painful to handle. So, you shove them aside, out of your attention, and just try to hang in there. The trouble with not attending to your emotions is two-fold:

First, our emotions constitute information that is sometimes crucial in solving problems. Situational Reconstruction is an information-rich, problem-solving task. If you try to do it without all the relevant information—in this case, your emotional reactions to the stressful circumstance—you may not come up with the solution that will work. It's a little like playing solitaire with an incomplete deck of cards—at some point, you will get stuck and be unable to reach the solution.

Second, pushing our emotions aside involves using the same mental process that inhibits our imagination. How can you engage in the imaginative aspects of Situational Reconstruction, which ask you to become a novelist about your own life, if you are trying very hard not to experience your emotional reactions?

So, here are two good reasons why it is better to know about your strong emotional reactions if you are having them. Keep in mind that emotions are information, and that knowledge is power. Knowing about your emotions cannot weaken you. It's up to you whether and how you express your emotions around others. They need not know your emotional reactions just because you do. But, if you know your emotional reactions, you are more likely to understand the stressful situations that arouse them and be able to figure out what to do.

Introduced by Gendlin in 1973, the **Focusing** technique is how we explore ourselves to see if there are strong emotional reactions to the stressful circumstance that we have been hiding from ourselves. It is a way of temporarily pushing aside the familiar ways we have of understanding the stressful circumstance in order to make room for listening to the messages that our bodies are trying to give to us. We listen to these messages without rushing to judge them in order to see whether there is some new, previously unrecognized insight in them.

For most people, Focusing is hard. It's different from how we usually function. But we promise you, the more you try it, the better you will get at it. As a way into the technique, go on and read about the emotionally based insights Cesar and Sandra came up with.

CESAR'S BREAKTHROUGH

THROUGH FOCUSING

Young, capable, and dynamic, Cesar was rising rapidly through the managerial ranks of his large corporation. Spurred by a sense of good fortune, he and his wife bought a remarkable home in what had been a great neighborhood, then it had become a slum, but was now on the verge of regentrification. That wonderful old home would appreciate greatly in value as soon as the neighborhood improved.

Imagine how he felt coming home after work to the new place that first evening, only to find a gang of hoodlums camped out on his front walk. It was their turf. Anger welled up in him, and he could barely get past them into the house without trying to kill them. His excitement and enthusiasm were shattered. This turn of events was the stressful circumstance with which Cesar needed to cope.

His first efforts at Situational Reconstruction were fruitless. He was too preoccupied to be imaginative. No methods came to mind as to how the situation could be even worse or better. He was unable to compose stories, and no perspective or understanding emerged. Clearly, he needed to try Focusing to see if he could free up his imagination.

As he started Focusing, his anger was, of course, omnipresent. But finally, he managed to put it aside, not dwell so much on it, and tried to listen to the messages his body was giving him. He realized the tightness in his chest and shortness of breath as he reflected on the stressful circumstance. That wasn't anger. Can you imagine what emotion Cesar found underneath the anger? Perhaps you guessed it: Fear! Despite his macho upbringing as a Latino, Cesar discovered that the gang frightened him. To his credit, he could admit this "unmanly" reaction to the others in his group training session.

Returning to Situational Reconstruction, he found that this newfound emotional insight made all the difference. He was no longer stuck. Indeed, the fear reaction was not only natural, but very valuable as well. In terms of how the situation could have been worse, he imagined what would have happened if he had acted on the anger without the tempering effect of the fear. There were more of them than he could handle, or they might have had guns, or they might have returned the next day to prey on his wife and infant son when he was far away at work. He began to be thankful for the fear that had kept him prudent. And, as he imagined ways in which the situation could have been better, the fear helped him formulate win-win solutions. The hoods lived there too, so he couldn't just vanquish them. Rather, he had to find some way to make things better for them as well as for his family. This sense of perspective and understanding led to an impressive action plan, which you will hear about later. Can you anticipate what it was?

SANDRA'S INSIGHT THROUGH FOCUSING

The oldest child in her family, Sandra was going to a local college while living at home with her parents. Although she was a student in good standing, her advisers often told her that she could be doing far better than she was. Her younger brother had just been admitted to a prestigious college in another city, and her family was making a big deal over him.

Then one day, Sandra heard that her parents had given her brother a car to take to college. She angrily said to her parents, "I'm tired of you treating me, like a nobody, while Jim gets all your support and admiration." Her parents countered defensively, "But he'll need a car to travel back and forth from out of town, and he's going to have such a great career. You're so jealous of him because you aren't doing well at college. Why don't you leave school and just get married?" This disastrous confrontation was the stressful circumstance that Sandra tried to cope with.

Her initial effort at Situational Reconstruction was painful. It was hard for her to think of ways in which the stressful circumstance could be worse, as she already felt that "they hate my guts. Now I gave them a reason to think of me as stupid and rigid. Who knows what they're thinking about me? And, I can't even leave their home because I don't have money." Nor could she get into ways in which the situation could be better.

She was stuck, unable to achieve perspective and understanding, so her next task in coping was to try the Focusing technique. Perhaps the strong emotional reactions not completely understood were obstructing her imagination. Certainly, Sandra felt her anger at her parents as she initially focused her attention on her body and asked what it was about the stressful situation that was bothering her. But as she set this aside, and other emotions surfaced, she found she felt tiny, hurt, and abandoned, like no one cared about her. Although she had her eyes closed for this exercise, the tears began running down her cheeks. Many images from her childhood flooded her mind, and it was hard to catch her breath. Sandra remembered growing up with a passive mother, a domineering father, and four brothers. Her brothers were always the ones who counted, who were supposed to amount to something, whereas she was passed over, pushed into the background, only a girl. The hurt had never gone away.

She realized in a flash of insight that she had bought into this image of herself as inadequate and unimportant a long time ago. By her behavior, she had conformed to her inconsequential place in the family. In a paradoxical way, she had been expecting to be passed over and contributed to this by not being assertive. Having confronted her parents this time was actually a step forward, and their argument was at least an attempt at communication about the problem.

Now Sandra was ready to tackle Situational Reconstruction again. The disastrous confrontation seemed the result of pent-up emotions on both sides. But it was, she also saw, positive in the sense of something that could clear the air and enable more constructive communication. Maybe it should have happened long before. As she recognized more and more that she had contributed to the problem by not being assertive and failing to pursue her own talents and goals, Sandra realized that she had to change and take the lead in helping her parents see her differently. She recognized that her parents were not terrible, but they just bought into the conventional fiction that males have the great careers, while females are the homemakers. They did not hate her so much as they were being creatures of their culture. Once she understood the conflicted communication with her parents as a limitation perspective, Sandra could begin to imagine more constructive ways to help her parents understand the ways in which she felt overlooked by them. And, of crucial importance, she realized that she would have to break out of the lost, passive, hurt mold of her childhood and take the initiative in her career and life. She began formulating ways to be more assertive at school and to influence her parents to change their views of her.

Clearly, with Focusing as the opening wedge, Sandra was no longer stuck in Situational Reconstruction. She emerged from her second effort at this technique with sufficient perspective and understanding to formulate and carry out an action plan.

HardiCoping Exercise 3: Focusing For Emotional Reactions

In order to try this exercise, you will need to have in mind a current stressful circumstance that you want to work on. If you got stuck doing Situational Reconstruction, use the stressful circumstance that was involved. If you did not get stuck, then just pick another stressful circumstance from your list in Exercise 1.

What you need to do first is read through the six steps described below until you can do them from memory. This is necessary because reading the steps as you try to go through Focusing will distract you from sinking into yourself (which is what the steps call for). Once you can remember what you have read pretty well, then push your workbook away, sink into yourself, and go through the steps.

Step I Get in a comfortable position. You may want to close your eyes so as not to be distracted.

Step 2 Direct your attention inward to the center of your body, your chest and abdomen, where you usually feel things.

Step 3 Ask yourself the question, "What is it about the stressful circumstance that I am facing that stands in the way of my feeling really good right now?" The first few answers that come to mind will probably be familiar, conventional ways of understanding the problem. Recognize and accept them, but put them off to the side of your attention and continue to direct your full attention to your body. Just try to experience what the problem feels like in your body, without rushing to put words to it.

Step 4 After you have felt your body's reaction to the problem for a while, and the familiar, conventional ways of understanding it have been put aside, then try to find a label for the feeling that is different, that

somehow seems right for you. A label can be a word, a phrase, or even a picture.

Step 5 When you have a label that seems right for you, then "resonate" by alternating your attention to the bodily feeling, then the label, then the feeling again, then the label again. This is to see if the label is really accurate. If, while you are resonating, any changes occur in the label, the bodily feeling, or both, let that happen. When no more changes happen, your Focusing effort is over.

Step 6 What have you learned about your emotional reactions to the stressful circumstance? Jot down some notes as to how Focusing for emotional reactions went for you:

Step 7 If you were stuck in Situational Reconstruction before you tried Focusing on this stressful circumstance, write down here how your second attempt at Situational Reconstruction went. Were you able to be imaginative enough to go through the steps? If you got more perspective and understanding, detail what it is. Do you feel more relief?

_____

_____

_____

_____

EXERCISE END

Compensatory Self-Improvement: Regaining Momentum

Suppose you got stuck in Situational Reconstruction and gained no emotionally based insight while Focusing. Or suppose you indeed gained an insight through Focusing, but it didn't get you unstuck when you tried Situational Reconstruction again. What do you do then?

Through focusing, you showed that strong emotions are not contributing to your inability to solve the stressful problem. This means that something else prevents you from solving the problem. It may be that, as the problem stands right now, there's little you can do to change it. We call these unchangeable problems givens. The HardiCoping process has a way to go still

In our lives, at one time or another, we each will encounter unsolvable stressful circumstances, no matter how hard we try. At such times, the Hardi-Coping process ensures that we get beyond bitterness or self-pity, about the world. Your Hardiness lowers, by thinking, the world shabbily treated you, so you no longer have to care. If bitterness and self-pity increase, you try less to solve living problems and are less successful in transforming future stresses. What must you do then to bypass bitterness and self-pity, if you've encountered a circumstance that resists change?

That's where the third technique of HardiCoping comes into play. We call it **Compensatory Self-Improvement**. The idea is that at the very time when an unchangeable stressful circumstance, a given, has laid you low, you must find some alternative problem to work on using the tools of Hardi-Coping. This alternative problem must relate to the one you cannot solve. On balance, you recognize that although you can't fix every problem, there are certainly some that you can work on and actively solve. Working on the alternative problem thus compensates for the inability to fix the original problem. It assures that you have an opportunity to continue to improve yourself through HardiCoping. Compensatory Self-Improvement is a good way of **regaining momentum** lost through the inability to transform the original stressor.

DAVID'S TRIUMPH THROUGH COMPENSATORY SELF-IMPROVEMENT

David's stressful circumstance is that his wife suffers from breast cancer, and he does not know how long she will live. As a Senior Executive in a major corporation, he had lived his life solving problems. In addressing this family problem, he had obtained for his wife the best medical treatments available. But, he was still uncertain as to what the future would bring.

He could not get very far with Situational Reconstruction. Relatively unimportant details kept distracting him. Because his wife could not lift heavy weights after her surgery, he felt he had to do all the shopping, cooking, and cleaning. This, on top of his work responsibilities and evening teaching at the local junior college, left little time for anything else. He simply could not get involved in the imaginative requirements of Situational Reconstruction, getting stuck.

Through Focusing, David did uncover an emotional reaction he had been avoiding. Fear! This man who had worked hard his whole life long, anticipating a comfortable retirement in which there would be time and means to do all the things that had been set aside earlier, now feared that his wife would die and leave him alone in his old age.

He was quick to try Situational Reconstruction again, armed with this emotional insight. But try as he might, there was no way he could find to ensure that his wife would remain alive for any acceptable period of time. It was out of his hands, he had to

admit. He had confronted a given and had to protect himself against becoming bitter about the world or sinking into self-pity.

In turning to Compensatory Self-Improvement in order to regain momentum, David had initial difficulty in finding some other stressful problem, related to the given, that he could hope to solve instead. But the emotionally based insight obtained through Focusing helped in the end. David realized that he had been losing himself in busy work (he could easily have hired household help to shop, cook, and clean) in order to avoid his mounting fear of being alone in old age. Indeed, he had detached himself from his wife through busy work, thereby not having to talk about the problem of her breast cancer. After all, with that kind of talk, he risked facing the fear. Feeling abandoned, his wife had sunk into depression, feeling alone in her hour of need, and he had failed to recognize this.

The problem to be worked on through Compensatory Self-Improvement emerged from this line of thinking: Though he could not keep her alive, he could do something to improve the psychological quality of their relationship for however long that proved possible. With a mixture of sadness, determination, and relief, David brought his formidable problem-solving skills to bear on this compensatory task. After a surprisingly quick return to Situational Reconstruction, David was ready to formulate and carry out an action plan to improve their psychological relationship. You will hear about what happened later.

BETTY'S DEVELOPMENT THROUGH COMPENSATORY

SELF-IMPROVEMENT

Betty's stressful circumstance hit when her boyfriend of two years announced that he had fallen in love with another girl. He felt confused and wasn't sure whether he wanted to persist or break off with Betty. Betty wanted him to stay, despite her shock at his disloyalty. She loved him still. She proved resourceful in doing Situational Reconstruction. Far from getting stuck, she found ways in which the problem could be worse (e.g. death of her boyfriend or his being sure about breaking with her) and better (e.g. if this had never happened or if he was sure he wanted to stay with her). She was able to construct convincing stories about how these alternatives could come about. In all this, she discerned things she could do to improve the relationship and developed sufficient perspective and understanding with which to plan a decisive course of action.

The action plan involved the goal of recapturing intimacy and romance for the relationship, and there were many articulated steps along the way. These steps included spending more quality time together, talking through problems as they arose, re-experiencing each other in a variety of ways, and, of course, enlisting her boyfriend's active cooperation in all these endeavors. She tried very hard, and he did try to cooperate.

Despite these heroic efforts, however, his preoccupation with the other girl persisted. Soon, Betty's attempts to turn the disaster to their advantage exhausted her; she had to admit whether the relationship that persisted thus far was really out of her hands. At that point, it was time to turn to Compensatory Self-Improvement, despite her exhaustion and demoralization, lest bitterness and self-pity erode her hardiness.

The alternative problem Betty chose to work on was her phobia of skiing. The way this problem compensates for and relates to the relationship problem was that her boyfriend was an inveterate skier, and her fear of this sport had been an obstacle all along. In the early days of their relationship, Betty had tagged along on skiing weekends. But in the evening, when the skiers were relating their exploits on the slopes, all she could contribute was news of the soap operas she had been watching on television in the lodge. Soon she had stopped going along, and this symbolized the erosion of their romance. So at the very time when Betty felt most defeated, she had to struggle to overcome a phobia she had left unsolved even when the relationship was good.

Through a combination of Situational Reconstruction and Focusing, she gained considerable understanding of this skiing phobia, and a clear sense of what she could do to overcome it. Despite her overall sadness at her relationship problems, she began to feel excited at the prospect of overcoming the phobia as clarity about how to do this emerged from her mental coping efforts. Soon she was ready to carry out the plan. Can you guess what happened? You will find out later.

Some of you have already encountered unchangeable stressful circumstances in this course, and the rest of you have not. Even for those of you who have not, it is useful to think through what kinds of stressful circumstances are likely to be unchangeable, or givens.

HardiCoping Exercise 4: Regaining Momentum

31

Through Compensatory Self-Improvement

Sometimes, no amount of Situational Reconstruction and Focusing will resolve a stressful circumstance. Try as you may, you remain stuck and unrelieved. If you have already tried to resolve the problem and failed, then we say that you have encountered a given of your experience: something that you cannot change, at least not with your current resources.

If you cannot change a problem, the next best thing is to accept it serenely. This involves recognizing that, although you obviously do not control everything, you can still feel a general sense of Commitment, Control, and Challenge (that is, hardiness) rather than feeling bitter or full of self-pity. The clue to this is that you do not have to control every last thing in your world in order to feel good about yourself and that world.

Right at the moment when you have to accept a stressful circumstance as unchangeable, it is helpful to also see yourself as generally effective. That's what Compensatory Self-Improvement is all about. It comes into play after you have struggled unsuccessfully with a problem using Situational Reconstruction and Focusing. As you are trying to accept the unchangeable problem, you identify some other problem (hopefully even related to the first) where you can make changes, and you use your energies in trying to resolve it. You are, in effect, saying to yourself, "Here is a problem that I just have to accept, but I also have signs that I can resolve other problems." This Compensatory Self-Improvement helps you to accept the unchangeable serenely. The key to this is that instead of giving in to self-pity and bitterness because you cannot change a problem, you do the hard work of changing some other

problem. On balance, you still emerge with a sense of Commitment, Control, and Challenge. And, at some other time, you may even find it easier to return to the original problem in a manner that will change it.

Step 1 Begin by identifying some stressful circumstances that you strongly doubt you can change. You may have already identified some of these unchangeable circumstances or givens when you did HardiCoping Exercise 1, Identifying Acute and Chronic Stresses. Circumstances I feel are unchangeable, and thus are givens, include:

_____

_____

_____

_____

Step 2 Why do you feel the givens you listed in the preceding step are unchangeable?

_____

_____

_____

_____

Step 3 Now see if you can list some stressful circumstances that are related to the givens that you might be able to change with effort. The stressful circumstance that you decide to work on is related to the original given that produces it--think, for example, of David's related stressor, or perhaps like in Betty's example, the changeable stressful circumstance was related in another way.

_____

_____

_____

Step 4 Select one of the givens that you identified in Step 1, and while you are trying to accept it as a given, work on reconstructing a stressful circumstance that you deemed related to the original stressor. Use the tools of Situational Reconstruction and Focusing to do this. My given is:

_____

_____
_____
_____

My stressor that relates to the original problem and is more changeable is:

_____
_____
_____
_____

There's a danger in the notion of Compensatory Self-Improvement that some of you may have skirted very close to. That danger is to accept too easily, too uncritically, that a particular stressful circumstance is unchangeable. "Oh, my family has always been that way, there's no changing that," we may say. Or, "That's just the way the world works—it's naive to think otherwise." Sometimes our problems go unsolved not because they are givens, but because it would be painful to solve them. This is a waste of your life. It is not to be confused with HardiCoping.

EXERCISE END

Third HardiCoping Checkpoint

Please check in with your Hardiness Trainer at this point to evaluate your learning thus far.

Summary Concepts And Terms

> CLASH OF WILLS
>
> COMMONPLACE

COMPENSATORY SELF-IMPROVEMENT

EXTERNAL FORCES

FIVE FORMS OF PERSPECTIVE

FIVE FORMS OF UNDERSTANDING FOCUSING

GIVENS

IMPROVEMENT

MANAGEABILITY

MISUNDERSTANDINGS

PERSONAL LIMITATION

REGAINING MOMENTUM

SITUATIONAL RECONSTRUCTION

UNPREDICTABILITY

VICTIMIZATION

TIME

Test Your Knowledge

To test what you learned so far, see if you can correctly answer the following questions. Remember, the more information you have to think about what happens to you, the more building blocks you have to generate creative solutions to everyday living problems. This, in turn, strengthens your HardiAttitudes.

Commitment. The more information you seek to learn about yourself and the world, the more you demonstrate your belief that you are worthwhile and important enough to gather information that helps you.

Control. The more information you gather about yourself and your world, the greater your ability to influence the direction of your life.

Challenge. The effort you apply in learning the Hardiness skills shows that you regard the time spent in developing yourself as a normal challenge of life.

For the answer key, See "Questionnaire and Test Your Knowledge Answer Keys" on page 259.

1. There are _____ forms of perspective.

2. When you perceive a stressful situation as an example of a circumstance that happens in most people's lives, your perspective is _____.

3. When you perceive a stressful situation as neither the best, nor worst, thing that has or will ever happen, your perspective is _____.

4. When you view a stressful situation as something that can be changed, your perspective is _____.

5. When you can see a definite end point to a stressful situation, your perspective is _____.

6. There are _____ forms of understanding.

7. When you recognize that your lack of ability, patience, or skills factored into how you handled a stressful circumstance, you show an understanding of a _____.

8. Which kind of understanding involves competition, a desire to win at all costs, between you and another person? _____.

9. The kind of understanding that involves a miscommunication is _____.

10. The kind of understanding that involves the scapegoating of yourself is _____.

11. The kind of understanding that involves something outside of your control is _____.

12. The HardiCoping technique that involves thinking through alternatives is called _____.

13. The HardiCoping technique that involves exploring emotional reactions is called _____.

14. The HardiCoping technique that involves accepting that some things cannot be changed, and thus, you need to regain coping momentum is called _____.

15. A circumstance that cannot be changed is called a _____.

16. The kind of perspective that involves uncertainty is _____.

Learning Goals

- Do you understand how the five useful forms of perspective and understanding prepare people to solve stressful problems?

- Do you see how the focusing technique helps to reduce strong emotions that interfere with the problem solving process?

- In the problem-solving process, can you determine when it's time to turn to Compensatory Self-Improvement to regain problem solving momentum?

CHAPTER 4   *HardiCoping: Planning Action*

"Without a purpose, nothing should be done."
Marcus Aurelius

Once you complete HardiCoping's mental part, it's time to turn to the actions that follow it. HardiCoping's mental process is very important because it frees us to solve the problem through renewed perspective and understanding that lowers our tension and frustration. But, just by changing how we think about a problem only gets us so far.

To get more comprehensive relief, we need to decisively act to transform the stressful circumstance out there in the world, where it began. Take, for example, performing poorly on a school or work assignment. By understanding what led you to perform poorly on the assignment, you may feel somewhat better. But, lasting relief comes when you put into action a plan for improving your performance on subsequent assignments. In the steps that follow, you will learn how to translate the mental insights of HardiCoping into decisive action steps.

Formulating A Plan

Goal Setting

In HardiCoping's first action step, you determine your action plan's main goal. Whether your goal is simple or complex, concrete or abstract, it's important that it expresses the perspective and understanding you gained by doing HardiCoping's mental process. Be clear about your goal, before you take action. An impulsive, ready, aim, and fire approach makes it likely that you will miss your target, despite all the effort.

By now, you have gained perspective and understanding concerning one stressful circumstance, by doing HardiCoping's mental processes. You reached this point through Situational Reconstruction or through its supplementation with Focusing. Or, perhaps, HardiCoping's mental process led you to a circumstantial given, which necessitated Compensatory Self-Improvement.

Whichever your route, you are now ready to formulate a main action plan goal, based on your Hardi-Coping process. Take a moment to think through the goal that once realized, will help you to turn around your stressful problem. You can write down your thought process, in Part 1, the HardiCoping Exercise 5 that follows, Formulating an Action Plan.

Steps To The Goal

Once, you formulate a main action plan goal, you outline the steps to realizing it. Usually goals are complicated enough that you can't just reach them with one step. Once again, it's important to think through the steps, before you take action. Just what concrete things can you do that will bring you even closer to that overall action plan goal? The more your steps relate to your goal, the greater your ability to carry out steps to transform the stressful situation from undermining to advantageous. You can formulate the steps to the goal in Part 2, the Hardi-Coping Exercise 5 that follows.

Establishing A Time Line

You now need a timeline for carrying out the steps of your action plan's main goal. It's important that you estimate accurately how long it will take you to realistically carry out these steps. Also, you may be tempted to drag out your time line, if some of the steps seem difficult or trying. We can also slip into naïve optimism. Here, we may naively take on too much and undermine our coping process, believing that it's easy to satisfy the steps to our goal. You can establish your steps' timeline in Part 3, the Hardi-Coping Exercise 5 that follows.

HardiCoping Exercise 5, Formulating An Action Plan

Part 1: What is the goal of your action plan? Be as specific as you can.

_____
_____
_____
_____

Part 2: What are the steps you will take that lead toward the goal? (Put them down in the order in which you will take them.)

_____
_____
_____
_____

Part 3: For each step, indicate when you will take it, and how long it is likely to take to complete.

_____
_____
_____
_____

How do you feel about your action plan? Can you think of any additional ways of increasing your likelihood of success in carrying it out? Write them down here:

_____

_____

_____

_____

If, in the process of carrying out your action plan, one or more of the steps doesn't seem to work, can you be prepared with contingencies? Write down how you might regroup, and try again, if necessary.

_____

_____

_____

_____

Summary Concepts And Terms

- Goal Setting
- Goal Steps
- Time Line

Test Your Knowledge

To test what you learned so far, see if you can correctly answer the following questions. Remember, the more information you have to think about what happens to you, the more building blocks you have to generate creative solutions to everyday living problems. This, in turn, strengthens your HardiAttitudes.

Commitment. The more information you seek to learn about yourself and the world, the more you demonstrate your belief that you are worthwhile and important enough to gather information that helps you.

Control. The more information you gather about yourself and your world, the greater your ability to influence the direction of your life.

Challenge. The effort you apply in learning the Hardiness skills shows that you regard the time spent in developing yourself as a normal challenge of life.

For the answer key, See "Questionnaire and Test Your Knowledge Answer Keys" on page 259.

1. In addition to perspective and understanding _____ is required for more comprehensive relief from HardiCoping.

2. The first action step of HardiCoping is _____.

3. Goal setting requires thinking through the _____ that bring you closer to your goal.

4. In an action plan, once you decided upon a goal and devised its steps, your next task is to develop a _____.

5. Taking action makes you feel you can influence your world. This HardiAttitude is _____.

6. Taking action signifies you believe you are worthwhile and important enough to do something about your life problems. This HardiAttitude is _____.

7. Taking action shows you believe skill development prepares you to face change positively and to regard life transition as grist for the mill. This HardiAttitude is _____.

Learning Goals

- Do you see how important goal setting is to formulating and implementing an action plan?

- Do you appreciate how by clearly defining a main action plan goal, you can more easily define the steps to carry it out?

- Do you understand the importance in formulating a manageable time line for carrying out the steps to your plan?

CHAPTER 5

HardiCoping: Carrying Out the Plan

Now that your action plan is complete, it is time to carry it out. Actually, the other HardiTraining program components may aid your efforts to carry out your plan. Your plan may involve improving your relationship to others. If so, Hardy Social Support knowledge and skills can enhance your coping effort's relational aspects. Or, perhaps your plan involves modifying eating, exercising, or relaxation habits. What you learn in the hardy relaxation, nutrition, and physical activity components can be quite helpful here. Practice in these other training components will increase the likelihood that you will successfully reach your action plan's goal.

How Feedback Builds HardiAttitudes

HardiCoping helps solve problems and decreases difficult situations stressfulness. This is a major reason for making HardiCoping a life habit. Another HardiCoping benefit, however, is that when you engage its problem-solving process, you build up self-esteem; this is what we call HardiAttitudes. Remember that Figure 1 on Page 4 in Chapter 1 has arrows running both ways that join the HardiCoping and HardiAttitudes boxes. There is a system here. HardiAttitudes motivate you to do the difficult work of HardiCoping. And, when you engage in this process, the HardiAttitude's of Commitment, Control, and Challenge grows in you. You can speed the process whereby HardiCoping builds HardiAttitudes by being especially sensitive to the feedback you get when you carry out your action plan.

Three Sources Of Feedback

OBSERVATIONS OF YOURSELF IN ACTION

What did you think of yourself when you implemented your action plan's steps? Did your attitude and behavior seem different than usual, perhaps, more constructive and better? Was it exciting, even maybe a little frightening to carry out these steps? When people decisively act, they like how it feels. Did you like seeing yourself this way? Did your new found self-confidence satisfy you?

OBSERVATIONS MADE OF YOU BY OTHERS

What did others think of you, as they observed you carrying out your action plan's steps? Did you seem different to them? If so, then how? Did they admire and appreciate your coping efforts? Or, were they threatened by your courage? Other's constructive observations of us hardily solving life's problems can be powerful feedback for strengthening our HardiAttitudes. So, become aware of how others see your new coping efforts. If your actions are well-planned and constructive, most people will value your efforts.

DIRECT REACTIONS TO YOUR PLANNED ACTIONS

What effects came about from carrying out your action plan's steps? Did you successfully produce changes in you, the circumstance, or others? Do you feel better off or worse from carrying out the steps?

What is it like to constructively influence a stressful circumstance's outcome? Most people feel relieved that there was something they could do to change the problem into an opportunity that strengthens their performance resources and furthers their development.

What is the process whereby HardiCoping builds up the HardiAttitudes of Commitment, Control, and Challenge in you? When you take the actions that follow from perspective and understanding, you are apt to feel more committed to, in control of, and positively challenged by, the problematic situation. This is true even if the circumstance remains somewhat stressful or if your actions are not completely successful. If you shrink back from stressful situations or avoid them altogether, HardiAttitudes vegetate. By proactively coping with stressful problems, you increase instead:

- Commitment: You involve yourself much more in daily living rather than hanging back.

- Control: You take steps that influence a stressful situation's outcome, which empowers you.

- Challenge: You find interest in your coping effort's effects. And, along the way, you open yourself up to learn from whatever happens.

Your coping efforts increase your three C's, especially with regard to the particular stressful circumstance on which you are working. If you use HardiCoping regularly, you will increasingly committ yourself to, stay in control of, and challenge yourself by the circumstances that form your life. By exercising HardiCoping, you increase HardiAttitudes and vice versa. Read the cases that follow to see how former HardiTraining trainees utilized feedback from carrying out HardiCoping actions.

People Who Formulated And Carried Out A Plan Of Action

Andy's Role Pressures

Do you remember Andy? By doing Situational Reconstruction, he gained perspective and understanding about his stressful circumstance. The goal of his action plan emerged. He worked to feel less overwhelmed by his schoolwork load, by organizing his time better, believing in himself more, and feeling more connected to school. The following steps came about, as what he needed to do to achieve his action plan's goal.

STEP 1. He needed to take his friends' and family's beliefs more seriously that he could be successful and that they supported his efforts.

STEP 2. He also needed to share his academic difficulties with his teachers, rather than seeing them as the enemy wanting to do him in.

STEP 3. Additionally, he needed to increase the hours he spent doing homework by scheduling social time with family and friends and work around academic responsibilities. He would worry less about failing school and stop wasting time feeling angry at his teachers.

He mentally rehearsed possible conversations that he'd have with his teachers, where he formulated questions, observations, and constructive ways to let them in on what he was doing. He also considered ways to tell family and friends how important they are to him, even though his new studying schedule might temporarily reduce how often he sees them. He then set about taking these steps in the order listed.

What feedback did Andy get from these efforts? He found his teachers surprisingly open to his suggestions. Further, Andy's fellow students reacted positively, in general. Most began to treat him like an in- rather than outsider. A few, of course, envied rather than supported him; they acted as if he sold himself out to his teachers.

By this time, however, Andy's self-confidence was so much better that he even tried to befriend the few people who resisted his attitude and behavior change. Andy's friends and family were surprisingly willing to support his efforts, even though, until his academic performance improved, it meant seeing him less frequently. They voiced to Andy their love and approval of him.

Andy, importantly, felt great about himself. He saw just how influential, competent, and constructive he could be once he tamed his own fears. The various feedback sources from carrying out his action plan deepened his Commitment (he once again valued his work and looked forward to each day), Control (he recognized just how much of a difference he could make), and Challenge (he really got into studying and learning from talking with the teachers). His HardiAttitudes grew stronger, and he became a more effective student, family member, and friend. And, additionally, his urges to overeat sweet and fatty foods and to drink wine diminished, which resulted in him steadily losing weight and keeping it off.

Barbara's Marriage

Through Situational Reconstruction, Barbara also developed enough perspective and understanding to develop an action plan. Its goal was to promote discussions with Bill that would lead to each making relationship compromises. By this, they could strengthen rather than destroy their love ties. The specific steps that she developed follow.

STEP 1. She wanted to talk with Bill in a loving way about how they both needed to compromise, if they were to stay together.

STEP 2. Additionally, she would work on accepting Bill's ways more, without detaching from him. She hoped through this, he too would become more accepting of her ways.

STEP 3. She also wanted them both to work on changing their ways in order to accommodate the other's needs and desires.

STEP 4. Finally, Barbara wanted to see if these steps would help them to fashion a life together.

Taking the first step was difficult for Barbara. They each slipped into defensiveness and self-justification modes at times. Despite this, Barbara used the her HardiTraining group's continuing social support to fashion interaction ground rules. Bill accepted them. These ground rules included valuing each other's viewpoints as being important and valid.

The second and third steps really expressed the old adage that loving involves more giving than receiving. Once they got into this interaction mode, their relationship got easier and easier for them. Before long, Bill was more organized and decisive, and Barbara was more laid back and accepting. The fourth step followed naturally from the others, and soon, they were talking about marriage.

In terms of feedback from her efforts, Barbara found that she could remain deeply involved in a relationship, even though it was not initially perfect (Commitment). Further, she recognized through Bill's reactions and her own observations that she could be as influential in personal relationships as in her schoolwork (Control). Finally, as the process of taking decisive actions unfolded, she felt really thrilled by what she was learning about herself, Bill, and their relationship and looked forward to the future (Challenge). Right after they graduated from college, they got married. When last heard from, Barbara was pregnant and ecstatic about it.

Sandra's Personal Triumph

Focusing in Sandra's quest to solve her home problem was significant. Through it, she realized that she had long ago bought into her parents' belief that because she was female, it was less important for her to develop her talents than it was for her brothers. By appreciating why and how she held herself back in life, she was able to formulate a decisive action plan. Her action plan's goal was to proactively use her talents and capabilities to improve her schoolwork and to simultaneously encourage her family to accept her as her brothers' equal. The following are the steps she took along the way.

STEP 1. She would counteract her ingrained tendency to passively give in to others' attitudes and dictates, by maintaining that the past is gone, along with the attitudes and feelings that she once let rule her.

STEP 2. She would also double her efforts to do well in college and to use its career counseling service to develop a career path that fit her talents.

STEP 3. And, when her schoolwork improved, she would take time to lovingly rather than destructively bring this to her parents' attention.

Although this was difficult at first, Sandra found that it became easier as she got into it. Throughout the day, Sandra examined her behaviors for passivity or new efforts to make a difference. When she behaved passively, she resolved to change that in the future. Soon, she worked up the courage to become more proactive. Her grades improved, she engaged herself more in schoolwork, and she interacted more with her teachers. Through career counseling, she began to work out for herself a career in law. She patiently and carefully communicated to her parents and siblings the ways in which she improved and her new career direction. When they reacted with disbelief, she persisted without expressing anger or defensiveness. When they expressed admiration, she accepted it without criticizing them for not having reacted that way earlier in her life. Soon, her parents bragged to their friends and extended family about their daughter's new confidence and resolve.

By now, the feedback you get by carrying out an action plan, and how it works to increase your HardiAttitudes, may be an old story to you. If that's so, then it's good. Sandra saw herself implementing changes and being valued by others for doing so. She involved herself in schoolwork as never before (Commitment), accepted her more influential role (Control), and looked excitedly toward every new day (Challenge).

By now, the role of feedback in increasing HardiAttitudes may be an old story to you. If so, good. Sandra saw herself implementing changes and being valued by others for doing so. She involved herself in schoolwork as never before (Commitment), accepted her more influential role (Control), and looked excitedly toward every new day (Challenge).

Cesar's Emergence As A Social Leader

Cesar came a long way from the angry homeowner railing out at neighborhood delinquents. Having needed Focusing to become unstuck, he was then able to find perspective and understanding. The goal of his action plan was to rid himself and his family of the threat posed by the delinquents. But he recognized that the only way to accomplish this was to pursue a win-win solution, as reflected in the steps he formulated. The steps were as follows.

STEP 1. He would explore what could be done to help the delinquents aspire to a more socially central and constructive life.

STEP 2. And, because this task was bigger than one person, he would enlist other interested adults to help him.

There were many substeps in this ambitious plan. First, Cesar went to the other middle-class people who were also buying into the neighborhood. They too were troubled about delinquency and agreed to help. Together, they visited the parents of the delinquents, most of whom still lived in the neighborhood. Many of these parents were worried about their youngsters sinking into criminality and danger but felt at a loss for what to do about it. All these adults banded together as a community organization. Those who could do it, contributed money to rent a storefront for the youngsters to use as a club house, and time to be big brothers and sisters, for the youngsters.

Of course, as the lives of the youngsters improved, and they had some real chance to join in the benefits of the larger society, they posed less of a neighborhood threat. The city's area square blocks really became a neighborhood. People cared about each other. Some of the youngsters and their parents became dear friends of Cesar and his family.

When last heard from, Cesar was giving talks in other troubled neighborhoods about how to overcome the problems of delinquency by win-win solutions. Can you imagine how Cesar felt as he carried out his action plan and received feedback from these efforts? Would it surprise you to know what a boost in commitment, control, and challenge he experienced?

David's Turnaround

Even David's insight into his fear, garnered through Focusing, did not get him unstuck in his attempts with Situational Reconstruction to ease the stress brought by his wife's breast cancer. He was confronting a given that he could not change and had to pick another related problem to work on instead in order to avoid bitterness and self-pity. That alternative problem was the deteriorated psychological state of their marriage. He could gain enough perspective and understanding of this alternative problem through Situational Reconstruction to emerge with an action plan.

The goal of his action plan was to recapture the intimacy and romance of his marriage. The steps involved were:

STEP 1. David wanted to talk with his wife about how and why they had drifted apart.

STEP 2. He further wanted to spend quality time doing mutually-interesting things together again.

They not only talked about how the cancer threat had pulled them apart but also considered problems that had existed in their marriage long before the cancer. As David found that his fear lessened through talking about it straightforwardly with his dear wife, her depression lifted at having been forsaken. They began going out to dinner, seeing friends, and doing a host of things that had been pushed into the background.

Two months later, at the alumni reunion of his HardiTraining group, David expressed himself to the others this way: "Well, my wife and I have been planning a trip around the world. I have accumulated so much vacation time it isn't funny, and we're going to use five weeks of it in the summer. We've been reading travel books, talking to friends and our travel agent, making plans. All the golf courses I want to play on are on the itinerary, and she'll tag along with me. All the museums she wants to see are on the itinerary, and I'll tag along with her. It's going to be great."

Then there was a reflective silence, following which he said, "You know, I don't even know if we will actually get to go—it depends on her condition. But I want you to know that the fun has been in the planning." David is doing wonderfully from the point of view of HardiAttitudes.

Betty's Blossoming

Once Betty failed at resolving the stresses of her boyfriend's romantic interest with another girl through Situational Reconstruction and Focusing, she too had to regain momentum through Compensatory Self-Improvement. The related problem she threw herself into was to overcome her phobia of skiing.

The goal of her action plan was to complete a skiing course at the local resort. Although this sounds simple, it was going to be difficult for her, given her depleted emotional state and her tremendous fear of the slopes. The following are the steps she formulated.

STEP 1. Betty would sign up and pay for the course.

STEP 2. She would attend the course sessions.

STEP 3. She would rely on her Hardiness Trainer and HardiTraining group for social support, whenever the going got rough.

STEP 4. Betty would also pass the skiing test. This, to her, marked a successful course completion.

In the first two steps, Betty badly needed not only the encouragement, but also the assistance of her HardiTraining group and Hardiness trainer. She had a mass of reasons why she couldn't afford the price of the course and was too busy to attend the sessions. When she did attend, she felt embarrassed when she would start to shake in fear as they mounted the heights. But we kept her at it, and soon it became easier for Betty to fulfill the steps of the action plan.

She even began to anticipate the skiing class sessions with a complex of fear and excitement. Then she actually began to be able to ski, and this was a real boost to her enthusiasm. Everyone in the skiing class gave her enthusiastic feedback. She was overwhelmed with excitement when she passed the skiing test and successfully completed the course. Soon, she was actually going on skiing weekends by herself, meeting others, and enjoying the newfound skills. The tremendous boost to her HardiAttitudes spilled over into all areas of her life. She had never felt so self-reliant and strong. And, of course,

her former boyfriend began to find her more attractive.

Now that you've completed reading the examples of people who carried out a decisive action plan to improve their lives, it's time for you to carry out yours. Remember, be sensitive to the feedback you receive and what it means to you. After you do this, be sure to write down your experiences to share with your Hardiness trainer.

HardiCoping Exercise 6, Using The Feedback You Got From Carrying Out Your Action Plan

DESCRIBE WHAT IT WAS LIKE CARRYING OUT YOUR ACTION PLAN:

_____

_____

_____

_____

FEEDBACK: OBSERVING YOURSELF SOLVING PROBLEMS: WHAT DID YOU THINK AND FEEL ABOUT YOURSELF AS YOU TOOK THE STEPS OF YOUR ACTION PLAN?

_____

_____

_____

_____

FEEDBACK: OBSERVATIONS OTHERS MADE OF YOU SOLVING PROBLEMS: WHAT DID THEY THINK AND FEEL ABOUT YOUR EFFORTS AS YOU TOOK THE STEPS OF YOUR ACTION PLAN?

_____
_____
_____
_____

FEEDBACK: THE EFFECTS OF CARRYING OUT YOUR ACTION PLAN: WHAT CHANGES DID YOU BRING ABOUT AS YOU TOOK THE STEPS OF YOUR ACTION PLAN?

_____
_____
_____
_____

Rate yourself on a scale from 0 to 100%

HOW SATISFIED ARE YOU WITH YOUR EFFECTIVENESS? _____

HOW MUCH HAS THE SITUATION DECREASED IN STRESSFULNESS? _____

HOW COMPLETELY IS THE PROBLEM RESOLVED?

_____

If your answers are 50% or more, you are doing great. Congratulations! If you are not satisfied with your efforts, don't give up. You may need to revise your action plan and try again. Perhaps you learned some things by trying this plan that provides a basis for revising it. If not, your Hardiness trainer can probably make suggestions. If you keep trying, you will succeed.

Using the feedback from all three sources, pinpoint the differences carrying out the action plan makes in your HardiAttitudes:

Commitment. On a scale from 0 to 100%, how much more do you feel involved or invested in, rather than distant or separate from, the problem you are trying to solve? _____.

Control. On a scale from 0 to 100%, how much more do you feel you can influence, rather than just give in to, the problem you are trying to solve? _____.

Challenge. On a scale from 0 to 100%, how much do you feel you are learning through your efforts to solve the problem, rather than just being disrupted by it? _____.

Remember: The more you react to stressful situations by developing perspective and understanding, and by carrying out action plans, the greater your sense of Commitment, Control, and Challenge will be even if you do not solve every problem every time.

EXERCISE END

Fourth And Final HardiCoping Checkpoint, Where Do We Go From Here?

At this point, you check in with your Hardiness Trainer to evaluate your learning thus far. Discuss your progress in formulating and carrying out your action plan. You are now on your way in the exciting adventure of HardiCoping. Remember, it's not the number or magnitude of stressful circumstances that does you in. Rather, it's failing to cope with them in a hardy way.

Summary Concepts And Terms

THREE FEEDBACK SOURCES:
OBSERVATIONS OF YOURSELF IN ACTION
OTHERS OBSERVATIONS OF YOU
FEEDBACK YOU GET FROM TAKING ACTION.

Test Your Knowledge

To test what you learned so far, see if you can correctly answer the following questions. Remember, the more information you have to think about what happens to you, the more building blocks you have to generate creative solutions to everyday living problems. This, in turn, strengthens your HardiAttitudes.

There are five questions on this quiz. Go back through the reading material to make sure you got the answers right. For the answer key, See "Questionnaire and Test Your Knowledge Answer Keys" on page 259.

Commitment. The more information you seek to learn about yourself and the world, the more you demonstrate your belief that you are worthwhile and important enough to gather information that helps you.

Control. The more information you gather about yourself and your world, the greater your ability to influence the direction of your life.

Challenge. The effort you apply in learning the Hardiness skills shows that you regard the time spent in developing yourself as a normal challenge of life.

1. The effects of your action plan is a form of feedback. Which kind? _____ _____.

2. What you think about yourself when you take action is the form of feedback called

   _____.

3. Observing yourself taking action builds the HardiAttitude of _____, because taking action involves you rather than waiting for things to change on their own.

4. Observing yourself taking decisive steps to solve your problems builds the HardiAttitude of _____, because you behave like you can positively influence your world.

5. Observations of yourself, others, and the direct effects of your action plan increases your interest to learn what comes when you engage yourself in the world. This builds the HardiAttitude of _____, because you regard change as grist for the mill.

Learning Goals

- Do you appreciate the relationship between the three major HardiCoping techniques of Situational Reconstruction, Focusing, and Compensatory Self-Improvement?

- Do you see how the three feedback sources builds up HardiAttitudes in you?

TABLE 1. **HardiCoping Decision Tree**
(Jensen, K. UVSC, 1998)

SITUATIONAL RECONSTRUCTION
WERE YOU ABLE TO PUT THE STRESSFUL CIRCUMSTANCE INTO A BROADER PERSPECTIVE? DID IT DEEPEN YOUR UNDERSTANDING OF THE PROBLEM?

Yes	No
If yes, then you develop an action plan and take action.	If no, do Focusing for emotional information.
If yes, try Situational Reconstruction again.	Did you access information through, Focusing that helped you to find relief this time, through Situational Reconstruction?
Did your second try at Situational Reconstruction help you to get unstuck?	No, then chances are your stressful circumstance is a given. Go to Compensatory Self-Improvement.

If yes, you develop an action plan.	If no, then chances are your stressful circumstance is a given.	Do Compensatory Self-Improvement again, using the tools of Situational Reconstruction.

Hardy Social Support

What Is Hardy Social Support?

Social interaction need not be a source of stress and strain; it can be a source of support instead. The right kind of social support can help motivate you to cope effectively with stress and to carry out a healthy lifestyle. Social support can decrease the likelihood of performance ineffectiveness.

What exactly is the right kind of social support that motivates and supports Hardi-Coping efforts? Research shows that there is a specific kind of social support that buffers people against stress, strain, and performance insufficiencies. When faced with stressful circumstances, hardy social assistance and encouragement supports your efforts to turn adversity to opportunity, vitalizing your performance and health.

This HardiTraining component forms three key areas of knowledge and skill sets that motivate you to engage in HardiCoping. These areas include Conflict Management, Communication, and Giving and Getting Social Support.

Conflict Resolution Skills

In this section, you learn about social conflict. Social conflict involves different attitudes or opinions toward a person, situation, or event that creates tension within you, or between you and others. Conflict disrupts interpersonal harmony. It can unsettle you biologically, mentally, and emotionally. Hardy people restore interpersonal harmony by HardiCoping efforts. If you are hungry or tired, you eat or sleep to restore biological harmony. When there is interpersonal conflict, Hardy people exercise the social support ideas and skills of this component to positive problem effectively and restore personal harmony.

Hardy Communication Skills

In this section, you learn basic communication principles and skills that are the basis for clear communication and social interaction. Poor communication skills can limit your ability to successfully negotiate conflict and to give and get adequate the social support you need to cope well. The more you mature in the hardiness process, the more you appreciate the importance of communicating well. Also, what you put out into the environment influences strongly what you get back. Confusing communications can lead to interpersonal misunderstandings and estrangement.

You do not have to literally speak a different language to have communication difficulty. To some degree, we all speak a different language in the ways we've learned to express ourselves. When your communication adequately expresses what you really want to say, the listener can respond in a way that makes you feel heard. To truly be intimate, you need good communication skills. Through a variety of techniques, Hardy Social Support trains you to communicate effectively. A specific set of communication resources helps you to get on line.

Giving And Getting Social Assistance And Encouragement

The knowledge and skills you learned thus far help you to give and get the kind of social support that encourages HardiCoping and the HardiAttitudes of Commitment, Control, and Challenge. We call this Hardy Social Support giving and getting encouragement and assistance for one's coping efforts.

These key areas of knowledge and skills help you to give and get the kind of social support that makes you feel **assured**. You feel:

Assisted Communicating clearly increases the probability that others can assist you because they understand what you want.

Secure You can bring about the support you need through Hardy Messenger Skills.

Satisfied Your Hardy Social Support skills increase the probability that your efforts result in win-win solutions to conflict.

Understood The message you put out in the environment matches your inner thoughts, needs, and feelings. Your messenger translation was effective.

Respected Your hardy direct support-giving skills make you a valued ally to your family, friends, and colleagues. Others trust and respect you because your message is clear.

Encouraged You can give and get the support you need.

Desirable Hardy Social Support skills, and the direct results you get from using them, enhance your self-esteem that further builds your HardiAttitudes and motivates your sense of yourself as a social being.

With Hardy Social Support, you feel assured of meaningful and supportive social, familial, and work relationships. Through constructive attitudes and skills, you become an invaluable friend, family member, colleague, and life partner.

In the section that follows, we address the quality and quantity of your social interactions that either inhibit or enhance your hardiness. You can review your HardiSurvey III-R® scores as you read through this section. Think about your work support and family support scores and how they relate to your overall hardiness, stress, and strain scores.

Your Social Support Network

Functions Of Social Support

For many, it is difficult to establish a solid social support network. This is especially true today. We work longer because of technological advancements and globalization pressures, which decreases the time we spend with other people. Loneliness plagues many of us, today.

There are those who still feel lonely despite a filled up social calendar. Perhaps, you can recall a time yourself when, either through conflict or dissimilar interests, the social interaction dissatisfied you.

The quality of relationship that you give to and get from others influences your HardiCoping efforts. In this section, you think through the quantity and quality of your social network. What types of friendship do we provide to others or do others provide to us? Do you get your friendship needs met by family members rather than coworkers or vice versa? Do you have people in your life who you can

turn to for emotional support? If you actively participate in daily life, you have many opportunities to satisfy your social needs.

The are five **friendship support functions** that we can get from and give to others.

MENTOR FRIENDSHIP

This is social support that is based upon your or another person's knowledge and experience. A partner who champions your growth as a person, professional, parent, or spouse, and offers whatever resources he/she has to further your development in these areas, provides you with mentor friendship.

MATERIAL FRIENDSHIP

This is social support that is based upon help that provides goods or services, such as food, money, transportation, baby-sitting, clothing, or a place to live.

EMOTIONAL SUPPORT FRIENDSHIP

This is social support that is based upon understanding and empathy and can involve love. A friend, for example, appreciates, respects, and supports your life struggles both within and outside the relationship.

ACTIVITY FRIENDSHIP

This social support function is the sharing of specific activities with people in our lives. Book clubs, sports, movies, and restaurants are just some of the things we like to share with people in our social network.

WORK OR SCHOOL FRIENDSHIP

This is social support that comes from friends, family, teachers, employers, or coworkers that is based upon teamwork efforts toward school, work, personal or family goals.

It is important to evaluate the ways in which you give and get friendship, because you may be missing some types of friendship that are important to your well-being. Intimate relationships usually satisfy at least four of the five friendship support areas. Most of us, however, vary in the kind of friendship we give to, and get from, others.

Some relationships, such as the one we have with our auto mechanic or bank representative, may not require emotional support. However, other more intimate relationships with family and friends need emotional friendship or else the relationship weakens. Relationships in general satisfy us more when they provide at least four out of the five friendship areas. Also, your core values determine to some degree the areas of friendship that you value. If, for example, you want emotional friendship from a sibling, and it is missing, you most likely suffer. In addition, if you desire mentorship at work, and you have none, your job becomes less satisfying, and this can negatively impact your health and performance.

What Makes Social Interactions Stressful?

To improve your social interactions as well as your social support network, you need to understand the general reasons why social interactions become stressful. Stressful social interactions can be a potent source of strain. They can sap your motivation to do HardiCoping and to take care of yourself. Chronic dissatisfaction with your social experience can lead to insufficient performance, illness, weight loss or gain, and unhappiness and apathy about life.

Reasons For Social Stress

There are five general reasons why a social interaction may become conflicted. If any of these potential sources for social stress take place, you need to acknowledge and skillfully navigate them or else social conflict results. The five reasons include:

- Someone may expect something of you that: a) you don't know about, b) you don't want to give, or c) you don't know how to manage, and thus feel incapable of adequately managing the problem.

- You may expect something of others that: a) they don't know about, b) they don't want to give, or c) they don't know how to manage, and thus feel incapable of adequately managing the problem.

- There may be a confrontation between you and another person that you don't like and run away from.

- There may be misunderstandings that pile up.

- You, or a person you are in a relationship with, may be too preoccupied with other problems to show attention and caring.

When a relationship involves these sources of stress, the probability of conflict increases significantly. When you listed chronic stresses in the HardiCoping component of this HardiTraining workbook, some of the mentioned relationships were most likely conflicted. As you can imagine, if you have a number of conflicted social interactions—daily, weekly—that leave you feeling misunderstood, under-appreciated, and put-upon, the world can begin to feel like a hostile place. Due to a lack of supportive relationships, you can actually begin to question whether your life has any meaning. When social interactions go sour, it is time to get to work on your conflict management skills.

Hardy Social Support Exercise 1, Identifying Your Social Support Network

In this exercise, you evaluate your current social support network in various areas in your life. You further evaluate the functions these social support networks provide you. In doing this, you get a clear picture of your life relationships and if they are capable of enhancing your coping efforts and well-being. Although most of us know if we are lonely, or if a relationship troubles us, it's rare for us to evaluate carefully the quantity and quality of our social network. We give you this opportunity now. There are three parts to this exercise.

Part A. Think about some people in your life who socially support you. Jot down their names. See if you can come with at least five people. Some of you will have less and others more.

Name

_____

_____

_____

_____

_____

_____

_____

_____

_____

Part B. Review the list of supportive friendships that you created in part A. Now, you will evaluate each person for the relationship area that characterizes the type of relationship (family member, friend, boss, colleague, church member, coworker, or other), and one or more of the five supportive friendship functions the person fulfills (mentor, material, emotional, activity, and work). Some people fulfill more than one friendship support type, this is especially true the more intimate and deep the relationship connection. You will also rate, across all supportive functions, how satisfied you are with the support you are getting in this relationship.

Relationship 1:

Name:

Relationship Area:

_____

Mentor Friendship 0   25   50   75   100%

Material Friendship 0   25   50   75   100%

Emotional Friendship 0   25   50   75   100%

Activity Friendship 0 25 50 75 100%

Work Friendship 0 25 50 75 100%

Relationship 2:

Name:

Relationship Area:

Mentor Friendship 0 25 50 75 100%

Material Friendship 0 25 50 75 100%

Emotional Friendship 0 25 50 75 100%

Activity Friendship 0 25 50 75 100%

Work Friendship 0 25 50 75 100%

Relationship 3:

Name:

Relationship Area:

Mentor Friendship 0 25 50 75 100%

Material Friendship 0 25 50 75 100%

Emotional Friendship 0 25 50 75 100%

Activity Friendship 0 25 50 75 100%

Work Friendship 0 25 50 75 100%

Relationship 4:

Name:

Relationship Area:

Mentor Friendship 0 25 50 75 100%

Material Friendship 0 25 50 75 100%

Emotional Friendship 0 25 50 75 100%

Activity Friendship 0 25 50 75 100%

Work Friendship 0 25 50 75 100%

Relationship 5:

Name:

Relationship Area:

Mentor Friendship 0 25 50 75 100%

Material Friendship 0 25 50 75 100%

Emotional Friendship 0 25 50 75 100%

Activity Friendship 0 25 50 75 100%

Work Friendship 0 25 50 75 100%

Reflect upon your responses to Part B of this exercise.

Are you satisfied with the support you get from the people you list in this exercise? Rate how much. I am _____% satisfied.

Least 0 10 20 30 40 50 60 70 80 90 100% Most

Part C. If you found that you are dissatisfied with your social support experience, answer the following questions. that highlight personal tendencies that may contribute to your social support experience and satisfaction.

Circle the percentage that applies to you.

1. Do you feel confident in your ability to express your observations, thoughts, needs, and feelings to people?

   No 0 10 20 30 40 50 60 70 80 90 100% Yes

2. Does your inability to manage conflict in relationships stop you from getting certain kinds of social support from others?

   No 0 10 20 30 40 50 60 70 80 90 100% Yes

3. Are you hesitant to provide certain functions of social support to those around you?

No 0 10 20 30 40 50 60 70 80 90 100% Yes

4. Are you better at providing some functions of social support than others?

No 0 10 20 30 40 50 60 70 80 90 100% Yes

5. Are you more comfortable receiving some functions of social support than others?

No 0 10 20 30 40 50 60 70 80 90 100% Yes

6. Are you more comfortable receiving social support from one area of experience over another (e.g. family, work, significant other, or church)?

No 0 10 20 30 40 50 60 70 80 90 100% Yes

7. Do you fear developing meaningful relationships with those who have some kind of authority over you?

No 0 10 20 30 40 50 60 70 80 90 100% Yes

8. Do you believe certain functions of social support (mentor, emotional, financial, activity, work) are taboo in certain areas of living experience (e.g. family, employment, significant other, church, or school)?

No 0 10 20 30 40 50 60 70 80 90 100% Yes

Your awareness of your current social support network prepares you for the training to come. As you learn the skills that help you to get and give meaningful and satisfying social support, please think about your ratings in this and how your new skills might improve your current situation.

EXERCISE END

First Hardy Social Support Checkpoint

Please check in with your Hardiness Trainer at this point to evaluate your learning thus far.

Summary Concepts And Terms

FRIENDSHIP SUPPORT FUNCTIONS: MENTOR, MATERIAL, EMOTIONAL, ACTIVITY, AND SCHOOL/WORK

ASSURED

FIVE REASONS FOR SOCIAL STRESS

Test Your Knowledge

To test what you learned so far, see if you can correctly answer the following questions. Remember, the more information you have to think about what happens to you, the more building blocks you have to generate creative solutions to everyday living problems. This, in turn, strengthens your HardiAttitudes.

Commitment. The more information you seek to learn about yourself and the world, the more you demonstrate your belief that you are worthwhile and important enough to gather information that helps you.

Control. The more information you gather about yourself and your world, the greater your ability to influence the direction of your life.

Challenge. The effort you apply in learning the Hardiness skills shows that you regard the time spent in developing yourself as a normal challenge of life.

For the answer key, See "Questionnaire and Test Your Knowledge Answer Keys" on page 259.

1. You call interactions with others that motivate you to cope effectively with sources of stress _____.

2. Differing attitudes or opinions toward a person, situation, or event that create tension between you and another person are called _____ _____.

3. The word that describes how you feel when you use the Hardy Social Support techniques is _____.

4. Social Support based upon mutual enjoyment of certain activities is _____.

5. Social Support based upon your or another's knowledge and experience is _____.

6. When someone expects something of you that you don't know about, or want, or there is a confrontation between you and another that makes the social relationship stressful, this is called _____.

Learning Goals

• Do you understand the Hardiness definition of social support?

• Do you know the three techniques that comprise Hardy Social Support?

• Do you know the five things that make a social interaction stressful?

CHAPTER 7 *Stressful Social Interactions*

There are times when, despite your best intentions, a social interaction goes awry. Stressful social interactions can result in interpersonal conflict. If you want to avoid such conflict, you must possess effective conflict resolution skills to bring about constructive solutions to problems that satisfy your goals and aims.

Ineffective Ways To Manage Conflict

We sometimes interact with people whose inadequate social skills cause conflict between them and us. If we possess effective conflict resolution skills, we can do a lot to sidestep problems that arise in these situations. There are some personal attributes and characteristics that can contribute to our inability to effectively manage social conflict.

- When you get so emotionally aroused that it disorganizes your thoughts and ability to reflect upon circumstance, this causes you to impulsively act.

- When you lack the necessary skills to effectively manage conflicted social interactions.

- When your attitude about social conflict causes you to respond maladaptively to it.

Sometimes we behave more constructively when the relationship is of the sort that is easily broken. At work, for example, it is important for us to preserve the relationship because we can easily be terminated. Also, with friends we put our best foot forward and make attempts to take into account the other person's needs so that they don't drop us. Unfortunately, with family, sometimes we make the damaging assumption that the special blood or kinship ties means tolerating behavior that no one besides your family would tolerate.

Let's turn our attention now to the attitudes and skills you need to learn and build in order to turn interpersonal conflict from a social disaster into an opportunity for Hardy Social Support. You begin by taking a minute to jot down some words you generally associate with conflict.

_____

_____

_____

_____

Across several cultures, the most common associations to conflict included: fight, anger, pain, war, impasse, destruction, fear, mistake, avoid, lose, control, hate, loss, bad, unnecessary, negative, and wrongdoing. History and folklore show that when there is conflict, people are killed, imprisoned, exiled, beaten upon, segregated, or isolated. We have learned many destructive ways of reacting to conflict.

In order to cope more effectively with conflict, you first need to review your attitude toward conflict and change it if necessary. Hardy Social Support encourages the kind of social interaction that endorses and facilitates human relatedness, and embraces conflict as one more opportunity for professional and personal development. There is both an illness-producing and a health-enhancing view of conflict. Take a moment to examine these differences in viewpoint.

Views Of Conflict

Hardiness Inhibiting

1. Conflict is a negative experience to be avoided at all costs.
2. Conflict is a war between two immovable forces.
3. Conflict is an event that is so terrible that it defines, and thus can destroy, the entire relationship.
4. Conflict involves opinions and values that need to be defended against.

Hardiness Enhancing

1. Conflict is an expression of different observations, thoughts, needs, and feelings that can lead to improved understanding, compromise, and a more satisfying relationship.
2. Conflict is a normal aspect of the relationship that can clear the way for healthier interactions that work better for both parties.
3. Conflict is an isolated event that does not define the entire relationship.
4. Conflict involves a difference in opinions and values that when handled with respect and tolerance can increase understanding and meaning for both parties.

Hardy Social Support Exercise 2, Ineffective Conflict Management Questionnaire

Before you proceed, complete the following questionnaire. Each question asserts a tendency, attitude or behavior about how one manages social conflicts. Decide if a question is true or false about you. You then read through the next section on Ineffective Conflict Management Styles, and next evaluate your answers to see which style(s) may apply to you (See "Questionnaire and Test Your Knowledge Answer Keys" on page 259.). Six of the thirty questions that follow highlight one of the five ineffective styles. The more true items that you endorse in a particular style category, the more likely you are to resort to its behaviors when stressed.

1. In a social conflict, I keep my feelings inside and don't say what bothers me. True False

2. People see me as easygoing, but I surprise them occasionally with sudden anger. True False

3. When someone troubles me, I stay away from him or her. True False

4. When people get upset with me, I tell them to lighten up. True False

5. I tell people they are ridiculous when they make a mountain out of a mole hill. True False

6. At work, I prefer not to socialize with subordinates. True False

7. In a conflict, you give away power when you don't negotiate. True False

8. In a conflicted situation, I bargain until I get my way. True False

9. I do not like being told I'm wrong by someone who clearly has less education and experience than I do. True False

10. In a conflict, I will not say I'm sorry unless the other person says it as well. True False

11. I believe everyone must give something when there's conflict. True False

12. When I manage an activity, I want others to just follow what I say.   True False

13. Social conflict is always messy. True False

14. In social conflicts, I often raise my voice. True False

15. I'll do whatever it takes, including threat, to get a person to do what I want. True False

16. I threaten abandonment, if I don't get what I want in a conflicted situation. True False

17. I walk away when a social interaction bothers me. True False

18. I stop listening and talking when I hear something that troubles me. True False

19. When someone confronts me, I act as if I don't know why he/she is making such a big deal out of it. True False

20. I expect associates to address me by my title. True False

21. I laugh when someone says something that threatens me. True False

22. My friends tell me that I am sarcastic. I tell them they should learn how to take a joke. True False

23. Conflict always involves anger. True False

24. Agreement is the most important thing in conflict. True False

25. Staying with the content in a conflicted interaction is more important than dealing with underlying feelings. True False

26. I believe people in authority should not be confronted. True False

27. I play the martyr when I'm bothered by something a person does or says. True False

28. I don't like people whom I manage to ask about my personal life. True False

29. I call names and swear if I do not get my way. True False

30. It is best to ignore rude or aggressive behavior. True False

QUESTIONNAIRE END

Five Ineffective Conflict Management Styles

There are five ineffective ways to manage conflict that can lead to ineffective performance, morale, conduct, and health. We'll review these ineffective ways, now.

Conflict Withdrawer

Some people believe that if they withdraw from conflict and pretend that it did not happen, it will go away. Withdrawers are so afraid of conflict that they have managed to limit the range and intensity of relationships just to make sure they avoid conflict. Some Withdrawers pretend there is no conflict because they don't have the skills necessary to resolve it. Let's look at different types of conflict Withdrawers.

THE CASE OF
AMY: CONFLICT
WITHDRAWER #1

Amy was very depressed. She sought therapy because she had just divorced her third husband. She was bitter because all her relationships had ended so miserably. Lonely and discouraged, she began to count the reasons why her relationships didn't last.

The first husband, she reports, came from a different social and economic background than hers, and this, she believed, got in the way of their relationship. The second marriage was to a rebound husband, she stated. Scared and lonely, she married him too soon and did not know he was "the kind of person that he turned out to be." The third husband,

she states, was uninterested in parenting her children. This she could not cope with.

Amy thought she had bad luck when it came to men. She did not see that her lack of self-awareness, inability to speak her mind, and emotional dishonesty factored into the relationship problems. Actually, Amy's short-term marriages, regardless of her rationalizations, show her lack of skill to cope effectively with relationships and associated relationship conflict. Learning emotional honesty and working through conflicts in her relationships would have deepened her as a person. This would benefit her, her spouse, and her children. It may have been true that these men weren't the best matches for her, but with better conflict resolution skills, she would have at least grown more in each relationship, helping to make her next relationship decision more thoughtful and mature. Also, to think that best matches just like soul mates happen magically is fairy tale stuff. People become best matches and soul mates only when they are developmentally mature enough to work through relationship difficulties.

THE CASE OF
TOM: CONFLICT
WITHDRAWER #2

Tom described himself as a "wimp." He felt under-appreciated and overworked both at home and at his job. As his boss piled on more and more work, he reminded Tom about the tough job market and how grateful people should be today to have a good job. Tom describes himself as a creative person who enjoys helping his children with homework and taking them on outings. At home he enjoys remodeling and home repairs. He feels his wife does not appreciate his talents. The only time Tom gets feedback from his wife, according to him, is when he either hasn't paid the bills on time or hasn't organized his home office.

Tom has built up personal resentments for several years now. He avoids confronting his boss and his wife because he views conflict as unfriendly and unpleasant. He stated, "If I tell my boss I feel under-appreciated, he may think I'm criticizing him." Tom is clearly the kind of person who avoids conflict because he regards it as a problem that is detrimental to everyone involved. Whatever reason a person may find to withdraw from rather than cope with conflict, it is never productive. Rather, conflict withdrawing:

- Prevents involved parties from opportunities to learn better coping skills.

- Leads to the harboring of unexpressed feelings and relationship pressures.

- Stops the parties from clarifying their relationship and working to improve it

Leveling The Playing Field

This ineffective way of managing conflict involves a process in which each person involved must give up the same amount, no matter what the disagreement is about. This conflict management technique does not consider people's views, needs, and feelings, to say nothing of claim legitimacy, insisting instead that each person must concede equivalent ground. Many parents use this conflict management technique when dealing with their children. It does not teach personal responsibility.

THE CASE OF ELIZABETH

Elizabeth managed conflict through leveling. Her two teenage girls were at the age where they did not get along well. There was one phone line in the house, and after school each day, each girl wanted to spend long hours on the phone with her friends. Elizabeth wanted to find a solution to this problem so, from four to seven each day, she permitted each girl to have 90 minutes talking to friends with 30 minutes allotted per friend. If Suzie had the first 30-minute phone call, Tami got the next 30 minutes, and vice versa. Every 30 minutes they rotated who got to use the phone. Elizabeth thought this compromise would solve the problem. What she did not take into account was that the girls still did not like each other, and the compromise did not increase their ability to take each other's feelings and needs into account. The only thing the girls learned was that sometimes you have to give up something to get what you want; an arithmetic of concessions. Some of the leveling the playing field problems include:

1. People who use this social conflict strategy never learn that it's okay to say, I'm sorry or to attend to others' feelings and needs, without demanding something from them. Leveling the playing field does not promote intimacy; maintaining control is the issue.

2. People who use this social conflict strategy consider dispute facts more important than relationship.

3. People who use this social conflict strategy define agreement as more important than anything else.

4. People who use this social conflict strategy misunderstand what it means to have win-win social-interaction solutions. We only really win when we learn how to address others' concerns without manipulating situations for false empowerment.

Emotional Bullying

Emotional bullying is another kind of ineffective conflict resolution that disrespects the other person's position and needs. Some youngsters learn, through modeling others' behaviors, that conflict is a battle that must be won for fear of losing advantage and power. People who manage conflict in this way are bullies.

But beneath the bully's tough exterior is often a person who is very afraid of being taken advantage of. Others probably took advantage of them in their childhood. To protect themselves, they learned that the best defense is an offense. As a result, they have not learned the coping skills for constructive conflict resolution and are not aware that conflict can actually be growth-promoting rather than growth-inhibiting.

For those of you who are familiar with the TV show *Titus,* you know too well the kind of solutions Papa Titus finds to problems. Because he is into emotional bullying, he never entertains the accomplishments of Titus or his brother, but instead focuses only on winning and maintaining his power in the relationship, and this often means destroying the psychological health of his sons. The family values and ways of interacting show that the important thing to the family is advantage and power. Papa Titus is an extreme example, but all of us can think of a time when someone we knew used this strategy for conflict management.

THE CASE OF MARISSA

Marissa was 24 years old and one year into her first marriage. In her early twenties, she had dated a man who was verbally and physically abusive to her. Further, during her childhood, she witnessed her alcoholic father beat her mother every time he was unhappy about something. Marissa had a history of relationships with people who were emotionally out of control, and who dominated others to gain advantage and power in relationships. She vowed to never let anyone take advantage of her again. Fearful that she was too passive to handle tough relationships, she developed an aggressive, problem-solving style that helped her with ruthless people. This style kept her from being verbally and physically abused, but prevented the kind of closeness where both persons' needs and feelings are considered and valued. Marissa was so caught up in protecting herself that she had no time to consider others' needs. Her tendency to be preoccupied with self-protection limited her awareness of other people's feelings.

Her first year of marriage was rocky. Because she was so busy defending her relationship territory, she managed conflict in ways that denied her husband the right to have his needs considered. She feared others taking advantage of her, which made her socially aggressive at times. She pushed others away from her, even those who had her welfare in mind. Fortunately, Marissa was in psychotherapy, which helped her to work through her dominating interactional style. Through this process, she became aware that she had become her own worst enemy; she was the aggressor that she feared others to be.

Hiding Behind A Mask

Hiding behind a mask is another ineffective conflict management technique. Some hide behind social masks in order to avoid experiencing and dealing with conflict. In a conflicted situation, it's a problem when you mask yourself in your role as boss, employee, parent, child, doctor, patient, teacher, or student in order to protect yourself from facing the conflict honestly. These social masks only protect you from true human relatedness. Hiding behind a mask during confrontation usually serves to frustrate and demean the other party, and deprives you both of true intimacy. Have you ever had a person tell you, "You'll do it because I told you so?" Or, "Because I'm teacher, parent, or spouse, it's my way." Ouch!

THE CASE OF MARTIN, THE MASKED MAN

Martin, chief financial officer of a large manufacturing company, is valued by his company for his financial skills, but unappreciated by his department staff because of his authoritarian ways. The staff members' anonymous reports indicated that interacting with him frequently made them feel stupid, inferior, and like children. They found him uninterested in them as people. When staff members made attempts to confront his rude behavior, they reported he responded with anger or an icy silence. His department members felt undermined and hopeless. As long as Martin was playing the role of boss and punitive parent, his staff felt they had no other options but to quit. Martin's employers could not risk losing such valuable, long-term employees so they moved to rectify this situation. The human resource department sent Martin for professional executive coaching. Executive coaching revealed Martin's belief that the business environment was not a place in which to develop relationships. He believed in his own authority and felt others just had to accept this. In order to please his employers, he worked superficially on his atti-

tude, but deep down inside, he believed he did not need to change.

Martin had a lot to learn about relationships in general. In Martin's childhood, it's highly probable that someone behaved toward him in a masked role, as he now behaves toward others. Assuming the masked role of boss was his attempt to avoid the personal risks inherent in relationships. He feels that taking the mask off means losing authority ground. Disguising his true self through the boss role means he does not have to recognize others' need for respect. But most importantly, the mask hid extreme emotional vulnerability. Further, his mask hid his poor social skills. As you can see, hiding behind a mask undermines conflict resolution because it:

- Unproductively exploits power differentials in relationships.
- Stops people in less socially powerful roles from making contributions.
- Restricts ways of resolving the conflict, and thus inhibits intimacy.
- Creates unnecessary hatred of the person hiding behind the mask.

Conflict Trivializing

A person who manages conflict by finding the quickest, easiest way out of the problem trivializes the situation on hand. A quick fix is a way to avoid opening up the conflict because it might show one's vulnerabilities or lack of effective problem-solving skills. In this process, the person minimizes the conflict, rather than taking it seriously. Let's take a look at a quick fix to a social conflict.

THE CASE OF
MARJORIE AND
SAMANTHA

Marjorie and Samantha are good friends. For several years, every time they plan to do something socially together, Samantha shows up late or changes the plans at the last minute. Many of these times, Marjorie had cleared her day at considerable effort in order to be free to spend time with her friend. Marjorie began to realize that her friend's lateness pattern was chronic. She felt irritated and wondered if Samantha valued their friendship. Marjorie began to see Samantha socially less and less, and to commit to social engagements with her only when it was convenient. Deciding never to go out of her way for Samantha protected Marjorie from being hurt.

Marjorie had put a quick fix on the problem by arranging to care less (decreased social time spent with Samantha), so that her feelings would not get hurt. She did not give Samantha the opportunity to realize the problem and react to it. So, Marjorie failed to use this conflict as a way to deepen their relationship by expressing her needs and feelings and letting Samantha do the same. Conflict trivialization does not work because it:

- Glosses over a problem, which can actually worsen it because it remains unresolved.

- Deprives the parties to the problem of the chance to learn better coping skills and deepen the relationship.

- Decreases your self-esteem because, somewhere deep inside, you know the problem hasn't been solved due to your not being brave enough to confront it openly.

Hardy Conflict Management Techniques

A Constructive Mind-Set Goes A Long Way

The information and techniques that follow help you to successfully manage social conflict. A constructive mind-set is the first step in finding solutions to stressful social problems that preserve the integrity of the relationship. When you start off on the right foot, you are more apt to generate perspective and understanding that leads to constructive solutions. The following relationship principle helps you to do just that.

IN THE SERVICE
OF THE
RELATIONSHIP
PRINCIPLE

How often do you find others, or yourself, verbalizing interest in furthering a relationship, but behaving in ways that result in its ending rather than improving? If you wish to further a relationship, you need to maintain attitudes about it that service its health and longevity. You begin by accepting the assumption that two parties make up a relationship whole. This relationship entity can be an association between you and a meaningful other, a family member, your employer, your academic institution, your church, or some other person or institution.

If you want to preserve and enhance a relationship, whether it is related to school, work, friendship, or family, you must behave in ways that positively service it. If you want a plant to grow, you nourish it with water and minerals. You nourish a relationship with thoughts, feelings, and behaviors that help it grow in a meaningful way, if you wish to preserve it. This principle is a useful framework that guides your social interactions by helping you to respect the needs, values, goals, feelings, and interests of those who make up the relationship. It helps you to consider others' realities, as important to them as yours is to you. Mutual respect helps you to find satisfying social conflict solutions, which makes all parties feel, heard, appreciated, and valued. When you behave constructively, your sincerity shows. The In the Service of the Relationship Principle leads to social experiences that strengthens hardiness in you and your social community. Three key actions sustain this principle. These include:

Empathy. You sincerely attempt to understand the conflicted situation. You further step into the person's shoes by acknowledging that he/she, like all others, desires appreciation and understanding. You approach the interaction with the knowledge that all people desire authentic recognition by another.

Generosity And Kindness. Even if the social interaction is confusing or challenging, you remain open to, and generous and kind toward, the communication and the person. You acknowledge personhood beneath the communicated message and orient your responses toward this.

Responsibility. You position yourself to take fifty percent responsibility for a conflicted social interaction problem. No matter how outrageous you perceive the problem to be, you attempt to maintain this performance-, morale-, conduct-, and health-enhancing social interaction stance.

When you exercise this principle, you convey that:
- Your personal and community values center you; from this center, you act responsibly.

- You work to resist unfair and destructive conflict management strategies, no matter how conflicted a social interaction becomes.

Responsible action assures that, in social conflict you respond to others empathically, generously, and kindly. Conflicted social interactions do challenge our ability to exercise this valuable social principle, especially when tensions run high. Disappointment, fear, anger, and hurt can be so strong for involved parties that it temporarily suspends our desire to behave responsibly. If we get our emotions under control, we do a lot to defuse unproductive thoughts and emotions; this is the first step to positively servicing social relationships. Now, in this less-charged atmosphere, you are more likely to find hardy resolutions to social problems.

This assures that you respond socially with empathy, generosity, kindness, and responsibility. It can be challenging to try to maintain the above principle in a conflicted situation when tensions can run high. Emotions of disappointment, fear, anger, and hurt can be strong for all participants. The first step in implementing this principle is to find ways to get the emotions under control, to defuse the situation, to decrease the tension. Once the atmosphere is less charged, it is more likely that a conflict resolution will be found.

THE CASE OF KAREN

In this case, Karen's short-sighted perspective and understanding undermined her stressful situation coping efforts and compromised her work relationships. Karen regards herself as a valuable employee of the construction firm, for which she works. She's worked overtime whenever needed, and her performance reviews always highlighted her energetic and capable ways. Her company valued her talent and saw her as highly dependable. In the last year, however, things changed. Karen's personal stresses created conflict between her and her employer.

Karen's current romantic relationship stresses her. Her employer sees this problem as undermining her work performance. Work superiors noted Karen's lengthy personal phone calls, absenteeism, and moodiness as examples of her deteriorating work performance. Karen, however, does not see it this way. She maintains that "As long as I do my job, they shouldn't care about my personal life." Karen further disliked her company's contradictory company policy message. "They promote a family atmosphere, yet are intolerant of my personal problems." This outraged her.

Karen couldn't wait to "give them a piece of my mind." They are "hypocrites," she states. "I dislike working for an unsympathetic employer." As soon as possible, she'd tell them what she thought about this situation. Her employer began to lose patience with her and became more upset by Karen's unproductive work relationship behaviors.

Karen clearly did not let the In the Service of the Relationship Principle guide her during this stressful time. She focused solely on her perceptions, needs, and feelings, but not those of her employer. She sabotaged work relationships by rationalizing her hurt and anger with flimsy justifications. This harmed her work future, with this employer. She burned relationship work bridges, which increased her potential for poor performance reviews or getting fired. It seems, her stressful romantic relationship undermined her judgment much more than she realized. Karen needed to broaden her perspective and deepen her understanding of this stressful work situation. This would have served her well on many levels.

1. She would be able to cool down, thereby reducing out of control emotions, which confirmed her employer's misgivings about her.

2. She would also more accurately evaluate her employers' perceptions, needs, and goals. Then, she could take action that would positively service her relationship to her employer.

Thus, by broadening your perspective and deepening your understanding of a social conflict, you cool down and work positively to resolve the problem. HardiCoping tools help you to do this.

In Situational Reconstruction, you describe the conflict, then think through how it could become worse and how it could become better, and finally consider what steps you can take to stop it from becoming worse and help it to become better. Thinking through alternatives can lead you to a broadened perspective and deepened understanding of the conflict.

If Situational Reconstruction does not by itself lead to perspective and understanding, it can be supplemented with Focusing, which is another HardiCoping technique that helps you realize the emotional reactions you are having to the conflict. Recognizing your emotional reactions often frees you to find perspective and understanding.

In any event, broadened perspective helps you to cool down, and deepened understanding helps you to decide on constructive courses of action. HardiCoping can help us appreciate how assumptions and expectations others and ourselves bring to situations may clash, producing conflict. It can alert us to how the way we perceive ourselves, others, relationships, and situations have much to do with our upbringing. During our childhood, adolescence, and adulthood, we have accumulated a variety of beliefs and attitudes that lead us to perceive what happens to us in certain ways.

For example, if you grew up in a family that was boisterous, expressive of feelings, and argumentative, you might view the television sitcom *Roseanne* as a slice of American life and find the episodes entertaining. In contrast, if you were raised in a family that valued emotional reserve and socially polite behavior, you might perceive this sitcom as shocking and evidence of what's wrong with American life.

Because we perceive something in a certain way, we tend to think it is that way, and we often base our behavior on that perception. Confusing your perception with actual reality causes strain for you and others. Karen, for example, reacted to her employers' limits on her behavior as insensitive and hypocritical. Karen's parents were often insensitive and hypocritical; thus she tended to perceive authority figures, such as employers, as doing the same thing to her. Karen was so ready to tell her employers off that she did not take the time to find out what they really were thinking and feeling. Nor did she give sufficient weight, in her angry reaction, to their previous approval and support of her.

It is time now for you to take the first step of Hardi-Coping by using Situational Reconstruction, supplemented by Focusing, if need be, to begin to resolve a social conflict you are having. But remember to search for a solution that positively services the relationship.

Second Hardy Social Support Checkpoint

Please check in with your Hardiness Trainer at this point to evaluate your learning thus far.

Summary Concepts And Terms

BULLY

CONSTRUCTIVE MIND-SET TO SOLVE SOCIAL PROBLEMS

EMPATHY

FIVE INEFFECTIVE CONFLICT MANAGEMENT TECHNIQUES

GENEROSITY AND KINDNESS

IN THE SERVICE OF THE RELATIONSHIP PRINCIPLE

LEVELER

MASK-HIDER

RESPONSIBILITY

TRIVIALIZER

VIEWS OF CONFLICT

WITHDRAWER

Test Your Knowledge

To test what you learned so far, see if you can correctly answer the following questions. Remember, the more information you have to think about what happens to you, the more building blocks you have to generate creative solutions to everyday living problems. This, in turn, strengthens your HardiAttitudes.

Commitment. The more information you seek to learn about yourself and the world, the more you demonstrate your belief that you are worthwhile and important enough to gather information that helps you.

Control. The more information you gather about yourself and your world, the greater your ability to influence the direction of your life.

Challenge. The effort you apply in learning the Hardiness skills shows that you regard the time spent in developing yourself as a normal challenge of life.

For the answer key, See "Questionnaire and Test Your Knowledge Answer Keys" on page 259.

1. Give three reasons why you might manage conflict ineffectively:

   * _____
   * _____
   * _____

2. Name five ineffective conflict management styles:

   * _____
   * _____
   * _____
   * _____
   * _____

3. When you exploit power differentials in a relationship, you are a _____ and _____.

4. The person who finds the quickest way out of a conflict in order to manage it is a conflict _____.

5. When you behave in ways that recognize your, as well as another person's, interests, you express which relationship motto?

   _____.

6. The two HardiCoping techniques that help you to resolve social conflict are _____ and _____.

7. Which ineffective way of managing conflict insulates the parties involved from pressure to learn better coping skills, exacerbates the problem, and prevents the persons involved from clarifying their relationship?

   _____.

8. When you define agreement as the most important thing in resolving conflict, you solve problems through _____.

Learning Goals

* Do you appreciate the differences between a hardiness inhibiting and hardiness enhancing view of conflict?

* Do you understand how the five ineffective conflict management styles undermine your HardiAttitudes and HardiCoping efforts?

* Can you identify if, at times, you use one or more of the ineffective conflict management styles?

Hardy Communication

Communicating Whole Messages: Message IRA

To communicate effectively, you need to engage rather than offend, clarify rather than confuse, and stimulate discussion rather than shut it down. This is particularly true as your social world increases in complexity.

All communications mean to impact. Whether it is a person or a situation, we speak to cause action of some sort. Even the wave of your hand to say hello communicates your wish to be acknowledged. What you say, and how you say it, influence your social experience, positively or negatively. In general, there are two major reasons why we communicate. When we communicate, we intend to:

- Convey an intent or purpose through our observations, thoughts, needs, and feelings; this is our message intent, and

- In certain circumstances, to bring about relationship intimacy.

Your ability to construct a communication that adequately supports your message intent determines the level at which you satisfy these two communication goals. We call this process the Message IRA. This is a Message's Intent and the Relevant message components needed to support it. If we then successfully convey what we mean, we have message Accuracy.

Message Intent

All communications have a purpose, reason, or intent, no matter how simple they may be. Even a wave hello communicates some purpose. We may wave to acknowledge a social acquaintance or friendship. Our wave hello can mean many different things depending upon our desires. All verbal and non-verbal communications thus act upon the environment.

If we want to clearly convey our communication intent, we need clear verbal and non-verbal messages. This is especially true during stressful social interactions when our purpose or reason for communicating is complex.

Message Components

When you leave out important aspects of a communication that would add to its clarity, it confuses others. There are four modes that we process experience that can help us to structure a communication in ways that highlight its intent. Through our observations, thoughts, needs, and feelings, we communicate. Which message aspects are relevant to your message depends upon your message intent. Telling your garage mechanic, for example, that you were overcharged by fifty dollars for your last tune-up most likely does not require an expression of deep feelings. You might feel differently, however, if this service station regularly overcharged you.

Because daily communications usually revolve around a division of labor at work, school, and at home, we need to make extra sure we communicate in a way that does not contribute to our and others' stress levels. When you use what is needed to support your message intent, you communicate with whole messages. The following distinctions between observations, thoughts, needs, and feelings help you to think about the various components of a message that contribute to making it whole.

OBSERVATIONS

We frequently use observations about a person, situation, or event to express message intent. For instance, "I withdraw socially at parties," "I get depressed when you arrive home late every night," or "When you pick up after yourself, I feel appreciated," link observations with thought, feeling, or behavioral outcomes to clarify a message.

THOUGHTS

Unlike observations, which often include feelings, thinking statements usually beginning with "I think" imply but do not include feeling words. Thinking statements comment about your belief, attitude, or interpretation about your or another person's behavior, situation or phenomenon. Take for example, Shawn's statement about Lucas: "Lucas always comes out smelling like a rose." Do we know how Shawn feels about this aspect of Lucas? Shawn may feel amused, disgusted, or unmoved by this idea. Shawn's statement suggests a range of possible feelings, but at this point, it's only a stated idea or interpretation about Lucas' behavior. Shawn may also add, "Lucas is socially superficial." We still do not know what Shawn feels, until he adds a sensory expression that illustrates his position. I like, dislike, enjoy, amused, disgusted, unmoved, are sensory expressions that point to Shawn's feeling position on his statements about Lucas.

FEELINGS

Feeling expressions often begin with I feel or I am, and they often accompany thinking statements.

Feelings label sensory experience. Staying with the example mentioned above, Shawn states, "I'm impressed with Lucas' resourcefulness. I like, even envy this attribute." Now we know Shawns' personal take on his statements about Lucas. We still do not know Shawn's message intent, the purpose for this communication. He needs to say more. Remember, feeling statements describe a sensory experience that highlights a physical, mental, or behavioral state, like feeling sad, happy, content, disappointed, nervous, frustrated, or mad.

NEEDS

A need is a requirement, wish, or expectation that you have for yourself, another person, or a situation. "Can you," "Will you," "I need for you," or "I want from you," directly express the messenger's wish for a behavioral shift in a person or circumstance. Need statements are very important when you wish to stimulate action.

Message Accuracy

Language allows us to share interpersonal experience. As we grow in our capacity to accurately express ourselves through our observations, thoughts, needs, and feelings, we deepen our connection to others and find true joy in interpersonal relating.

Hardy Social Support Exercise 3, Communicating Whole Messages

Part A In this exercise, we practice the social support skills that you have learned thus far. You learn how to evaluate a message for its intent and the message components that support it (IRA). You have three opportunities to decipher a message intent from three message scenarios. Each message scenario provides you with the message sender's thought process as well as what was actually communicated. You discern the accuracy of the sender's message by evaluating if the message conveyed what the messenger really wanted to say. By appreciating how a message sender either failed or succeeded in constructing a message, you learn how to do it yourself.

Note: Skillful messengers really understand how to describe their observations, thoughts, needs, and feelings. The more complex your message, the greater the need to make distinctions between the message components.

Message Scenario 1

Sarah, a 25-year-old graduate student, has been frustrated with her "sloppy" roommate, Jane. She feels angry at coming home each day to Jane's clothing scattered throughout the apartment. Although she's quite fond of Jane on other grounds, if the sloppiness doesn't change, Sarah wants her to move out. Sarah feels sad by the thought that she may lose this friendship.

Begrudgingly, she decides to talk with her roommate about this problem. This is Sarah's message to Jane: "Jane, why don't we clean the apartment today? I have a lot of energy and have nothing better to do. After we clean the apartment, we can get a bite to eat." Sarah, trivializing the matter, laughs as she states, "I hate cleaning but someone's got to do it."

Let's analyze this message for intent, relevant message components, and message accuracy. You do this by analyzing Sarah's thought process against what she actually said.

Decipher from Sarah's thought process what she would like to have said (use observations, thoughts, needs, and feelings to evaluate her intent). Can you come up with three things she wanted to express to Jane?

_____
_____
_____
_____

Relevant components? Did Sarah's message completely convey her intent (again, use her observations, thoughts, needs, and feelings to determine this)?

_____
_____
_____
_____

Evaluate the successfulness of Sarah's message by comparing her real intent (thought process), observations, thoughts, needs, and feelings against what she actually said.

Least 0 10 20 30 40 50 60 70 80 90 100 Most

Now, based upon your rating in number three, estimate the likelihood of Sarah's message to deepen intimacy between her and Jane.

Least 0 10 20 30 40 50 60 70 80 90 100 Most

Estimate if you think Sarah's actual communication strengthened her HardiAttitudes of Commitment, Control, and Challenge.

Least 0 10 20 30 40 50 60 70 80 90 100 Most

Message Scenario 2

Suzanne, a 50-year-old financial analyst, travels a lot for business. Her long-term travel agent, Mary, has begun to make mistakes frequently on Suzanne's travel plans. This situation frustrates Suzanne. She needs special diabetic meals and dislikes sitting in anything other than an aisle seat. She knows Mary's recent work problems stem from the stress of her divorce proceedings. Suzanne feels badly for Mary and, in general, has felt well served by her. She cannot, however, avoid dealing with the meal situation because of her diabetic condition. But she can survive if she gets something other than an aisle seat. Suzanne knows she needs to talk to Mary about this situation. This is Suzanne's message to Mary:

"Mary, how are things going with you? I know these past few months have been quite difficult on you, and you've felt pressured. You've been so great in handling all the details of my traveling plans for so many years. But recently, many of my plane meals have been non-diabetic. Because of my health condition, I need to ask you to please remember to get me diabetic meals when traveling. It's really so important." She laughs as she states, "I can live occasionally with getting something other than an aisle seat, but my meal is a non-negotiable."

Let's analyze this message for intent, relevant message components, and message accuracy.

Decipher, from Suzanne's thought process, what she would like to have said (use her observations, thoughts, needs, and feelings to evaluate her intent). Can you come up with three things she wanted to express to Mary?

_____
_____
_____
_____
_____

Relevant components? Did Suzanne's message completely convey her intent (again, use her observations, thoughts, feelings, and needs to determine this)?

_____
_____
_____
_____

Evaluate the successfulness of Suzanne's message by comparing her real intent (thought process), observations, thoughts, needs, and feelings against what she actually said.

Least 0 10 20 30 40 50 60 70 80 90 100 Most

Now, based upon your rating in number three, estimate the likelihood of Suzanne's message to deepen intimacy between her and Mary.

Least 0 10 20 30 40 50 60 70 80 90 100 Most

Estimate if you think Suzanne's actual communication strengthened her HardiAttitudes of Commitment, Control, and Challenge?

Least 0 10 20 30 40 50 60 70 80 90 100 Most

Message Scenario 3

John is a 40-year-old married man. He comes home one Friday evening to find a house full of friends for his 40th birthday. His spouse planned this party without him knowing about it. Everyone he would have wanted to be there was, and the party prepara-

tions and food were wonderful. He felt like the luckiest guy in the world to have Karen for a spouse. She's a wonderful mother, a professional, and a great cook to boot! He thought he would marry her all over again.

He felt deeply loved and appreciated. This is John's message to Karen after the party:

"Karen, when did you find the time to do all of this? It was so great to see all my friends and family. The house looked beautiful, and the food was excellent. Thanks honey, you're the best."

Let's analyze this message for intent, relevant message components, and message accuracy?

Decipher, from John's thought process, what he would like to have said (use observations, thoughts, needs, and feelings to evaluate his intent). Can you come up with several things he wanted to express to Karen?

_____
_____
_____
_____

Relevant components? Did John's message completely convey his intent (again, use his observations, thoughts, needs, and feelings to determine this)?

_____
_____
_____
_____

Evaluate the successfulness of John's message by comparing his real intent (thought process), observations, thoughts, needs, and feelings against what he actually said.

Least 0 10 20 30 40 50 60 70 80 90 100 Most

Now based upon your rating in number three, estimate the likelihood of John's message to deepen intimacy between him and Karen.

Least 0 10 20 30 40 50 60 70 80 90 100 Most

Estimate if you think John's actual communication strengthened his HardiAttitudes of Commitment, Control, and Challenge?

Least 0 10 20 30 40 50 60 70 80 90 100 Most

Part B Take a few minutes to think about a message that you want to convey to someone. Choose a message that has some element of stress in it for you. Remember that a stressful communication does not always involve confronting or verbalizing disappointment to another person. Saying something intimate like, "I love you," can also be stressful. Write down the nature of the situation and the person(s) involved. Also, note which of the five reasons for social stress enters into your communication.

Now think about the goal(s) of the message you want to convey. What's your message intent or goal? Is there more than one goal? Write down the intent(s) of your message.

_____
_____
_____
_____

Next, think about which message components are relevant in this situation (observations, thoughts, needs, and feelings). Write them down.

_____
_____
_____
_____

Part C Finally, develop a message that accurately conveys your observations, thoughts, needs, and feelings about the situation. Reflect upon the difference between an observation, thought, need, and feeling to assure message accuracy.

_____
_____
_____
_____

Rate your success at developing the IRA aspects of your message.

Least 0 10 20 30 40 50 60 70 80 90 100 Most

Did you make successful message component distinctions when expressing your observations, thoughts, needs and feelings?

Least 0 10 20 30 40 50 60 70 80 90 100 Most

HARDY SOCIAL SUPPORT EXERCISE END

Hardy Social Support Exercise 4, Tracking A Communication for Understanding

In this exercise, you learn how to track a message for maximum understanding of it. The more complicated the message, the greater the degree of tracking skill you require for complete understanding. For example, hearing your daycare person tell you that she needs you to return home by 6:00 P.M. does not require high level tracking skills. Hearing, however, from the same person that she is dissatisfied with her employment because of inadequate pay and is considering leaving, requires greater message tracking sophistication, especially if you wish to service this relationship.

We concern ourselves with messages that involve some level of stress, and consequently require greater tracking sophistication on our part. *Note:* The most stressful messages fall broadly into one or more of the five social stress areas (See "Reasons For Social Stress" on page 54.).

Part A There are three message scenarios that follow. You first evaluate the messenger's communication. Evaluate if any of the four broad intent areas mentioned above are relevant (observations, thoughts, needs, and feelings), and then write down your answer. Next, you examine the receiver's response, which has already been provided for you, to see if it relates accurately to the expressed communication.

Message 1 Naomi's message to her 19-year-old son Shawn

"Shawn, the other day you borrowed my car and returned it to me without gas. This irritates me. I don't mind lending you my car, but feel it is unfair for you to leave the gas tank on empty. This is not the first time you have done this. This means much more to me than a full tank of gas. I want to see that our relationship matters to you and that it is not one-sided. The rule for the future is, whatever gas you use, you replace."

What is Naomi's message intent or main idea?

_____
_____
_____
_____

Which message components did she use in her communication?

Observations _____
Thoughts_____
Needs _____
Feelings _____

Evaluate the following narrative to see how Shawn heard his mother's message.

"It sounds like I made you feel disrespected. I'm sorry about not refilling the tank. I guess it was sort of thoughtless of me. I know that my action does not demonstrate it, but I really do appreciate you, Mom, and your generosity in lending me your car. I'll make a real effort to make sure this doesn't happen again."

Can we clone this teenager? Because we have all been teenagers, you probably chuckled at the unlikelihood of this response. If, however, you actively attend to the message IRA and nothing more, this healthy, hardy response becomes more the norm than an irregularity.

Message 2 Jim sends the following message to his wife, Patricia

"Pat, I notice you're spending a lot of money lately at the health club. I love that you exercise and enjoy the club's amenities, but your monthly bill exceeds what we have allocated for this expenditure in the monthly budget. Do you think you could try to stay within the parameters of our financial plan? If we really want to go to Paris in the spring, we have to try to stay within our budget. Will it be possible to do this? I want you to continue enjoying yourself; just see if there's any club activity you can cut down on. I'll leave that up to you."

What is Jim's main idea or message intent?

_____
_____
_____
_____

Which message components did he use in his communication?
Observations_____
Thoughts_____
Needs:_____
Feelings_____

Evaluate the following narrative to see how Pat heard Jim's message.

"I'm frustrated that I have to give up a club activity to make our budget work, but if that needs to be done, I guess I should do it. You know I hate to feel hemmed in, especially because of limited money. I grew up that way. But it's a reality, I know. Perhaps we need to talk more about the trip to Paris in spring. At this point, I guess I haven't considered it strongly enough to curb my spending. I need to think about all of that. I'm glad you appreciate how much I enjoy the club experience. It has been very good for me. I'm disappointed, but I will make it work."

How did Pat hear Jim's message? Did she consider the IRA of his communication? Take a few minutes to write down your thoughts.

_____
_____
_____
_____

Message 3 Sharon sends the following message to her coworker, Martha

"Martha, I'm glad we've become friendly. I enjoy your company, and you've made this work environment pleasurable. But lately, our talks have been taking up more of the workday. If we could limit our talks to our lunch hour, I'd really appreciate it. I'm so busy that I can barely get my work done, and that makes me feel stressed. I hope you understand."

What is Sharon's main idea or message intent?

_____
_____
_____
_____

Which message components did she use in her communication?
Observations_____
Thoughts _____
Needs _____
Feelings_____

Evaluate the following narrative to see how Martha heard Sharon's message.

"Sharon, I didn't know you felt that way. Why didn't you let me know sooner? You shouldn't let all that work get to you. Relax, you're too serious!"

How did Martha hear Sharon's message? Did she consider the IRA of Martha's communication? Take a few minutes to write down your thoughts.

_____
_____
_____
_____

Part B You need a partner for this part of the exercise. You practice taking turns delivering and receiving a message. The message deliverer attempts to effectively convey his/her message intent and relevant components. The receiver of the message, on the other hand, attempts to effectively track the message's intent and relevant components, and to create a response that directly relates to this message. The receiver then answers the questions to evaluate how well he/she tracked the message on hand.

The sender and the receiver then take turns sending and receiving a communication. The receiver listens to the sender's message and then formulates a response that attempts to address the IRA aspects of the communication. The receiver then answers the following questions and reviews each answer with the message sender to evaluate if he or she felt heard and understood.

What was the message sender's main intent or idea?

_____
_____

Which observations, thoughts, needs, and feelings did the message sender use to support his/her main intent?

_____
_____
_____
_____

Did you track the communication effectively? In other words, how well did your response correspond to the message IRA?

_____
_____
_____
_____

Does listening in this way increase in you the attitudes of Commitment, Control, and Challenge?

Very Little 0 10 20 30 40 50 60 70 80 90 100 A Lot

Learned Ideas

Learned ideas are deeply stored templates about us and the world, and the interaction between the two, that filters perception and influences functioning. During childhood and adolescence, social interaction taught you how everything works. Your parents, siblings, schoolmates, friends, teachers, and relatives are just some of the people who influenced the models you built about life. We use these stored models to evaluate our present environment. Ideas about authority, trust, control, people's motivations, religion, family, political beliefs, career choice, and general life depend upon your past experience in these areas.

The quality of your past social interactions strongly influences the way you think about such ideas. If, for example, you perceived your parents as loving, kind, and trustworthy in meeting your needs, your ideas about authority figures will generally follow suit. If, on the other hand, you learned that people get their needs met through competition and aggression, you may perceive people who solve problems cooperatively, and with social interest, as naive.

There are two ways in which learned ideas can operate:

A Springboard For New Learning

Your learned ideas are harmless if they are flexible enough to permit new information about yourself, a person, or a situation to enter in without alarming you. You can comfortably take in new information and decide how to integrate it into your belief system, because you are not overly invested in seeing yourself in one way versus another. You develop and mature as your childhood ideas continue to refine themselves to fit who you are in the world today.

A Steel Trap

A learned idea that closes down your ability to take in new information about yourself, the world, and the interaction between the two, operates to inhibit your personal development. On automatic pilot, you stop thinking and processing information. In a time warp, you experience the learned idea like an alien invasion that controls your perception and your thinking. You begin to highlight those aspects of the situation that confirm the learned idea, and reject those aspects of the situation that disconfirm the learned idea. You do this because your reality is threatened. This can trigger a deep emotional response in you that inhibits your ability to see and hear openly.

Interpreting through Learned Ideas

People who listen through a learned ideas lens, listen more for how a communication impacts them, rather than for understanding the communicator's message and point of view. This takes them out of the present moment and into their minds, where they are most apt to distort what they see and hear. For example, a friend cancels an outing with you because she's ill. She just wants to communicate to you that she's not well and needs to cancel. You, on the other hand, think she found something else she'd rather do than spend time with you. This is your "I'm unlovable" learned idea, rather than your friend's simple need to cancel. You distorted what you heard because of personal insecurities.

When you interpret what others say through a learned idea lens, you move far away from the face value of a communicated message.

THE CASE OF JACK AND MARIA

The following case example illustrates how learned ideas can undermine a work-related relationship. Jack believes his supervisor Maria treats him unfairly. According to Jack, he sees her as demanding, controlling, and expecting too much from him. She reminds him of his demanding mother. At 10:00 A.M., Jack gets a message that he's to meet with Maria today at 2:00 P.M. He thinks, "I'm in trouble over this work deadline that I failed to meet." Jack's anger grows throughout the morning, and by the time it is 2:00 P.M., he is furious. He's furious that he has to put up with such garbage, especially from this woman.

Maria: "Hi Jack, come on in and sit down. How are you?"

Jack: "Fine."

Maria: "Jack, I called this meeting because I need you to work on this special project. It's very important, and we need to complete it in one week. Our competitors just introduced fat-free French fries to the market. We need to immediately get out a product that competes for sales in this particular market. We'll pay you for overtime on this, if necessary."

Jack: "I'm already working on the winter menu project. I can only do so much! Why do I always get these fire drill projects handed down to me? What's wrong with Susan, can't she handle it? It's unfair. You must think that I'll do anything?

Maria: "Jack, I'm surprised. I didn't know you felt this way. I rely on you because you have the skills to do a good job on these kinds of projects. Your creative approach to past sales promotions has been excellent. I know you sometimes need more time on projects, but your work output is well worth it. I thought overtime compensation would offset the distress of the time pressure."

How did Jack's past learning contribute to the stressful interaction with Maria? Jack heard, "Here it comes again, she's about to dump another fire drill job on me. She must really disrespect me, because I'm always the one whom she selects for this bottom of the barrel kind of job. She thinks she can placate me with overtime compensation."

The recipient of this kind of social interaction always feels confused. Jack needed to bring himself, and his H.G. Well's time machine, back to the present. Jack took a basically harmless message to meet Maria at 2:00 P.M. and ran with it. He imposed his conflicted history with his mother on Maria. This prevented him from hearing that Maria trusted his ability and respected rather than devalued him. Maria saw such projects as an opportunity for Jack to shine, rather than a bottom of the barrel job for lackeys. We find it's not Maria, but rather Jack, who thinks of himself so poorly.

Your past trains you to think about yourself and the world in a specific way. These ideas help you to organize and think about your experience, and to formulate meaning. Flexible learned ideas help to define us. Rigid learned ideas, on the other hand, can stifle our growth. Early learning determines, to some degree, how flexible or rigid a learned idea becomes to us. We all learn to run away from a dangerous tiger because we know we could be eaten alive. At the most basic level, learned ideas can be consensually shared in terms of survival. There are

learned ideas, however, that are more subjective. Jack's fear of not measuring up to a person's standards is unique to him.

All of us have learned ideas about ourselves in relation to the world that have interfered with our ability to see and hear clearly. This always brings about interpersonal conflict, because the recipient of such an interaction feels misunderstood and unheard.

Emotional Triggers

How do you know when you are letting learned ideas guide what you hear? You begin to compare and contrast what you hear with what you already know. You seek to preserve what you know by discounting the unfamiliar and threatening. You are defending a way of being, rather than listening. The following two emotional triggers warn you that a deeply entrenched learned idea has taken hold of you.

All Good, All Bad Characterizations

When you begin to polarize people and situations into all good or all bad dimensions, an emotional trigger is on the rise. Such dichotomies distort perception and logic, which results in superficial characterizations of others and events. There are various ways in which we split people into all good, all bad dimensions.

PIGEONHOLING

This is when you prejudge a person. You shut down the opportunity to hear purely when you prematurely frame a person or situation with negative labels. We are most apt to do this when we do not want to solve a problem. In these situations, we define others unidimensionally. "Italians are emotional," "Women are hysterical," "Capitalism is bad," are examples of negative stereotypes that shut down our ability to think.

OVERREACTIONS

Learned ideas can cause us to overreact to a communication, especially if the learned idea conflicts with the message. When your reaction exceeds the message intent, an overreaction is on hand. Overreactions bewilder the message sender and are painful to everyone involved in the interaction.

CUT-AND-PASTE LISTENING

Cut-and-paste listening can result in hearing only the negative aspects of a message, or hearing only the positive aspects of a message. Whichever is on hand, cut-and-paste listening is an attempt to modify what is heard. When we rewrite a communicated message, we do not want to hear what others observe, think, feel, or need from us because it conflicts with our way of thinking about ourself and the world. It takes a lot of emotional strength to hear the unedited version of a communicated message. When you do this, you dare to take in new information about yourself and the world that helps you to adapt to life changes and leads to intimate relating.

A Need To Be Right

This person listens strategically so as to better position his argument. He twists facts by cutting and pasting communications to avoid being wrong. To him, communicating is like arm wrestling; whoever has the most muscle wins. Sadly, this person mistakes being wrong and/or having to say I'm sorry as a weakness, rather than a strength.

These three emotional triggers block listening and undermine the HardiAttitudes of Commitment, Control, and Challenge. A fragile sense of your unique talents, skills, and self-worth can rouse these emotional triggers.

Hardy Social Support Exercise 5, Identifying Learned Ideas

In this exercise, you identify ways in which you think about yourself that, when challenged, threaten you. First, answer the following set of questions.

Step 1. Think about a time when another person described you in a way that challenged you. For example, Tom's parents called him the creative child and his sister the intellectual. His sister got much better grades than Tom, which made him feel inferior to her. Today, he reacts strongly to anyone's description of him that may suggest he's intellectually inferior.

a. Use the above example to think through ways in which you think about yourself that, when challenged, threaten you. Jot it down.

_____
_____
_____
_____

b. Where did you learn to think about yourself in this way? In other words, which relationships influenced this aspect of your learning?

_____
_____
_____
_____

Step 2. Jot down some comments that someone might say to you that challenges the learned idea that you identified in Step 1. For example, Tom may write: A friend calls me "dummy" when I take a wrong turn while driving. I answer a question in class and my teacher says it is not well thought out. Now, you try it.

_____
_____
_____
_____

Knowing yourself is your first line of defense against learned ideas that can trigger an unwanted emotional response. Self-awareness takes the air out of an emotional trigger, because it prepares you for whatever comes your way.

EXERCISE END

Hardy Social Support Exercise 6, Listening To Positively Service The Relationship

Daily, you listen to various messages from teachers, supervisors, family members, friends, and others with whom you engage socially. The In the Service of the Relationship Principle can inhibit negative emotional reactions to what you hear by reminding you of your overall relationship objective: to understand and to relate. The next time a stressful communicated message comes up, try to discipline yourself by letting the In the Service of the Relationship Principle help you to listen. When listening, it is also helpful to keep in mind the five reasons for social stress (See "Reasons For Social Stress" on page 54.). This helps you to organize

what is happening, which has the effect of decreasing tension.

Jot down the specifics of the communicated message and the social interaction. Which of the five reasons for social stress is relevant in this situation? Which aspect of the communicated message felt stressful to hear?

_____
_____
_____
_____

How well did you listen? What was it about the communicated message that stimulated a learned idea that threatened you? Did you let the In the Service of the Relationship Principle discipline your listening? Was this hard to do?

_____
_____
_____
_____

Were you able to positively service the relationship by listening well?

No 0 10 20 30 40 50 60 70 80 90 100 Yes

Did this exercise help to increase or maintain in you the HardiAttitudes of Commitment, Control, and Challenge?

No 0 10 20 30 40 50 60 70 80 90 100 Yes

If an emotional trigger was fueled by the interaction, were you successful in keeping it at bay?

No 0 10 20 30 40 50 60 70 80 90 100 Yes

Which, if any, of the three warning signs threatened to sabotage your listening? Endorse an item by placing a check mark next to it.

All Good, All Bad Dimensions.

- Pigeonholing ____
- Over-reaction ____
- Cut-and-Paste Listening ____

A Need to Be Right. ____

EXERCISE END

Third Hardy Social Support Checkpoint

Please check in with your Hardiness Trainer at this point to evaluate your learning thus far.

Summary Concepts And Terms

ALL GOOD, ALL BAD CHARACTERIZATIONS: PIGEON HOLING, OVER REACTIONS, CUT AND PASTE LISTENING

A NEED TO BE RIGHT

EMOTIONAL TRIGGERS

INTENT

INTERPRETING THROUGH LEARNED IDEAS

LEARNED IDEAS

MESSAGE ACCURACY

RELEVANT COMPONENTS: OBSERVATIONS, THOUGHTS, NEEDS, AND FEELINGS

SPRINGBOARD FOR PERSONAL DEVELOPMENT

TIME WARP

WHOLE MESSAGES: IRA

Test Your Knowledge

To test what you learned so far, see if you can correctly answer the following questions. Remember, the more information you have to think about what happens to you, the more building blocks you have to generate creative solutions to everyday living problems. This, in turn, strengthens your HardiAttitudes.

Commitment. The more information you seek to learn about yourself and the world, the more you demonstrate your belief that you are worthwhile and important enough to gather information that helps you.

Control. The more information you gather about yourself and your world, the greater your ability to influence the direction of your life.

Challenge. The effort you apply in learning the Hardiness skills shows that you regard the time spent in developing yourself as a normal challenge of life.

For the answer key, See "Questionnaire and Test Your Knowledge Answer Keys" on page 259.

1. There are two general reasons why you communicate. What are they?

   _____ and

   _____ .

2. The aspect of a communication that helps you to think through what is needed to effectively communicate is called the message _____ .

3. The acronym for a whole message is

   _____ .

4. "Lucas always comes out smelling like a rose" is an example of a _____ message component.

5. An idea you have about yourself that can threaten you when challenged is a _____.

6. When you insert or delete aspects of a message that someone communicates to you, you listen by _____.

7. When you listen to a communicated message for what you already know and think, you listen by interpreting through _____.

8. When you manage stressful communications by lumping people into predetermined categories, you listen by _____.

9. If you want to make sure a learned idea does not undermine your ability to listen, you use the _____.

10. When you listen to another person's communication to find ways in which he or she is wrong, you listen to be _____.

Learning Goals

- Do you understand how a message's intent is made clear by message components?

- Do you understand learned ideas and how they can further or inhibit your listening ability and personal development?

- Do you appreciate the ways in which emotional triggers undermine listening?

- Can you identify learned ideas that trigger emotional responses in you?

Assistance and Encouragement

Giving And Getting Social Support

Your learning thus far helps you to give and get assistance and encouragement that enhances your performance and health. There is a specific type of assistance and encouragement that motivates HardiCoping and the strengthening of HardiAtti-tudes. You learn here that you can help other people to cope with stressful circum-stances. When you provide Hardy Assistance and Encouragement, you motivate other people in their HardiCoping efforts. There are two ways in which we can get from, and give to, others social support.

Hardy Encouragement

EMPATHY

You let the struggling person know that you understand his/her struggle. You con-vey that how the person feels matters to you and do not impose what you would think, feel, or do in a similar circumstance. But most importantly, you empathize with the kind of difficulties life throws our way and with the kind of efforts involved in coping transformationally with such challenges.

ACCEPTANCE

You let the person know that you care about him/her no matter what happens with his/her struggle. You convey that no matter what happens with his/her struggle, the most important thing is the effort involved in changing adversity into opportunity. You accept that the outcome of the coping effort is not always as important as the meaning derived from seeing oneself cope in a health-promoting way and building HardiAttitudes within oneself. By this, you make the person feel valued as one who is capable of coping transformationally with his/her life problems.

ADMIRATION

You let the person know you believe he/she can cope transformationally with the problem at hand. You admire the person's resources to change adversity into opportunity and verbalize confidence in his/her hardy capabilities during this time of need.

Hardy Assistance

We assist a person in his/her HardiCoping efforts by behaviorally:

GIVING TIME AND SPACE

You put other relationship matters you share with the person on the back burner to allow him/her time and energy to invest in the coping task at hand. You appreciate if the person cannot spend as much time with, or are as open to, you as usual, while he/she struggles in the coping task.

TAKING UP THE SLACK BY DOING WHAT WE CAN

You temporarily take upon yourself the burden of usually shared relationship matters that are too crucial to suspend altogether. The division of relationship labor may shift temporarily. You take up the slack by doing a larger amount of shared work or shouldering a larger amount of shared responsibilities, while the other person occupies him/herself with the coping process. In doing so, you give whatever information and resources are within your control, if that seems helpful to the coping person. But, you stay out of the actual coping efforts if that is what the other person wants. Perhaps you have knowledge or contacts that the person might find helpful. You offer these with no expectations as to whether the person should follow through on these suggestions.

ACT AS A SOUNDING BOARD

You go over the results of the person's coping efforts. You give supportive feedback and outcome evaluations as needed. You further listen sensitively to the results of the coping efforts and help the person evaluate feedback from observations of him/herself in action, and from the direct results of carrying out an action plan.

**Remember the *Reciprocity Principle*: "Do unto others as you want them to do unto you." We need to prepare ourselves to receive and to give encouragement and assistance whenever it is needed.

Dangers In Trying To Assist And Encourage

Sometimes, while trying to help, we encourage and assist in an ingenuine way. While we appear as if we want to help, our underlying intention says otherwise. When we react in a counterfeit way to other people's problems, we undermine their coping efforts.

Counterfeit Reactions

Some people choose to feel good about themselves by subtly and not so subtly putting other people down, in times of need. At such times, their ego gets the best of them. There are two forms of counterfeit reactions that can lead to regressive coping. This is when your reaction to the other person's problem makes them feel overwhelmed and incapable. It can lead them to deny or avoid the stressful situation through escapist activities that include drinking, drug use, binge shopping, and having affairs.

OVERPROTECTION

This counterfeit reaction happens when you rush in to take care of the other person's stressful problem. By doing this, you make the other person feel weak, passive, and incapable of managing living problems. When you protect others so completely, you make them dependent upon you. This is how you provoke regressive coping in them by undermining their self-confidence and opportunities for self-mastery experiences.

SUBTLE AND NOT-SO-SUBTLE COMPETITION

You subtly compete when you give advice in a way that makes the other person feel inferior to you. This kind of advice comes in the form of a lecture and most of the time has little to do with what the other person needs. You openly compete when you say things like, "Why do these problems always happen to you?" or "You must be asking for trouble because things like this never happen to me."

Whether you compete subtly or not so subtly, your reaction deprives them of the opportunity to learn through HardiCoping and leads them to doubt their capabilities. We can fall into the traps of overprotection and competition when we have hidden motives. Although we may overprotect them in the guise of concern, we really want to make sure other people continue to regard us as important to them. In the case of competition, we fear other's success takes away from our self-worth.

The Case Of Tanya And Sally

Tanya is a very bright, yet depressed, 18-year-old female who came from a very dysfunctional family. For such a young woman, she had a life already filled with many losses. Her emotionally unstable mother left her children and husband many years ago, and her father, through limitations of his own, decided he had no financial responsibility toward his children. Tanya was told she would be financially on her own at 18. The reality was she had to parent herself for as long as she could remember. Tanya was faced with a very difficult life challenge. At 18 years old, she had to secure full-time work to provide herself with shelter and food. She knew, without an education, her life would go nowhere.

Depressed and scared, Tanya could not see the light at the end of the tunnel. It was difficult not to succumb to bitterness and self-pity.

Sally, a 40-year-old female school counselor, saw Tanya's potential. During high school, Tanya would visit Sally seeking counsel for academic issues. Before long, they befriended each other, and Tanya slowly disclosed her difficult life situation to Sally. Sally did what she could (**assistance**) by sharing all the information and resources within her control to help Tanya. Sally herself had a difficult childhood and understood (**empathy**) the challenges Tanya had ahead of her. She conveyed to Tanya that she did not quite understand why some people have such hard beginnings, but that she knew by experience that through effort and persistence, things could get better. Sally shared with Tanya some of her past difficulties and coping efforts, and assured Tanya that she knew she was capable of making her life worthwhile and doing what she needed to do to get through this tough time (**admiration**). Sally often felt so emotionally moved by this young person's circumstance that it would stimulate her to want to overprotect Tanya. But she knew this kind of pampering would hinder, rather than help, this young woman with the huge task at hand. She, rather, encouraged Tanya to go to school even though she had to work. Tanya enrolled in a two-year college. During this difficult time, Sally often met with Tanya, making herself available as a sounding board (**assistance**) for Tanya's efforts to cope during this time. And, when Tanya elicited feedback, Sally gave it to her in regard to Tanya's coping efforts (how Tanya coped with working full time and taking three to four classes per semester, how she coped with loneliness, anger at her circumstance, and health problems as a result of all the stress). Although Sally assisted Tanya in many ways, she never treated Tanya as a victim. She conveyed by example and

encouragement that Tanya was capable of turning adversity into opportunity and that Tanya should settle for nothing less than this.

Well, Tanya graduated successfully from a four-year university, and due to her stellar school performance, she was immediately recruited into a job in her discipline with a very prestigious company. The combination of Tanya's courage, intelligence, and vision, and Sally's encouragement and assistance of Tanya's four-year efforts to cope, helped this young person to thrive during very difficult times.

Hardy Social Support Exercise 7, Giving And Getting Assistance And Encouragement

Step 1. Remember a time when you were struggling with a major or minor stressful circumstance and went to someone to whom you felt close for help. Put down what happened in the interaction between you and this other person:

_____

_____

_____

_____

a. As you reflect on what you got from the other person in the interaction, rate the following on a scale from 0% (none), 50% (some), to 100% (a lot):

Encouragement 0 25 50 75 100%

Assistance 0 25 50 75 100%

Overprotection 0 25 50 75 100%

Competition 0 25 50 75 100%

Copyright© 1999-2008, The Hardiness Institute, Inc.

b. What was the outcome of the coping effort, and was that understandable in terms of the ratings you have just made? Write down what you think:

_____

_____

_____

_____

Step 2. Remember a time when someone close to you was struggling with a major or minor stressful circumstance and came to you for help. Put down what happened between you and this other person:

_____

_____

_____

_____

a. As you reflect on what he/she got from you in the interaction, rate the following on a scale from 0% (none), 50% (some), to 100% (a lot):

Encouragement 0   25   50   75   100%

Assistance 0   25   50   75   100%

Overprotection 0   25   50   75   100%

Competition 0   25   50   75   100%

b. What was the outcome of the coping effort, and was that understandable in terms of the ratings you have just made? Write down what you think:

_____

_____

_____

_____

c. What generalizations can you reach about yourself and others with whom you interact when you think of you and them in terms of genuine assistance and encouragement and of the counterfeit form of these?

_____

_____

_____

_____

d. Is there need for change on your part or theirs? And, if so, how will you approach this change? (Think of what you've learned in previous social support exercises.)

_____

_____

_____

_____

Step 3. Now bring what you have learned doing Steps 1 and 2 into the present. Identify someone you know well who is currently struggling to cope with a stressful circumstance. Think of how you can give them encouragement and assistance (not overprotection or competition) to help them in their struggle. Carry out the actions that will give them your encouragement and assistance, and record your experiences below:

_____

_____

_____

_____

Step 4. Because you are going through HardiTraining, you are probably trying right now to do Hardi-Coping with a stressful problem in your life. Think of approaching someone you know to give you the encouragement and assistance that will support your difficult coping task. Plan a way to ask for assistance and encouragement, and carry it out. Record your experiences below:

_____

_____

_____

_____

a. What have you learned in doing Steps 3 and 4? Were you successful in giving and getting assistance and encouragement? If not, did you learn something that will help you do better next time you try?

_____

_____

_____

_____

EXERCISE END

Fourth And Final Hardy Social Support Checkpoint

It is time for you to contact your Hardiness trainer. Discuss your efforts at giving and getting the kind of assistance and encouragement that strengthens your HardiAttitudes and motivates HardiCoping.

Summary Concepts And Terms

ACCEPTANCE

ADMIRATION

BEING A SOUNDING BOARD

COUNTERFEIT REACTIONS

EMPATHY

GIVING SPACE

HARDY ASSISTANCE

HARDY ENCOURAGEMENT

OVERPROTECTION

SUBTLE AND NOT SO SUBTLE COMPETITION

PAMPERING

TAKING UP THE SLACK

Test Your Knowledge

To test what you learned so far, see if you can correctly answer the following questions. Remember, the more information you have to think about what happens to you, the more building blocks you have to generate creative solutions to everyday living problems. This, in turn, strengthens your HardiAttitudes.

Commitment. The more information you seek to learn about yourself and the world, the more you demonstrate your belief that you are worthwhile and important enough to gather information that helps you.

Control. The more information you gather about yourself and your world, the greater your ability to influence the direction of your life.

Challenge. The effort you apply in learning the Hardiness skills shows that you regard the time spent in developing yourself as a normal challenge of life.

For the answer key, See "Questionnaire and Test Your Knowledge Answer Keys" on page 259.

1. What are the three components of Hardy Encouragement?

   • _____

   • _____

   • _____

2. When you temporarily take upon yourself the burden of usually shared relationship matters that are too crucial to suspend altogether, you _____.

3. When you go over the results of the person's coping efforts, you assist by

   _____.

4. When you put other relationship matters you share with the person on the back burner to allow him/her time and energy to invest in the coping task at hand, you assist by

   _____.

5. The two dangers in trying to encourage and assist others include

   _____ and

   _____.

Learning Goals

- Do you understand Hardy Encouragement and Assistance?
- Do you understand the dangers in encouraging and assisting people in their coping efforts?

.

Hardy Relaxation

Tension And Stress

Change of any type can increase tensions within you that undermine your performance, morale, conduct, and health. Prolonged physical tension puts you at risk for depression, anxiety, attention and concentration difficulties, food and chemical addictions, and other stress-related disorders. And, because living changes disrupt what you know and how you do it, stressful living changes can make you feel insecure, which lowers your self-confidence. Teachers, bosses, or friends and family members' expectations can tax our already faltering resources. This can stir up in us competence and dependency anxieties and fears that when mismanaged, turn into strain symptoms.

Stressful changes, remember, are events or situations that pressure the body to adjust, by regulating arousal levels. Through adequate levels of central nervous system arousal, we can successfully meet the stress at hand. Most daily activities require adequate nervous system arousal to carry them out, like dancing, working on a school or work project, social interaction, eating, and exercising. Prolonged brain and body arousal, however, can strain us physically, mentally, and behaviorally.

By learning how to relax our body and mind, we can manage physical stress. In addition to HardiCoping and Hardy Social Support, relaxation tools help us to master stressful changes, by optimizing physical and mental arousal levels.

It is true that your body is your temple. Your ability to effectively solve problems, constructively and healthily interact, and approach life with confidence hinges upon how well you feel. The knowledge and skills you learn in this HardiTraining component help to calm and center you, as you work to solve daily living problems.

Take a moment to recall a time when you were stressed out or not feeling well. How were your social interactions during this time? Did you perform well in your activities? What conflicts arose due to this condition?

_____
_____
_____
_____

We behave and perform well when our physiological arousal levels are just right. If we are ill or too stressed out, our performance usually decreases. Let's learn about the stress and strain response and how they impact our performance and well-being.

Stress

As is detailed in the HardiCoping component, **acute stress** is a change that disrupts our usual routine, requiring us to make some kind of mental and behavioral adjustment. So, the situational change brings about a change in our normal living. Acute stress, thus, can involve:

• **A positive event**, like the birth of a new baby, a promotion at work, or graduating from school; or

• **A negative event**, such as the death of someone close to you, tax assessments, or physical illness in you or others in your life.

There is also what we call **chronic stress**. Here the problem is less the changes happening to you than the ongoing mismatch or conflict between you and your world. Thinking of yourself as a creative person but having a routine job is an example of this kind of stress.

As is detailed in the introduction to this workbook, **strain** is your mental, physical and behavioral response to the stresses in your life. You go into that well-known fight or flight mode of arousal to meet the danger of the stresses. Civilized people, generally, do not to fight or run away, which prolongs the arousal. Signs of prolonged arousal and strain are irritability, distractibility, tension, and cravings for sweet and fatty foods and alcohol. Further, if the strain state is intense and prolonged enough, you risk ineffective performance, leadership, morale, conduct, and health.

Performance Ineffectiveness

Mental Ineffectiveness. Chronic worry, self-doubt, burnout, confusion, depression, loneliness, concentration difficulties, suspiciousness, anxiety, and fear are just some of the mental breakdowns possible.

Physical Ineffectiveness. Chronic aches and pains, tension headaches, migraines, allergies, fatigue, gastrointestinal problems, diarrhea, and/or constipation are just some of the ways strain can show up. Hypertension, heart disease, stroke, cancer, and diabetes are just some of the physical breakdowns possible.

Behavioral Ineffectiveness. Examples includes: Disinterest in activities once enjoyed; disorganization that jeopardizes work and personal performance; social isolation; anger and crying outbursts; mood swings; insomnia; and many others. These behavioral breakdowns feed on each other, and if strain continues too long, it destroys your happiness and success. Obesity, chemical dependencies and eating disorders (anorexia, bulimia, and compulsive overeating) can take hold during this time.

There is one more important thing to understand about strain and its impact on your performance, and health. Although the disruptive changes and continuing conflicts in our lives are real enough, how overwhelming they are depends upon how we react to the situation. If we think of acute and chronic stressful situations as the end of the world and let them do us in, we are likely to show ineffective performance physically, mentally, and behaviorally. If, however, we put the stresses in perspective, gain understanding of them, and take needed actions, **HardiCoping** (see the HardiCoping component of this workbook) should keep us performing well and healthy. In addition, if we resolve the social conflict some stressful situations pose for us, we increase our ability to give and get **Hardy Social Support** (see the Hardy Social Support component of this workbook), which supports our HardiCoping efforts and keeps us successful and healthy.

The other thing we can do to keep ourselves successful and healthy despite mounting stressful situations is to practice Hardy Relaxation. That's what this HardiTraining component is all about.

Hardy Relaxation: Body and mind techniques that help you to bring about a physiological state of low arousal that research shows is critical to mental, physical, and behavioral well-being.

Most of you can recall times when illness or lack of sleep or skipping a meal caused crankiness, low energy and poor performance. Even subtle changes in your body state can negatively influence your mental, emotional and behavioral effectiveness. A relaxed body makes you feel confident, strong, and open to your environment. Engaging in the activities of HardiCoping and Hardy Social Support brings about a relaxed body. The more physically centered you feel, the more options you can generate during problem solving and the more apt you are to generate win-win solutions to social conflict. When you relax, understanding, compassion, and generosity increase in you, which supports your HardiCoping and Hardy Social Support skills.

To relax on a deep biological level, you need special skills. In the section that follows, you learn to increase your awareness of body strain versus body relaxation. This prepares you for the relaxation exercises that follow. The techniques that follow teach you how to bring about a state of low body arousal that decreases the strain response. This training helps you to develop skill in toning down arousal states so that even in difficult times, you remain calm, centered, and aware. In addition, cravings for alcohol and sweet and fatty foods diminish when you decrease body strain. This decreases the likelihood of performance and health deficits in you and, in turn, increases personal satisfaction.

Summary Concepts And Terms

ACUTE STRESS

CHRONIC STRESS

HARDICOPING

HARDY RELAXATION

HARDY SOCIAL SUPPORT

NEGATIVE STRESS

POSITIVE STRESS

STRAIN

Test Your Knowledge

To test what you learned so far, see if you can correctly answer the following questions. Remember, the more information you have to think about what happens to you, the more building blocks you have to generate creative solutions to everyday living problems. This, in turn, strengthens your HardiAttitudes.

Commitment. The more information you seek to learn about yourself and the world, the more you demonstrate your belief that you are worthwhile and important enough to gather information that helps you.

Control. The more information you gather about yourself and your world, the greater your ability to influence the direction of your life.

Challenge. The effort you apply in learning the hardiness skills shows that you regard the time spent in developing yourself as a normal challenge of life.

For the answer key, See "Questionnaire and Test Your Knowledge Answer Keys" on page 259.

1. Body and mind techniques that lower body arousal are called

    _____.

2. The birth of a new baby is an _____ and _____ stress.

3. Mental, physical, and behavioral responses to stress in your life are called

    _____.

4. A mismatch or conflict between what you have in life and what you want is a

    _____ stress.

Learning Goals

*   Do you understand how acute and chronic stress build to create a strain reaction?

CHAPTER 11

The Physiology of Stress

"Activity of the nervous system improves the capacity for activity, just as exercising a muscle makes it stronger."

Dr. Ralph Gerard

The Central Nervous System

In ancient times, people struggled daily with survival issues. Threat came from all areas of existence. If they did not get wiped out by other humans or by animals, they died of famine, environmental disasters, or by diseases from which there was no cure. Evolution designed our nervous system to meet the challenges of every day life. When our ancestors met an acute or chronic stressful situation, their central nervous system stimulated a widespread arousal or mobilization response to either fight or flee the situation on-hand. In less civilized days, flight or fight was literal. If our ancestors did not run away from the threat, or fight to kill, they could die. If they survived, when the threat ended, their bodies returned to normal functioning.

Today, we do not literally fight or flee threatening situations because we favor civilized behavior. Our biological response to stress, however, has not changed. In addition, technological advance brought with it a host of stresses to which our ancestors did not have to contend. The following section discusses how different body systems and organs interact to bring about an effective biological response to stress. You will gain respect for your body when you appreciate its effort to support you, even when you do not support it.

The Reticular Activating System

The infant is born with the reticular activating system intact. This system contains the brain stem and its various parts, and its life supporting functions make it critical to survival. In the first few weeks of an infant's life, heart rate, blood flow, respiration, and cardiovascular activity dominate. Infants emerge slowly as beings capable of thought and action when their central nervous system develops. These basic and involuntary functions occur outside our conscious control.

The Limbic System

The limbic system matures next. It consists of sub-structures that include the hypothalamus, hippocampus, septum, cingulate gyrus, the amygdala, and the pituitary gland. The limbic system plays a major role in the strain response because it is the store house for ideas and memories. These ideas and memories serve as templates for thinking about experience, and most importantly, influence what we regard as stressful. The limbic system influences, thus, how we perceive events by interpreting information in the context of stored ideas and memories.

The Neocortex

In the infant, the neocortex' neural networks are the last to develop fully. The neocortex contains the brain's frontal lobe. Abstract thinking, planning, delay of behavioral gratification, tolerance of frustration, imagination, and logic stem from frontal-lobe maturity. Through such functions, human beings interpret incoming sensory stimuli, assess what they need to do to address the demand, and organize their behavior around this evaluation. Har-

diCoping skills like problem-solving, imagining best and worse case scenarios, goal-development, action-plans, and feedback assessment stem from neocortex functioning. Luckily, through practice, you can strengthen thinking and action that exercises the capabilities of the neocortex.

The Peripheral Nervous System

The central nervous system directs the peripheral nervous system (PNS). Nerves outside the brain and spinal cord that services the limbs, muscles, skin and sense organs make up this brain system. The brain stem (reticular activating system) and the limbic system control peripheral nerves, which give rise to two PNS sub-branches.

THE SOMATIC BRANCH

This subbranch of the PNS carries sensory and motor impulses to and from the central nervous system. Sensory organs (ears, eyes, nose and skin) and muscles respond to external stimuli and our commands. We can consciously manipulate our sensory organs to take in more, or less of, a stimulus. If we want for example to stop seeing something, we just close our eyes.

THE AUTONOMIC BRANCH

This PNS branch regulates the body's internal environment. It controls respiration, heart rate, blood circulation, and some motor activities. In contrast to the somatic branch, we cannot directly manipulate this peripheral nervous system branch. In contrast to the somatic branch, we cannot directly manipulate this peripheral nervous system branch. While you can close your eyes to something offensive, you cannot, at will, change the diameter of your arteries and veins. Relaxation techniques help us to alter autonomic functioning to meet performance and health needs. The autonomic branch divides into two branches that essentially polarize in function.

The Sympathetic Nervous System

The sympathetic nervous system (SNS) increases brain and body arousal. Sympathetic **excitatory** chemicals and hormones turn the cardiovascular system into a pump so that these stimulating chemicals can reach the organs and body systems involved in arousal. The excitatory nerve chemicals, the **catecholamines,** include **dopamine**, **epinephrine** and **norepinephrine**. The most prevalent brain neurotransmitter is glutamate. **Glutamate** helps us to execute brain functions involved in learning, recall, and problem-solving. Sympathetic activation decreases blood flow and body temperature, increases breathing rate, depresses the digestive and immune system, to support brain and body arousal. These body systems shut down temporarily so that the body can produce changes in chemicals and nerve firing patterns necessary to body arousal.

Biological Effects Of Sympathetic Activity

1. Pupils dilate (fear response).
2. Saliva decreases.
3. Heart rate increases.
4. Veins, arteries, and capillaries constrict.
5. Bronchial passages dilate to increase air intake for increased energy.
6. Stomach and intestinal motility decrease.
7. Insulin decreases to raise blood sugar levels in the body.

8. The pituitary releases adrenocorticotropic hormone (ACTH).
9. Adrenal glands release noradrenalin and adrenaline.
10. Vascular constriction lowers temperature in peripheral body parts.

The Parasympathetic Nervous System

The parasympathetic nervous system (PNS) decreases brain and body arousal through **inhibitory chemicals** that dilate the body's arteries, veins, and capillaries. **Gaba-aminobutryic acid** is one such inhibitory nerve chemical that restores cardiovascular dilation with consequent body relaxation. **Acetylcholine**, another PNS nerve chemical, is critical to memory processes. The medical industry uses Acetylcholine-based medicines to treat degenerative diseases that deteriorate memory, such as alzheimers.

The parasympathetic nervous system dilates the vascular system. This in turn increases blood flow and body temperature, normalizes breathing rate, rhythm, and depth, increases digestive and intestinal motility, activates pancreatic function, and boosts the immune system. These bodily changes show up in feelings of relaxation, assuredness, and well-being. The calming mental and bodily changes brought about through a low arousal response help you to feel better, decrease your food and alcohol cravings, and lower the likelihood of physical, mental, and performance breakdown.

Biological Effects Of Parasympathetic Activity

1. Constricts the pupils.
2. Increases salivary flow.

3. Decreases the heart rate through vascular dilation.

4. Returns the bronchial passages to normal size.

5. Increases stomach motility and intestinal fluids.

6. Stimulates insulin.

7. Stimulates acetylcholine.

8. Inhibits adrenal gland stimulating hormones.

9. Increases body temperature in peripheral body parts.

How Do The Various Body Systems Communicate?

Your nerves make up an information highway of neural networks that communicate through electro-chemical firing. Preparing to talk, walk, sleep, eat, take an exam, pick up a child, or go dancing, for example, involves complex sensory, motor, and musculature actions. Your neocortex evaluates how much brain and body arousal you need to execute a specific activity. It then alerts the PNS to inform its subordinate systems to make the necessary adjustments to support this task. The PNS' somatic branch makes necessary sensory and muscle adjustments, and its autonomic branch regulates heart and respiration rate, motor activity, blood pressure, body temperature, and hormone and neurotransmitter levels to stimulate a level of brain and body arousal conducive to the task on hand.

Cell And Nerve Functioning

The smallest unit of this nerve highway is a **neuron**, or the nerve cell. Neurons bathe internally and externally in **electrolytes**, a fluid environment made up of minerals, such as potassium, sodium, calcium, and chloride. In varying concentrations of each other, these minerals produce electrical energy

that fires chemicals and hormones throughout your nervous system.

At rest, potassium makes up a neuron's intra cellular fluid, whereas sodium makes up a neuron's extra cellular fluid. This slows down nerve firing while decreasing the output of excitatory and increasing the output of inhibitory chemicals and hormones circulating in your body. When your neocortex instructs body systems to electrochemically shift for arousal, electrolytes arrange themselves in varying concentrations of each other within and outside your cells. They call this shift an **action potential**. This speeds up nerve firing, increases the output of excitatory chemical and hormones circulating in your body, and energizes your brain and body for complex physical, mental, and behavioral activities. Relaxation skills influence autonomic functioning.

Consider, for example, that you just entered a cross walk and the light turns red. You must quickly decide to cross the street or stay put. You assess the risk on hand and then determine the time that you have to safely cross the street. What physical changes must take place so that you accurately judge the circumstance and then act quickly enough to carry out some action?

The central nervous system signals the peripheral nervous system to prepare for brain and body arousal. In turn the peripheral nervous system alerts its somatic and autonomic branch to make changes that support this activity. Your body assumes walking position, your eyes take in the surroundings, and in the meantime, a shift in intra- and extra-cellular fluids turn your vascular system into a pump that routes excitatory chemicals, stress hormones, and sugar and fatty acids to implement brain and body arousal. If all goes well, the neocortex functions adequately enough to make this assessment and you cross or stay put relative to this appraisal.

Optimal Versus Excessive Central Nervous System Arousal

The neocortex regards arousal-based activities as a fight or flight response. It considers friendly conversations, driving a car, skiing, exercising, or running away from a tiger an arousal-based activity. In each activity, the sympathetic nervous system stimulates enough brain and body arousal for the activity on-hand. The intensity of, or the threat involved in, the activity determines the amount of arousal.

The Case Of Tom

Tom, for example, has a social phobia, so that he perceives most social interactions as potentially dangerous. To Tom, a social interaction feels like a tiger is about to devour him. His body mirrors his perception of threat. High levels of circulating sympathetic nervous system chemicals, such as glutamate, adrenaline, and blood catecholamines, make his mind and heart race. He stutters, behaves awkwardly, and forgets what he wants to say. Excessive central nervous system arousal shows up in him as fear and social inadequacy.

The Case Of Susan

On the other hand, Susan, a sophomore in college, performs well in a testing situation. She performs well on examinations. Although she prepares ahead of time, it is her attitude about examinations that helps her. Susan, you see, is the child of two academic parents. She participated routinely in friendly yet competitive social, religious, and political discussions with her family. She is comfortable examining different points of view and enjoys when authority figures challenge her thinking. Exams are generally a "piece of cake" for Susan. She recognizes the pressure, but regards it as manageable.

One's perception of the stress is critical to the fight or flight process. Nerve mechanisms in the neocortex's limbic system, where learned ideas reside and emotions dominate, trigger an arousal response. In other words, the meaning you apply to a stressor determines your attitude about it and the way in which you cope with it.

Uninterrupted stress, or stress poorly managed, can increase your risk for cardiovascular symptoms and illness that includes hypertension, blood clots, heart pain, and irregular heart rhythms, stroke, and other debilitating disorders. HardiCoping and Hardy Social Support shifts your perception of the stress on hand. When you reconstruct a stress, you find innovative ways of thinking about it that brings relief to you. When you give and get assistance and encouragement for your coping efforts, social conflicts no longer seem daunting.

For optimal arousal, most normal activities require an average amount of sympathetic nervous system arousal. Too much or too little arousal can undermine your performance in such activities. Perception, drink and food intake, illness, and intensity of the stress influences central nervous system arousal.

Behavioral Effects Of Sympathetic Activity

OPTIMAL
SYMPATHETIC
AROUSAL

1. Increases physical, mental, and behavioral energy.
2. Heightens awareness and concentration.
3. Increases mental alertness.
4. Increases liveliness and confidence.
5. Opens you up to the environment.
6. Stabilizes your mood.
7. Enhances social interactions.
8. Orchestrates behavior meaningfully.

EXCESSIVE
SYMPATHETIC
AROUSAL

1. Decreases concentration and memory.
2. Increases mental disorganization.
3. Increases fear, worry, and hopeless.
4. Increases hypersensitivity and suspicion.
5. Increases insomnia.
6. Increases temper tantrums and impulsive behavior.
7. Disrupts social interactions.

Sympathetic nervous system dominance places us in a chronic state of brain and body arousal, which leads to strain and ineffective performance. We spend a large portion of our day modulating our biological response to stress. There are so many pressures today that stimulate excessive arousal reactions in us. Luckily, the parasympathetic nervous system branch of the autonomic nervous system complements the sympathetic nervous system

by restoring biological **homeostasis**. Let's review some of the positive effects.

Behavioral Effects Of Parasympathetic Activity

1. Increases feelings of well-being and relaxation
2. Increases deep sleeping, especially as arousal lowers
3. Increases concentration, as long as arousal does not get too low
4. Increases creativity and imagination
5. Increases compassion
6. Decreases panic, worry, hopelessness, and fear
7. Decreases temper outbursts, irritability, and anger

Do You Know How To Relax?

To reduce physical, mental, and behavioral strain, you may think that all you have to do is take a day off, go to the beach, ski, play a game of golf, or have a meal with friends. Think of the last time that you took a vacation. Did you worry about travel plans? Did you fret about work or school responsibilities while away from home? Did you overeat or walk more than you normally do? How about that game of golf or skiing trip, did you relax completely? If you played or skied competitively, you most likely did not. When you exercise, do you relax? Exercise may drain sympathetic chemicals and hormones, but it does not stimulate parasympathetic activity.

Pleasurable, relaxing activities are not always sufficient in toning down central nervous system arousal. These enjoyable activities can tone down sympathetic arousal, but deep biological relaxation at the cellular level requires specific activities designed to bring about a state of relaxation. These special relaxation activities lower body arousal and bring about a parasympathetic response. The good news is that if you practice them for just 15 minutes, twice a day, you restore your physical, mental, and behavioral health.

Summary Concepts And Terms

ACTION POTENTIAL

AUTONOMIC BRANCH

CENTRAL NERVOUS SYSTEM

ELECTROLYTES

EXCITATORY NEUROTRANSMITTERS: EPINEPHRINE, NOREPINEPHRINE, DOPAMINE

GLUTAMATE

HOMEOSTASIS

INHIBITORY NEUROTRANSMITTERS: GABA BUTRYIC ACID, ACETYLCHOLINE

NEOCORTEX

NEURON

PARASYMPATHETIC NERVOUS SYSTEM

PERIPHERAL NERVOUS SYSTEM

SOMATIC BRANCH

SYMPATHETIC NERVOUS SYSTEM

Test Your Knowledge

To test what you learned so far, see if you can correctly answer the following questions. Remember,

the more information you have to think about what happens to you, the more building blocks you have to generate creative solutions to everyday living problems. This, in turn, strengthens your HardiAttitudes.

Commitment. The more information you learn about yourself and the world, the more you demonstrate that you are worthwhile and important enough to gather information that helps you.

Control. The more information you gather about yourself and your world, the greater your ability to influence the direction of your life.

Challenge. You view the time you spend learning about ways in which you can enhance your everyday functioning, as a normal part of life.

For the answer key, See "Questionnaire and Test Your Knowledge Answer Keys" on page 259.

1. The smallest anatomy unit in the human body is the _____.

2. The term for an electrochemical firing pattern is

   _____.

3. Your neurons bathe internally and externally in a concentration of fluids made up of

   _____.

4. The biological term for nerve chemicals is

   _____.

5. Dopamine, epinephrine, and norepinephrine are _____ nerve chemicals.

6. The nervous system that consists of the brain and spinal cord is the

   _____.

7. The most primitive central nervous system structure is the

   _____.

8. The central nervous system structure that involves the brain part most instrumental in emotions is the

   _____.

9. The central nervous system structure that presides over planning, imagination and logic is/are the _____.

10. The _____ branch of the peripheral nervous system services the limbs, muscles, skin, and sense organs.

11. The _____ controls the peripheral nervous system.

12. The _____ branch of the peripheral nervous system carries sensory and motor impulses to and from the central nervous system.

13. The _____ branch of the peripheral nervous system regulates respiration, heartbeat, and blood circulation.

14. The _____ branch of the autonomic nervous system stimulates a fight or flight response to stress.

15. You cannot manipulate directly the _____ branch of the peripheral nervous system.

16. The two subdivisions of the autonomic branch of the peripheral nervous system are called the _____ and the

    _____.

17. The autonomic branch most involved in the relaxation response is the

    _____.

18. The autonomic branch that activates the brain, heart, and muscles through catecholamine release is the _____.

19. The autonomic branch that activates release of acetylcholine is the

    _____.

20. The autonomic nervous system branch constricts the vascular system is the

    _____.

21. The peripheral nervous system branch that causes vascular dilation is the

    _____.

22. The branch of the autonomic nervous system that dumps fatty acids and cholesterol into your system for energy is the_____.

23. When intestinal and salivary fluid motility increase and heart rate slows, the _____ nervous system dominates.

24. The autonomic nervous system branch that dominates when your pupils constrict and pancreatic function increases is the

    _____.

25. An increase in temperature in your hands, fingers, feet, and toes involves the _____ branch of the autonomic nervous system.

26. Mental disorganization, behavioral ineffectiveness, suspicion, hopelessness, insomnia, and temper outbursts surface when sympathetic arousal is _____.

27. You activate the _____ branch of the peripheral nervous system when you golf, exercise, or play tennis.

Learning Goals

- Do you have a basic understanding of the biology of stress and strain?
- Do you know the difference between the central and peripheral nervous system?
- Do you know the difference between the sympathetic and parasympathetic nervous systems?

- Do you understand the difference between optimal versus excessive sympathetic nervous system arousal?

- Do you know the behavioral effects of parasympathetic activity?

CHAPTER 12

Body Awareness

"The mind's first step to self-awareness must be through the body."

George Sheehan

The Relaxation Response

Many of us lose the ability to sense what our bodies need to stay healthy. Children, limited by immature thought processes, express need through body state. They coo and smile to show pleasure and cry to show displeasure. As our thought processes mature, we favor thinking over sensing. Our connection to our body recedes into the background of our awareness, and we begin to live outside of it. It knows what we need to stay healthy, if we just listen to our body.

Although we can easily recognize obvious body changes, we often have trouble recognizing subtle shifts in body state. When our tummy gurgles, we feel hungry. When we tire, we sleep. Body shifts that point to excessive sympathetic activity lead to strain symptoms long before we recognize it. It oftentimes takes symptoms like shortness of breath, cold hands and feet, indigestion, or a neck, back, or headache to recognize strain within us.

What happens when you see a good friend in the library? You chatter animatedly because you are happy to see your friend. Your excitement and energy points to a shift in body arousal. You do not, however, directly experience glucose and excitatory nerve chemicals flowing through your veins or an increase in sweat gland activity.

Think about what occurs inside you when you listen to a class lecture. You listen intently to understand the lecture material. Your body responds sympathetically so your brain can process the information quickly and in depth. You track the information well. Your body releases glucose and excitatory chemicals into your system although you did not directly experience this biological shift.

If you notice subtle shifts in body state, you can do something about it long before the symptoms become painful. This chapter enhances your ability to recognize subtle changes in your body happening daily. Every split second, your body adjusts to changes stimulated internally (fatigue, hunger, pain) or externally (class exam, social interaction). Through sensory awareness training, it is possible to track these biological shifts so that you can do something early on to turn strain around.

In 1975, Herbert Benson defined the **relaxation response** as a state of physical, mental, and behavioral low arousal. Brought about by relaxation techniques, like deep breathing, muscle relaxation, and meditation, the relaxation response calms and centers you, and heightens your sense of subtle body changes. You learn how to sense tension soon enough to turn it around. This is the relationship between heightened body awareness and enhanced performance, morale, conduct, and health.

Collecting Baseline Data

In the exercises that follow, you record symptoms before and after each practice session. Whenever you want to increase or decrease behavior, you first measure the behavior before you try to change it. That way, you can evaluate the outcome of your change efforts. **Baseline information** is the data

you collect prior to beginning a behavioral change program. If, for example, you want to decrease sugar intake or increase study time or the intensity of your exercise routine, you need to assess the quantity of this behavior prior to your effort to change it. Baseline information provides you with a point for behavioral comparison, and a change in the desired direction points to success.

The Case of Jan. Jan wants to see whether increasing the amount that she exercises will improve her mood. Her first step is to determine her current exercise level so that she can better plan her direction for change. Jan assesses she currently exercises for 20-minute sessions, 2 times per week. She decides to increase the number of times per week she will exercise to 3, rather than increasing the minutes per session. So, her intervention is an increase of 1 time per week that she exercises. Besides the fact that exercise is good for her, Jan really wants to know specific data as to the effects of increased exercise levels. She decides to complete a physical and mental well-being rating scale both before and after her increase in exercise. By comparing the pre- and post-intervention test completions, she can pinpoint whether an increased exercise level has had a significant effect on her physical and mental well-being.

In many of the exercises within this component, we ask you to collect pre- and post-relaxation data so that you can determine how much the relaxation exercises helped you. You first learn to identify biological signs that point to a shift in body state. The symptoms you learn about in the next exercise estimate level of sympathetic activity. Although by no means exhaustive, these symptoms are common signs of strain. If a symptom does not apply to how you feel right now, do not rate it.

Hardy Relaxation Exercise 1, Baseline Strain Ratings

For this exercise, See "Appendix A: Strain Rating Scale" on page 221. Use this rating scale to get a baseline rating of any strain symptoms that you may feel right now. You evaluate each item in terms of its presence within the last two hours. Do not rate it, if you do not have a listed strain item at this time.

We categorize the symptoms physically, mentally, and behaviorally. One equals a little true, two equals true, and three equals very true. The fewer strain items you endorse, the greater level of relaxation you should feel right now.

Body and mind awareness increase your ability to detect early signs of strain so you can cut these high arousal symptoms off at the pass, so to speak. Now that you have an appreciation for signs of strain, let's link them up to your daily life events. As you already learned, our past training conditions what we deem as stressful or non-stressful. The following exercise helps you to identify the exact nature of your stress.

EXERCISE END

Hardy Relaxation Exercise 2, Your Average Daily Relaxation Score

This exercise helps you to become sensitive to subtle changes going on in your body daily. For one day, you fill out the observation diary that follows. Write down hourly your activity, relaxation level, and the presence of any train symptoms. To refresh your memory of strain items, See "Appendix A: Strain Rating Scale" on page 221. If things remain constant from one hour to the next, indicate no change.

By closely observing yourself throughout the day, you heighten your awareness of bodily shifts that could lead to strain, at the day's end. Daily activities can range from stressful, like an exam, to non-stressful, like watching television or resting. If you feel well, just note it. There is no need to look for symptoms, if you have none. At the end of the day, calculate an average relaxation score, by summing your total relaxation level and dividing that number by the number of relaxation entries.

Observation Diary

Time	Activity	Symptoms	Relaxation Score
6 am			10 9 8 7 6 5 4 3 2 1
7 am			10 9 8 7 6 5 4 3 2 1
8 am			10 9 8 7 6 5 4 3 2 1
9 am			10 9 8 7 6 5 4 3 2 1
10 am			10 9 8 7 6 5 4 3 2 1
11 am			10 9 8 7 6 5 4 3 2 1
12:00			10 9 8 7 6 5 4 3 2 1
1 pm			10 9 8 7 6 5 4 3 2 1
2 pm			10 9 8 7 6 5 4 3 2 1
3 pm			10 9 8 7 6 5 4 3 2 1
4 pm			10 9 8 7 6 5 4 3 2 1
5 pm			10 9 8 7 6 5 4 3 2 1
6 pm			10 9 8 7 6 5 4 3 2 1
7 pm			10 9 8 7 6 5 4 3 2 1
8 pm			10 9 8 7 6 5 4 3 2 1
9 pm			10 9 8 7 6 5 4 3 2 1
10 pm			10 9 8 7 6 5 4 3 2 1
11 pm			10 9 8 7 6 5 4 3 2 1
12 am			10 9 8 7 6 5 4 3 2 1
		Average Relaxation Score	10 9 8 7 6 5 4 3 2 1

First Hardy Relaxation Checkpoint

What was your experience in doing relaxation exercises one and two? What signs of strain do you show when stressed? How does your body respond physically, mentally, and behaviorally to your daily activities? Are there certain activities that cause you strain?

Summary Concepts And Terms

BASELINE MEASUREMENT

Test Your Knowledge

To test what you learned so far, see if you can correctly answer the following questions. Remember, the more information you have to think about what happens to you, the more building blocks you have to generate creative solutions to everyday living problems. This, in turn, strengthens your HardiAttitudes.

Commitment. The more information you seek to learn about yourself and the world, the more you demonstrate your belief that you are worthwhile and important enough to gather information that helps you.

Control. The more information you gather about yourself and your world, the greater your ability to influence the direction of your life.

Challenge. The effort you apply in learning the hardiness skills shows that you regard the time spent in developing yourself as a normal challenge of life.

For the answer key, See "Questionnaire and Test Your Knowledge Answer Keys" on page 259.

1. Relaxation techniques bring about a _____ response.

2. _____ awareness alerts us to bodily changes.

3. _____ data gives you a point for behavioral comparison when changing behavior.

4. Muscle twitching, headache, nausea, and fatigue are _____ symptoms.

5. Rather than give in to it, you develop skills to help you manage stressful situations. You believe whatever comes your way is "grist for your learning mill." You build the HardiAttitude of _____.

6. You know through your own resources, you can influence a lot of what happens to you in life. You show the HardiAttitude of _____.

7. You believe you are important and worthwhile enough to engage fully in whatever you are doing in life. You show the HardiAttitude of _____.

Learning Goals

- Appreciate how body symptoms inform us as to changes in strain and relaxation levels

- Know how you can use baseline body states to determine the effects of relaxation interventions

- Appreciate how observing the way your body responds to various activities can benefit you in your daily living

The Science of Breathing

Introduction

Your life begins, when you can breathe on your own. Breathing's life-affirming aspects predate Christ. The Book of Genesis speaks to breath's life affirming significance, when it emphasizes God breathing life into the world. Since Ancient times, Eastern religions utilized breath control, as a self-awareness vehicle.

Breathing, more mundanely, supports every body function. It orchestrates heart rate and blood flow, among other vital body processes, like catalyzing food nutrients for body energy. Your breathing rate shifts, with activity level and stress, mood, and health changes. Upset and anxiety and fear that accompanies increased threat can increase your breathing rate and consequently, body arousal. This produces breathing-related body changes in the form of physical, mental, and behavioral symptoms.

What exactly happens when you breathe? Oxygen, taken in through the nose or mouth, descends through the **trachea** (windpipe), **bronchi** (windpipe branches to each lung), and **bronchioles** (thousands of tubes attached to each bronchi) to where it reaches the lungs' **alveoli** (air sacs). These air sacs further respiration by expanding. When it reaches the aortic artery, oxygen combines with blood to create energy. The oxygen-rich blood then travels throughout your body where it feeds every cell and organ. **Carbon dioxide** is the byproduct of this metabolic process.

Exhalation deflates the lungs. Residual blood and body fluid carbon dioxide then ascends the same system that initially brought oxygen into the body system. In regulating physiological processes, the oxygen and carbon dioxide exchange that accompanies inhalation and exhalation is vital to body functioning.

Two Types Of Breathing.

Breathing seems like the easiest thing we do, because it's most natural to our systems. But many of us have lost our ability to breathe correctly. Today, we culturally favor flattened tummies, lead stressful lives, and live in increasingly threatening times. In this defensive living mode, we misuse our most basic life-sustaining mechanism.

Infants breathe correctly. When they breathe, their tummies gently rise and deflate. An infant's immature skeletal and muscular system is incapable of interfering with her breathing mechanism. But, as the infant grows and engages fully in living, she too may begin to misuse her breathing mechanism. Breathing is a remarkable body mechanism for restoring physical, mental, and behavioral calm and centeredness.

Thoracic. Chest, or thoracic breathing, uses the ribcage and its muscles to expand the lungs. While it is true that ribcage expansion inflates the lungs somewhat, it is not the primary lung expander. Your lungs attach to your ribcage by a thin tissue. Your lungs, however, are organs, not muscles. The lungs do not inflate and deflate on their own. Rather, they expand and contract by muscles attached to them. Because of this, your lungs expand to the degree that your ribcage expands. Thoracic breathing is therefore shallow, with only some alveoli inflating.

Thoracic breathing can interfere with your body's ability to transform food nutrients into energy. This limits blood flow to the body's peripheral cells, internal organs, such as the pancreas, stomach, spleen, and liver, and the sensory organs. Poorly oxygenated blood also leads to low carbon dioxide blood levels, which changes your **blood pH** to dangerously alkaline. Inhalation and exhalation rate, rhythm, and depth are critical to maintaining a balanced pH level.

Diaphragmatic. Abdominal, or diaphragmatic breathing, is the deepest of all breathing. Your diaphragm muscle is the lungs' primary expander. This large muscle attaches to the lower third of your lungs, and when it expands, it contracts and pulls the lungs downward, increasing their ability to take in more air. The blood that mixes with inhaled oxygen resides in the lower third of your lungs. To get oxygenated blood, you need air to reach the lower third of your lungs. It is here wheremore alveoli inflate, and the lobes of the lungs expand to their fullest capacity.

Diaphragmatic breathing is the primary mechanism underlying relaxation techniques. Diaphragmatic breathing reduces the negative effects of prolonged sympathetic activity.

1. What is the oxygen and carbon dioxide relationship?

When it mixes with blood nutrients, oxygen produces a carbon dioxide byproduct. Decreased oxygen intake interferes with this process and can result in psychiatric- type symptoms, such as anxiety, hyperventilation, and suspiciousness. Body homeostasis hinges upon the ratio of oxygen and carbon dioxide in your system at any point in time. When your blood gases and blood fluids are not in proper ratio to one another, body processes go awry. Rapid, irregular, and shallow breathing disrupt the blood and carbon dioxide ratio.

What happens next? Tissue carbon dioxide level lowers. When this happens, oxygen over-binds to your red blood cells, which prevents it from distributing freely throughout your system. Low blood tissue oxygen leads to symptoms, such as increased irritability, numbness and tingling of hands, feet, mouth and tongue, stiffness, aches and cramps of muscles, spasms of hands and feet, twitching and, at the extreme, convulsions. This shifts the blood and body fluid toward an alkaline state. Calcium now dominates the concentration of minerals in your cells. Excess cellular calcium overstimulates your system because it saturates heart, muscle, and nerve receptors. Hyperactivity, muscle and heart spasms, anxiety and panic disorders, dizziness and confusion, fear and paranoia, and agitated depression can arise from this cellular pH condition.

2. Why is adequate body oxygen good for you?

Blood adequately saturated with oxygen balances the nervous system. Your veins and arteries dilate to a proper size that allows blood to flow freely throughout your body. Stress can constrict the blood vessels and lower blood tissue oxygen level, which aggravates disorders like migraine, epilepsy, and Raynaud disease.

3. Why do body passageways and air sacs dilate first with sympathetic arousal?

Sympathetic arousal activates breathing to help you fight or flee the stressful situation. In an effort to increase oxygen to the brain and body, air passage ways and air sacs dilate. The rest of your cardiovascular system, however, constricts. In contrast, parasympathetic activity dilates the entire cardiovascular system.

4. How does breathing contribute to the maintenance of blood and fluid pH?

Constant internal conditions maintain body homeostasis. The body's internal temperature must be 98.6°, the glucose level of the blood must not be too high or too low, oxygen (O_2) and carbon dioxide (CO_2) must balance, and the body's fluid pH must stay within a range of 7 to 7.4. The blood especially must maintain a constant pH level of 7.4. This balances your body's fluid concentration of sulphur, potassium, sodium, magnesium, and calcium. When body homeostasis is disrupted, your pH turns overly acidic or alkaline. An overly acidic pH is mostly sulphur and phosphorus dominant while an overly alkaline pH is mostly calcium, potassium, and sodium dominant. These conditions shift with sympathetic versus parasympathetic dominance. Sympathetic dominance tends to turn body fluid and blood too acidic. Diaphragmatic breathing balances overly acidic or alkaline blood and body fluids.

The lungs do 85% of the work in maintaining blood and body fluid pH. As mentioned, a prolonged overly acidic or alkaline blood and body fluid condition can result in a host of illnesses and degenerative disorders. You can tell when your body's pH turns too acidic because breathing rate increases. This occurs in diabetic and hypoglycemic glucose states. A major effect of prolonged blood acidity is central nervous system depression. When blood pH falls below 7, in the acidic direction, the nervous system depresses. In this condition, you become disoriented and, if prolonged, comatose. Your body, however, has so many regulating mechanisms that it would take excessive stress or illness to produce this condition.

5. Why is rate, rhythm, and depth of breathing so important?

The number of breaths you take per minute is your breathing rate. It is the volume of air that enters and leaves your lungs per minute. As your breathing rate increases, its rhythm, depth, and rate become irregular. Breathing rate accelerates with increases in sympathetic activity.

Normal Activity. Your breathing rate is between 12 to 15 breaths per minute in activities that do not require too much sympathetic arousal. Listening to a lecture, engaging in normal social interaction, or doing dishes are examples of normal activity. Body arousal is mild to moderate while engaging in such activities.

Vigorous Activity. Your breathing rate is between 15 to 18 breaths per minute in vigorous activity. A conflicted social interaction or finding out you just won the lottery are examples of vigorous activity. In this condition, you can run the risk of low tissue oxygen and blood fluid and blood gas imbalance. Body arousal is moderate to high while engaging in such activities.

Relaxed Activity. Your breathing rate is between 5 to 8 breaths per minute when relaxed. As we become more and more relaxed, our breathing rate slows, becomes more rhythmic, and deepens.

Hardy Relaxation Exercise 3: Where Do You Breathe?

In this exercise, you evaluate which type of breathing you use. Do not change a thing at this point. Just observe, and breathe as you normally do. Place one hand over your chest and the other hand over your tummy. As you breathe, notice which hand moves most outward. If the hand over your chest moves most outward, you are a thoracic breather. If the hand over your abdomen moves most outward, you are a diaphragmatic breather. Take a moment to write down your observations.

_____

_____

_____

_____

EXERCISE END

Hardy Relaxation Exercise 4: Breathing To Reduce Strain

You can evaluate this exercise's ability to reduce strain, by getting a pre- and post-baseline rating of your strain symptoms. If the exercise made a difference for you, the number and intensity of the pre-rating strain symptoms should decrease. For a baseline symptom rating, See "Appendix A: Strain Rating Scale" on page 221. Rate yourself on this strain scale, before and after the exercise.

Begin by lying down on the floor in a comfortable position; this stops your chest from taking over the abdomen's breathing role. Place your left hand on your chest and your right hand on your tummy just about two inches below your belly button. If you breathe diaphragmatically, the hand on your tummy will move up and down as you take air into, and release air from, your lungs. If, however, you breathe thoracically, the hand on your chest will move up and down as you inhale and exhale air from your lungs.

The Balloon Imagery Breathing Exercise

Imagine your stomach as a balloon that expands and contracts with respiration. See the balloon gently expand and rise as you inhale air. See the balloon contract and lower as you slowly release air from slightly parted lips. By controlling the rate of exhalation, you deepen relaxation. To control exhalation, exhale while you slowly release air from slightly parted lips. See your balloon slowly contract and lower, with the released stream of air.

Do you feel more relaxed after the diaphragmatic breathing exercise? If so, how does this experience contribute to your sense of commitment, control, and challenge? Summarize your experience below:

_____
_____
_____
_____
_____
_____
_____
_____
_____
_____
_____

EXERCISE END

Hardy Relaxation Exercise 5: Bringing The Autonomic

Nervous System Under Conscious Control

Alternate Nostril Breathing

By controlling the rate, depth, and rhythm of your breath, you can tone down the sympathetic nervous system. Controlled breathing dilates the body's cardiovascular system and induces biological changes that induce deep cellular relaxation. This yoga breathing exercise is great for calming your mind and body. Opening up the nasal passages permits inhaled air to fully and freely enter the lungs. This positively balances central nervous system functioning and produces a deep relaxation state. If you choose, you can get pre- and post exercise symptom ratings. **See "Appendix A: Strain Rating Scale" on page 221.**

1. Get into a comfortable sitting or lying down position.

2. Begin by closing off your right nostril and inhaling air through your left nostril. Imagine the inhaled air moving upward through your left nostril, downward through the lungs, as your stomach slowly expands and rises. Begin to exhale through the left nostril while imagining the exhaled air moving up and out of your lungs. Repeat this cycle for ten to fifteen inhalations.

3. Next, close off your left nostril and inhale air through the right nostril. Imagine the inhaled air moving upward through your right nostril, downward through the lungs, as your stomach slowly expands and rises. Begin to exhale through the right nostril while imagining the exhaled air moving up and out of your lungs. Repeat this cycle for ten to fifteen inhalations.

Describe your experience?

_____

_____
_____
_____
_____
_____

How can practicing this skill strengthen the attitudes of commitment, control, and challenge in you?

_____
_____
_____
_____

EXERCISE END

Second Hardy Relaxation Checkpoint

It's time now to check in with your Hardiness trainer, to share your experiences of hardy relaxation thus far.

Summary Concepts And Terms

ALVEOLI

CARBON DIOXIDE

BLOOD pH

BREATHING ACTIVITY LEVELS

BRONCHI

BRONCHIOLES

TRACHEA

Test Your Knowledge

To test what you learned so far, see if you can correctly answer the following questions. Remember, the more information you have to think about what happens to you, the more building blocks you have to generate creative solutions to everyday living problems. This, in turn, strengthens your HardiAttitudes.

Commitment. The more information you seek to learn about yourself and the world, the more you demonstrate your belief that you are worthwhile and important enough to gather information that helps you.

Control. The more information you gather about yourself and your world, the greater your ability to influence the direction of your life.

Challenge. The effort you apply in learning the hardiness skills shows that you regard the time spent in developing yourself as a normal challenge of life.

For the answer key, See "Questionnaire and Test Your Knowledge Answer Keys" on page 259.

1. When oxygen enters through your nose and mouth and descends through your trachea, bronchi, bronchioles, and alveoli, _____ has taken place.

2. When oxygen ascends through your alveoli, bronchioles, bronchi, and trachea, leaving your nose and mouth, _____ has taken place.

3. Your windpipe is called the

   _____.

4. The branches to each windpipe are called the

   _____.

5. Tubes that attach to each windpipe branch are called the _____.

6. The lungs' air sacs are called the _____.

7. Blood pumped from the heart to the lungs combines with oxygen to create _____.

8. When food nutrients mix with oxygen, the chemical byproduct is _____.

9. When you breathe _____ you use your ribcage.

10. When you breathe _____, you use your abdominal muscles.

11. When you breathe _____, you use the lower third of your lung.

12. The portion of your lungs where the blood resides is _____.

13. Breathing _____ is the best for relaxation.

14. Poorly oxygenated blood shifts your blood pH to dangerously _____.

15. Which three aspects of breath control help your body to maintain body fluid pH balance?

    • _____
    • _____
    • _____

16. When you breathe using your _____, you decrease the SNS and turn on the PNS.

17. Psychiatric symptoms, such as anxiety, panic, hyperventilation, and suspiciousness come about when your blood pH is in the _____ direction.

18. Blood pH shifts to alkaline when blood oxygen is low and blood carbon dioxide level is _____.

19. Increased irritability, numbness, tingling of hands, feet, toes, mouth, and tongue, muscle cramps, twitches, spasms, and aches result from a deficiency in which kind of blood gas?

    _____

20. A shift in intra- and intercellular mineral concentration can disrupt body fluid and blood _____.

21. A pH of _____ indicates a balance in blood and body fluids.

22. When your pH is acidic, the blood's mineral concentration is high in _____ and _____.

23. When your pH is alkaline, the blood's mineral concentration is high in _____, _____, and _____.

24. The autonomic branch that helps to balance blood gas and blood pH level is the _____.

25. The _____ do 85% of the work in maintaining your blood's pH level.

26. When the body's blood base shifts toward acidity, as in diabetes and hypoglycemia, the body will increase breathing _____ to balance blood oxygen and carbon dioxide levels.

27. Breathing 12 to 15 breaths per minute is associated with a _____ activity level.

28. Breathing 15 to 18 breaths per minute is associated with a _____ activity level.

29. Breathing 5 to 8 breaths per minute is associated with a _____ activity level.

30. The key to relaxation is _____.

31. Relaxation increases your confidence that you can positively influence the world around you. It builds the HardiAttitude of _____.

32. The practice of diaphragmatic breathing shows you believe you are important and worthwhile enough to exercise a skill that promotes well-being. This practice, then, builds the HardiAttitude of _____.

33. The practice of diaphragmatic breathing shows you believe skill development prepares you to face change positively and to regard life transitions as "grist for the mill." This HardiAttitude is _____.

Learning Goals

- Do you know the body structures involved in inhalation and exhalation?

- Do you know the value of diaphragmatic breathing in performance and health?

- Do you see how alternating your breathing rate can tone down sympathetic?

- Do you have a basic understanding of blood fluid and blood gas pH and how it influences your well-being?

CHAPTER 14

Progressive Muscle Relaxation

Activity-Related Muscle Movements

Muscle tension is a form of strain. The physiological researcher, Edmund Jacobson, located 1,030 muscles in the human body. He wanted to understand how much energy human beings waste per day in non activity-related muscle movements. When some people breathe, for example, they lift their shoulders, although this movement is unnecessary to the breathing task. Jacobson found that human beings expend too much of their daily energy in muscle movements peripheral to physical tasks. This can result in end-of-the-day muscular tension and pain that physically drains us.

How does muscle tension create pain? If you are anxious, upset, or worried, you are more apt to engage in physical movements that tighten your muscles and constrict your cardiovascular walls. This decreases blood flow to the tense muscle areas, which causes body pain.

You can prevent the pain that comes with muscle tension, by heightening your ability to note sensory differences when you are tense versus relaxed. Jacobson's muscle relaxation technique helps you to do this. As you develop in this skill, you readily note early signs of muscle tightening and use them as cues to relax. By relaxing tense and painful body muscles, you restore blood flow back to them.

Jacobson's research showed that we can self-regulate muscle tension by inducing a relaxation response.

Hardy Relaxation Exercise 6: Reducing Muscle Tension

Evaluate how relaxed you feel right now. Then, begin this muscle relaxation exercise.

Tense	Neutral	Relaxed
1 2 3	4 5 6 7	8 9 10

Step 1 Get In A Relaxed Position. Sit in a comfortable chair and make sure your whole back contacts the chair. Keep your feet flat on the floor, your legs uncrossed, and place your hands in your lap. Balance your head between your shoulders. Do not bend your head forward, backward, or to the side.

Step 2 Tighten And Relax Muscle Groups. After you feel comfortable, you begin to tighten and then relax your body's muscle groups. For each muscle group, you go through the following exercise instructions. You first tense the muscle group for 10 seconds and then relax the muscle group for about 20 seconds. You do this two or three times before moving on to the next muscle group, noticing what it feels like to tense and to relax that area of your body. In addition, notice the sensations for a few moments before you go on to the next muscle group. If you keep the rest of your body relaxed while focusing on a muscle group, it is easier to note the difference between muscle tension and muscle relaxation. You should pay special attention to muscle groups in which you carry tension.

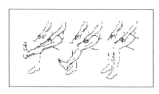

LEGS. Lift up your right leg, turn your toes inward toward you, and tighten your whole leg to its maximum tension. Notice where it feels tense (top and bottom and sides of thigh, knee, calf, front and back of foot, arch, and toes). Gradually relax and lower your leg until your foot is squarely on the floor, bending your knee as you relax. Make sure your leg goes back to the relaxing position. Notice how it feels to have those muscles switch from tension to relaxation, loosen, and then fully relax. Notice the difference in the way it feels. Repeat with the left leg.

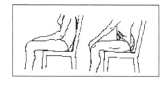

THIGHS AND BUTTOCKS. Tighten all the muscles below the waist including your thighs and your buttocks. You should feel yourself rise from the chair. You may notice that you have to tighten your legs a bit. Notice where it is particularly tense (top, bottom, and sides of thigh, muscles from the rear that make contact with the chair). Gradually relax and move back in your chair. Note how it feels to have those muscles switch from tension to relaxation, loosen, and then fully relax. Notice the difference in the way it feels.

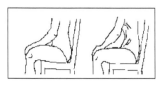

STOMACH. Tighten your stomach by pulling it in and making it as hard as a board. Notice where it feels tense (navel and the circle around the navel encompassing about 4 inches in diameter). Gradually relax your stomach to its natural position.

Notice how it feels to have those muscles loosen, release and then relax. Notice the difference between tension and relaxation in this muscle area. When this area relaxes, you may notice you breathing deepen.

CHEST. Tighten up your chest, constrict it, or pull it in. Notice where it feels tense (middle of the chest, and above and below each breast.) Gradually let your chest relax. Notice how it feels to have those muscles loosen, release themselves, and relax. Notice the difference between tension and relaxation in this muscle area.

ARMS. Put your right arm out straight, make a fist, and tighten your whole arm (from your hand to your shoulder) to its maximum tension. Pay special attention to those areas that are particularly tense (biceps, forearm, back of arm, elbow, above and below the wrist and fingers). Let it relax, release your elbow, and lower your arm until it rests in your lap and in a relaxed position. Notice how it feels to have those muscles loosen and relax. Notice the difference between tension and relaxation in this muscle area. Repeat with the left arm.

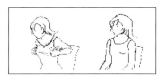

BACK. Move forward in your chair. Bring your elbows up and back; push them toward each other. Notice where it feels particularly tense (shoulders and down the middle of your back). Gradually relax by moving back into the chair while you straighten out your

arms and put them in your lap in the relaxing position. Notice the feeling as those muscles loosen, switch from tension to relaxation, and then fully relax.

NECK. Tighten your neck. Notice where it feels tense (Adam's apple, and on each side and the back of the neck). When you relax, you notice the difference between tension and relaxation in this muscle area. Notice how it feels to have those muscles loosen and then fully relax.

JAW. Clench your teeth and notice where your jaw feels tense (the muscles on the side of the face and also the temples). Then, let go. Notice how it feels to have those muscles loosen up and relax. Enjoy the difference between tension and relaxation.

TONGUE. Press your tongue up against the roof of your mouth. Notice where it feels tense (on the inside of the mouth and tongue, and the muscles just below the jaws). Slowly let your tongue relax by allowing it to gradually fall to the floor of your mouth. Notice the difference between tension and relaxation in this muscle area. Notice how it feels to have your lips loosen and relax.

LIPS

Pucker your lips and notice where they feel tense (upper and lower lips, and sides of the lips). When you note how it feels to be tense in this muscle area, gradually relax your lips and note the difference between tension and relaxation. Notice how it feels to loosen up and relax your lips.

SMILE. Place your mouth and face in a forced smile. The upper and lower lips and cheeks on each side should feel tense. Your lips should be tense enough that they are against your teeth. When you are through noting the tension in this area, let your mouth and face relax. Allow the side of each of your cheeks to loosen and relax. Let your whole face gradually relax and notice how it feels to have those muscles loosen and relax.

NOSE. Wrinkle up your nose (bridge and nostrils). Notice how it feels to be tense in this area. Then, relax your nose slowly, letting go of all the tension in this area. Notice how it feels to loosen up and relax the nose. Notice the difference between tension and relaxation in this area.

EYES. Close your eyes tightly. Squint them tightly and feel the tension above and below each eyelid and on the inner and outer edges of the eyes. When you are through noticing how it feels to be tense in this area, gradually let your eyes relax as you open them slowly. Enjoy the difference between tension and relaxation in this area.

FOREHEAD. Wrinkle up your forehead (if you wear glasses, remove them). Notice how it feels to hold tension in this area (over the bridge of the nose and above each eyebrow). When you are through noticing the tension, slowly relax your forehead and take a few seconds to notice how it feels to have those muscles loosen up and then completely relax. Enjoy the difference between tension and relaxation in this area.

Now that you have gone through this exercise, how do you feel?

Tense	Neutral	Relaxed
1 2 3	4 5 6 7	8 9 10

Compare your scores on the muscle relaxation rating scale before and after doing the muscle relaxation exercise. Do you feel more relaxed after the exercise?

_____

_____

_____

_____

Has your experience increased your sense of commitment, control, and challenge, those components of the HardiAttitude?

_____

_____

_____

_____

EXERCISE END

Third Hardy Relaxation Checkpoint

What was your experience in doing muscle relaxation? Where are you most apt to hold tension when you get stressed? When is it most apt to occur and under which circumstances? How does the muscle tension make you feel? How long does it last?

Summary Concepts And Terms

MUSCLE TENSION

Test Your Knowledge

To test what you learned so far, see if you can correctly answer the following questions. Remember, the more information you have to think about what happens to you, the more building blocks you have to generate creative solutions to everyday living problems. This, in turn, strengthens your HardiAttitudes.

Commitment. The more information you seek to learn about yourself and the world, the more you demonstrate your belief that you are worthwhile and important enough to gather information that helps you.

Control. The more information you gather about yourself and your world, the greater your ability to influence the direction of your life.

Challenge. The effort you apply in learning the hardiness skills shows that you regard the time spent in developing yourself as a normal challenge of life.

For the answer key, See "Questionnaire and Test Your Knowledge Answer Keys" on page 259.

1. _____ is an aspect of the strain response.

2. You practice muscle relaxation to study the difference between muscle_____ and

   _____.

3. The muscle relaxation exercise builds body awareness that gives you a skill to manage strain. This builds the HardiAttitude of

   _____.

4. The practice of muscle relaxation shows you believe you are important and worthwhile enough to develop a skill that helps you to manage strain. This is the HardiAttitude of

   _____.

5. The practice of muscle relaxation shows you believe skill development prepares you to face change positively and to regard life transitions as "grist for the mill." This builds the HardiAttitude of _____.

Learning Goals

- Understand the relationship between activity-related muscle movements and strain

- Appreciate how learning to distinquish tense from relaxed muscles helps you to prevent muscle strain

CHAPTER 15

Meditation

On Presence

*Eyes are just windows,
they can't see unless
you see through them.
How can a window
see? You have to stand
at the window, only
then can you see.*

Osho

Self-Reflection

Through meditative activities, we can relax and develop our ability to observe what's happening to us internally and externally. A heightened ability to reflect upon our experience leads to increases in self-knowledge. We can more accurately anticipate our reactions to people and situations and have insight into our motivations. Through this type of self-reflection, we are better able to direct our thoughts and actions in socially-constructive directions.

Self-reflection used to develop oneself psychologically and spiritually is not new. Since ancient times, reflective techniques, like prayer, meditation, and trance have been used to further human beings' spiritual practice. Meditation is a relaxation tool, or it can be used as a technique for developing self-knowledge by increasing one's self-reflective abilities.

By meditating, you can also ready yourself for the HardiCoping process. Distracting mental chatter interferes with putting problems into perspective so that you can begin to solve them. The calm and self-knowledge that grows with your meditation practice is particularly useful to the HardiTraining approach to managing life change.

Meditation For Relaxation

The **first meditation benefit** is stress reduction. When you meditate to relax, you want to clear your mind of nagging thoughts and worries that undermine your physical and mental calm. Before you try this exercise, review the following meditation conditions.

1. Do not meditate on an empty or full stomach. This is an unnecessary discomfort that can distract you. Make sure you are not over aroused by upset, caffeine, or sugary food and drink. It's difficult to meditate when you are overstimulated.

2. Do not over meditate. Meditate for a comfortable time frame. Your beginning sessions should be no more than 15 to 20 minutes per day. Prolonging your meditation session does little to advance your skill.

3. Choose a quiet, comfortable place to meditate. Reduced noise, dim lights, and loose clothing is best.

4. Sit comfortably in a chair or on the floor and rest your hands gently in your lap. You can also sit cross-legged on a floor cushion under your buttocks, so that both knees comfortably touch the floor. They call this the lotus position.

5. By turning your awareness inward, you tune out extraneous stimuli that disrupt your meditation practice. It's good, thus, to close your eyes, when you meditate.

THE CLEARING MIND MEDITATION TECHNIQUE

In this meditation technique, you use a **mantra** to clear nagging thoughts and worries from your mind.

What is a mantra? A mantra is a tool that focuses your attention and stops your mind from wandering. It can be a religious phrase, such as "Be still and know that I am God," or a vowel, like ohm, ha-sam, or may-am. An image can also serve as a mantra. You can, for example, imagine nourishing water slowly moving upward through the ground into a tree's roots, through its bark, to its limbs, and outward through its leaves. Or, watching your breath can serve as a mantra. Here, you might imagine inhaled oxygen entering your nostrils and descending through your lungs and bloodstream where its nourishes every body cell.

First, you choose a mantra. My mantra is:

_____.

Now, begin to quiet yourself. Close your eyes, and begin to silently repeat your mantra in your mind. Whichever mantra you are using, gently focus on it. If it is a specific phrase, vowel, or word, just silently repeat it in your mind. If it is an image, focus on it.

Continue to allow your mantra to quiet your mind, as it gently narrows your focus. Extraneous thoughts and images will come and go. When they do, let them go and return to your mantra. When you complete this exercise, ask yourself the following questions.

1. Do you feel calmer, focused, and/or centered?

2. Was it difficult to concentrate on your mantra?

3. Did you notice your breathing rate slow down as you concentrated on your mantra?

In the future, you can use this technique to help you become calm, focused, and centered prior to any event you regard as stressful. Just 10 to 15 minutes of this calming activity can enhance your well-being and performance.

Meditation For Mindfulness

The **second meditation benefit** is mindfulness. Many people let their minds dictate their thoughts. They let personal issues and concerns determine their focus. This self-involved, unmindful focus often heightens fears, anxieties, and emotions, and thus stress. It also can lead us to distort perception, as our internal world dominates our focus. When we are unmindful, we are more apt to respond poorly to living circumstances.

You can also meditate, then, to enhance your observation capabilities. By learning how your mind works, your self-observation abilities increase. The mind is an association machine; it makes connections between related and unrelated ideas. With or without us, our mind makes connections. A word, image, memory, or symbol stimulates association after association, and off and running, we go.

Like a computer, the mind stores information in complex information folders that organize your knowledge and experience. Much like computer files and folders, the mind's storage templates have names and labels that identity their subject matter. A thought, image, feeling, or activity acts like a computer search keyword. This process activates relevant, and sometimes not so relevant, stored information. The more mindful we are, the more easily we can observe what's relevant to our here and now needs and environmental demands. If we are unmindful, irrelevant information can more easily take us into unfruitful thinking pathways. Then, a chain of random associations can produce a running mental commentary that takes on a life of its own. Most people spend a great portion of their day letting their minds overrun them in this way.

THE CASE OF MARY

Mary is a good example of how an undisciplined mind can stress a person. While driving to school, another car almost smashes into the back of her car. Mary thinks about a time when her grandmother got into a car accident. She remembers how much fun she had as a child with her grandmother. She next wonders about a childhood friend who lived next door to her grandmother. She wishes they had remained in contact with each other. This makes her sad and feeling lonely. She wonders if her friend is successful. By the time Mary arrives at school, she is upset. She decides to skip class because she's in no mood to concentrate. If Mary were really the "captain of her ship," her day would not have had to turn out this way.

The experienced meditator learns how to observe the mind's associations without attaching to them. Experienced meditators do not turn these associations into dramas about themselves and life. In the above example, Mary attached the event. Mary turned this isolated event into the drama of her life. Because of this, she prolonged strain, missed an important lecture, and decreased her chance of getting a good course grade. Mary created a circumstance that fulfilled her story about herself; she is a victim.

Who is fooling whom? In mindful meditation, you develop the capacity to reflect upon the nature of thinking so you can begin to see that your thoughts do not define you. You have a choice in how your day proceeds. Mindful meditation practice helps you to develop the capacity to step outside of yourself.

Mindful meditation practice can deepen hardy perspective and understanding. With hardy perspective, you can pick and choose what you want to respond to. You move from reactor to actor. You are no longer a victim of whatever comes your way. Hardy understanding furthers your ability to step outside of yourself by deepening your appreciation for the complexity of any circumstance. The HardiAttitudes of commitment, control, and challenge increase within you as you experience yourself in this way.

THE I'M HAVING A THOUGHT MEDITATION TECHNIQUE

In this relaxation technique, you learn to observe your thoughts. Like Mary, our thoughts can sweep us away from one association to the next. A meditation tool called "I'm Having a Thought" trains your mind to stay on task. Whatever appears in your mind, a memory, or a random thought or image, you silently say to yourself, "I'm having the thought...", then you let it go and return to observing your breathing. For example, John observes his thinking when a thought enters his mind, "I'm tired." He says silently to himself, "I am having the thought that I am tired," and then returns to observing his breathing. You do this until the next thought or image arises where you repeat the process all over again.

Remember that thoughts come and go with our awareness or without it. Our minds rarely rest, and will resist this activity because we generally let them run freely. This technique quiets ideas that take us off track and away from our goals.

Mindful thinking does not imply an absence of thought, which would be difficult to achieve. It, rather, heightens your awareness of your thoughts so that you can decide what you want to respond to. You do not attach yourself to thoughts, emotions, and ideas that undermine your functioning. Attachment and emptiness are eastern terms for this phenomenon.

Despite such challenges, stick with it because meditation really works. Your session time should be no longer than 15 to 20 minutes, with beginning practice. With meditation, it is more important to practice daily and with consistency. Prolonging your practice session beyond your experience level will do little to increase your expertise at this skill. Your skill at observing your thinking may vary daily with your physiological arousal level. But, as you become your ship's master, you should experience more control over the various biological shifts that disrupt your calm and concentration. You'll begin to notice:

- Distracting thoughts lessen
- Detached observation increases
- Greater Awareness and Insight

Overall, do you see how meditation might help you in your daily living?

_____
_____
_____
_____

Can you see how being mindful can lead to an increase in your HardiAttitudes and aid your Hardi-Coping efforts?

_____
_____
_____
_____

Summary Concepts And Terms

SELF REFLECTION

MEDITATION SHORT-TERM GOAL

MEDITATION LONG-TERM GOAL

MINDFUL MEDITATION

Test Your Knowledge

To test what you learned so far, see if you can correctly answer the following questions. Remember, the more information you have to think about what happens to you, the more building blocks you have to generate creative solutions to everyday living problems. This, in turn, strengthens your HardiAttitudes.

Commitment. The more information you seek to learn about yourself and the world, the more you demonstrate your belief that you are worthwhile and important enough to gather information that helps you.

Control. The more information you gather about yourself and your world, the greater your ability to influence the direction of your life.

Challenge. The effort you apply in learning the hardiness skills shows that you regard the time spent in developing yourself as a normal challenge of life.

For the answer key, See "Questionnaire and Test Your Knowledge Answer Keys" on page 259.

1. The first meditation benefit is

   _____.

2. The second meditation benefit is

   _____.

3. The mind is an _____ machine.

4. Many ancient cultures use _____ to develop one spiritually.

5. A _____ is any religious phrase, non-sense vowel, or word that keeps your mind from wandering during meditation.

6. _____ thinking can distort perception and increase strain and social stress.

7. _____ _____ is excellent for silencing your mind.

8. The experienced meditator learns how to observe the mind's associations without _____ to them.

9. Mindful meditation deepens hardy _____ and _____.

Learning Goals

- Do you understand the differences between short- and long-term meditation?
- Do you see how meditation practice can help your HardiCoping efforts?
- Do you understand how meditation works to develop your observation skills?

CHAPTER 16

Imagery

"Imagine where you will
be tomorrow, and it will
be so."

Gladiator. Dreamworks
Films (2000).

What Is Imagery?

Although we use words to voice our internal and external experience, **imagery** is our most basic information-processing tool. Think about how many times per day you get lost in your imagination. Sometimes we visualize an event so strongly that it seems like we are there physically. If the imagined scene is unpleasant, we can feel agitated. And, if the imagined scene is a happy one, we feel relaxed and pleased.

Advertising agencies understood what Aristotle meant when he said, "The soul never thinks without a picture." If we see McDonald's golden arches ahead of us, we know a hamburger and French fries are a bite away. And, we don't leave home without American Express because we believe it can solve some of our problems. Long before we thought in words, we thought in images, and we still use imagery to organize information easily into memory.

When you combine physical relaxation with images that represent a desired physical, mental, or behavioral condition, you can actualize your living goals. You do this by using your five senses, sight, sound, smell, touch, and taste, to imagine the desired condition. The more sensory modes you use to think about something, the more lifelike, it becomes. If, for example, you want an image to relax you, you need to visualize a relaxing scene using as many of the sensory modes as you can. You *see* yourself, for example, at a beautiful blue stream surrounded by lush greenery, you *scoop up* the water while the sun's rays *warm your back*. When the wind *rustles* the trees, a fragrant *smell* envelopes you. With practice, your body begins to associate this visualized state with physical, mental, and behavioral relaxation, so that you can return to this condition whenever you want.

Frequently Asked Questions

1. Is imagery safe?

   Imagery is quite safe. It is a skill that utilizes our natural tendencies and encourages learning.

2. Isn't imagery hocus-pocus stuff?

   It is not hocus-pocus or mystical. Your mind processes information in the above mentioned five senses. When you relax through deep breathing, the rate at which your nerves fire slows down. This shifts your nervous system from sympathetic to parasympathetic dominance. Your brain's nerves begin to fire at a rate between 8 to 7 brain wave cycles (alpha hertz cycle). In this condition, your awareness widens and allows you to focus openly on multiple stimuli. The opposite happens with sympathetic dominance. In this condition, your brain's nerves begin to fire at a rate between 13 and 8 cycles per minute (beta hertz cycle). You need to be in an alpha brain hertz cycle for imagery to work.

3. What can I expect to experience?

   Practicing imagery in a relaxed state can increase body sensations, like tingling. It is also common, in such a state, for the body to shift into the background of your awareness. There can also be a sense of time distortion. A half-hour, for example, can seem like ten minutes.

4. What if I don't come out of the imagery exercise?

   You will always come out of a state of relaxation. There is nothing about relaxation techniques that override your will.

The following imagery techniques help you to cultivate a state of mind or a particular skill or resource. By using your imagination when relaxed, you can bring about behaviors that create the circumstance you wish to fulfill. The aforementioned frequently asked questions informs as to how imagery actually works.

Imagery For Performance Enhancement

Read over the Safe Place imagery script that follows. When you feel you know it well enough, breathe diaphragmatically to relax. As your relaxation deepens, begin to visualize a place that feels safe, comfortable, and peaceful. Once you complete visualizing the safe place, the exercise is over. Take a few minutes to complete the question that follows and then move on to the Hardy Person Imagery Script.

The Safe Place Imagery

"Now that you are comfortable and becoming more relaxed, we want you to transport across time...across space...to a place that to you means peace, comfort, safety and happiness. This is the first place in your experience that means this to you. Begin to experience all the sensations of peace...comfort...safety...and happiness...as you begin to look at all the things there are to see...and listen to, the sounds there are to hear...and smell. All the aromas..., touch and taste, whatever there is to experience it deeply. Knowing that as you experience all the parts of this special place, the feelings of peace...comfort...safety...and happiness...are being drawn inside of you. Draw these feelings into every part of your body so that every part of you knows these feelings. Each moment you spend experiencing this safe place, these feelings become stronger...and more of a part of you.

Just take a few minutes to enjoy the feeling of relaxation. You can return to this safe place again by seeing the safe place in your mind's eye.

How did you experience the Safe Place Imagery exercise? Do you find yourself even more relaxed? How do you feel with regard to the HardiAttitudes?

The next imagery exercise encourages you to experience yourself as a hardy person fulfilling your living goals. To realize your life dreams, you imagine yourself as you want to be. As writer and artist Pamela Vaull Starr once said, "Reach high, for stars lie hidden in your soul. Dream deep, for every dream precedes the goal."

The Hardy Person Imagery

When you are feeling very relaxed imagine yourself as you want to be...who are you...what do you look like...what are you doing...let your desires about yourself and your life unfold from within. See yourself as capable, healthy and vibrant. Imagine wellness...as a radiant light that surrounds and protects you. Draw more...and more...of this light into your body...your mind...your whole being. As you fill more...and more...with this radiant, resilient light....let your desires unfold. Imagine who you want to become...what you want out of life...see yourself doing and being it. What do you look like...what are you wearing...are you conversing with people...whatever it is imagine it deeply...if you can dream it....you can be it. Just spend a few minutes to stay there...enjoy this powerful image of yourself and know that by remembering this hardy image you can recapture these feelings any time you desire. In just a moment, the exercise will be over.

How did you experience the Hardy Person Imagery exercise? Do you find yourself even more relaxed? How do you feel with regard to the HardiAttitudes?

Fourth And Final Relaxation Checkpoint

To complete this final checkpoint, you practice one of the relaxation techniques in this component. You describe why you chose this particular relaxation technique, how it worked for you, and your experience practicing it.

In addition, please discuss the ways in which the information you learned in this component can strengthen the HardiAttitudes of commitment, control, and challenge. Finally, you discuss the ways in which the concepts and skills in this component helps you to solve stressful problems.

Summary Concepts And Terms

> IMAGERY
>
> SAFE PLACE IMAGERY
>
> HARDY PERSON IMAGERY

Test Your Knowledge

To test what you learned so far, see if you can correctly answer the following questions. Remember, the more information you have to think about what happens to you, the more building blocks you have to generate creative solutions to everyday living problems. This, in turn, strengthens your HardiAttitudes.

Commitment. The more information you seek to learn about yourself and the world, the more you demonstrate your belief that you are worthwhile and important enough to gather information that helps you.

Control. The more information you gather about yourself and your world, the greater your ability to influence the direction of your life.

Challenge. The effort you apply in learning the hardiness skills shows that you regard the time spent in developing yourself as a normal challenge of life.

For the answer key, See "Questionnaire and Test Your Knowledge Answer Keys" on page 259.

1. _____ is our most basic way of processing information.

2. Imagery often accompanies _____ exercises.

3. Imagery utilizes your _____ modes to process the information.

4. The brain wave cycle that is best for imagery is the _____ wave.

Learning Goals

- Do you understand how deep breathing can enhance the imagery technique?

- Do you understand why imagery scripts should utilize the five senses?

CHAPTER 17

Nutrition Basics

"Intake of proper food is important as it determines our thoughts, words and actions."

Atharva Veda

Nutrition And Stress

Good nutrition is especially important to your performance and health, during periods of prolonged stress and strain. A life transition, like going to school or job retraining requires that you have sufficient physical and mental energy to deal effectively with stress. You can expend lots of physical and mental energy, running between work, school, family, and social commitments. This can leave you little energy for work or play. For optimal physical and mental performance, you need a continual energy store. By sound nutrition habits, you can maximize performance and energy to effectively cope with life's pressures.

In stressful times, we often crave fatty and sugary foods to overcome fluctuating energy levels. Although initially satisfying, within hours, this short-term relief diet can lower blood sugar, increase physical exhaustion, mental confusion, and mood swings, and decrease self-confidence.

During stressful times, when we most need a sound diet, we often eat nutrient deficient foods. People undergoing a life change are particularly vulnerable to poor eating habits, which leads to physical, mental, and behavioral symptoms. Nutrient deficient diets increases fatigue, moodiness, and attention concentration capabilities. This can place us at risk for alcohol, drug, and food dependencies.

What do you do, if your energy runs low? You most likely get a cola or candy bar, to lift your energy level. In the short run, you feel better, but long term, these habits deteriorate your performance and health. This can lower your self-esteem, which increases your risk for addictions, as you attempt to self-medicate physical, mental, and behavioral symptoms.

This can also lead to excessive appearance preoccupations, which adds to your feeling out of control. Nutrient deficient food fads and unhealthy weight-loss diets may be one way you cope with such difficulties. Medical, learning, and psychiatric conditions that disrupt performance, like attention deficit disorders, anxiety and panic disorders, depression, and chronic fatigue syndromes, can be diet related.

In the HardiTraining program, nutrition is vital to HardiCoping, Hardy Social Support, and Hardy Relaxation and Exercise efforts. Sound nutrition helps your body and mind to run smoothly, so you can achieve your goals.

Twenty-First Century Nutrition Trends

By the end of the twentieth century, technology and science advances changed the way we live now. Many of these life streaming changes have deleterious effects on our health. Processed food is an example of this. More easily-stored foods that cook quickly oftentime have healthful fiber, vitamins, and minerals removed and harmful chemicals added to them. Despite this, processed food is Western society's primary food choice. Diets high in processed foods can cause or exacerbate chronic degenerative diseases, like type II diabetes, arthritis, cancer, and cardiovascular disease.

Although we work harder and exercise more today, on the average, most people eat daily larger food quantities, than at any point in history. By comparison with our ancestors, however, we expend much less energy fulfilling our daily activities. Our lives physically tax us less. We drive to the grocery store, sit and eat more, and walk, lift, run, and bend less. Our bodies also have to adapt less because of things, like better housing and heating. Just when conditions are such that we need less energy from food, we eat more rather than less. Overall, then, we consume more, exercise less, and consequently, store more fat than we burn.

Despite the many living amenities that streamline daily living, rapid living changes increase our stress. As we make the transition from an industrial to an information society, we all have to try to learn and use computers and keep abreast of the lightning changes they are bringing. We move around so much that the nuclear family hardly exists anymore. These changes pressure us. We try to cope and find social support, which makes it more difficult for us to relax.

The twentieth century has seen tremendous advances in medical technology and public health policy. Together, these advances have largely brought infectious diseases under control and, in this way, greatly increased how long we live. The paradox here is that, as we live longer, there is more time for us to develop the so-called degenerative disorders, such as arthritis, diabetes, heart disease, and cancer.

By learning to eat for life enhancement rather than for weight loss, you bypass these nutrition pitfalls. You need to learn the basics of food nutrients and metabolism and how food choices can either enhance or diminish your coping, social support, and relaxation efforts. Hardy people engage in more self-care behaviors, like sound nutrition. And, when you eat to enhance your health and coping efforts, the many benefits work to strengthen your HardiAttitudes.

Commitment. When you feel physically and mentally well nourished, you are more apt to regard yourself as important and worthwhile enough to engage fully in life.

Control. When you feel physically and mentally well nourished, you are more apt to take the necessary actions to influence the course of your life.

Challenge. When you feel physically and mentally well nourished, you are apt to regard adversity as opportunity and have the stamina to cope constructively with the situation at hand.

Food Nutrients

What Is Nutrition?

Webster's dictionary refers to nutrition as the "act or process of nourishing or being nourished." Nourishment refers to that which furthers, enhances, replenishes, restores, or balances biological functioning. Your body needs nourishment variety, to survive. Nourishment examples include eating, sleeping, physical touch, socializing, and time alone. Nourishment should do more than help you to survive; it should help you to thrive. You can eat in ways that bring about body repair, maintenance and growth, and energy levels, to further your living goals.

By taking in the sun's energy and environment gases, like oxygen, hydrogen, carbon, and nitrogen, plants make three distinct energy units. Together, these energy units, carbohydrate, protein, and fat,

are your body's **food nutrients**. Animal, dairy, grain, and vegetable food sources break down into these energy units, to aid your brain and body in repair, maintenance, and growth functions (Erasmus, 1986). Because they differ in molecular structure, they differ in energy output and cellular, organ, skeletal, and musculature function.

Food nourishment then refers to quantity and combination of food nutrients required to further body energy and structural development and maintenance. To evaluate food nutrients' role in metabolism, liken them to a car's structure and function. What you put into your car determines its performance and longevity. If you desire a high performing car, you put in high octane fuel. The same is true for your body. High stress, low octane foods can contribute to many disorders, like attention deficit disorder, premenstrual syndrome, depression, chemical and eating disorders, and phobias.

PROTEIN

Protein is the building block of body tissues and can be likened to the body frame of a car. Our muscles, internal organs (heart, kidney, lungs), bones, teeth, tendons, and ligaments are primarily protein. To continually grow, maintain, and repair these body components, you need protein.

Also, proteins form various chemical structures that make up your body's enzymes, hormones, and antibodies. These endocrine chemicals play a significant role in digestion, body fluid and acid balance, and immune functioning. If protein intake is sufficient, and there are no other biological difficulties, you have enough endocrine enzymes, hormones, and antibodies to protect you against illness.

Stress, strain, and increased activity level can significantly increase your need for protein at certain times. A protein, like a carbohydrate and fat, has a unique chemical structure. Proteins are a combination of oxygen, hydrogen, carbon and nitrogen. The various combinations of these molecules result in twenty different protein chemical structures called **amino acids**. These protein acids serve different body organs and systems (cellular, musculature, and skeletal), and are essential to your well-being.

Food categories that include animal (fish and meat), dairy, nuts and legumes, and plant proteins are the primary source for these essential amino acids. Animal proteins are more likely to provide all the essential amino acids than are those from plant sources. However, protein from all sources is very important. Balance, again, is important. Animal proteins provide all the essential amino acid proteins, but they also come with saturated fat that, in excess, can be deleterious to your health. Consequently, it is best to get your protein and essential amino acid requirements through a balanced intake from plant, animal, and dairy sources.

Carbohydrates and fat burn first in order to protect this protein store from being used. If there are no carbohydrates and little fat, then protein burns for body fuel. Seriously malnourished people become nothing but "bare bones" because a lack of sufficient nutrients causes the body to turn to the protein store in the muscles for metabolic fuel. Remember that protein serves as the body's building blocks. You need enough protein stored in your muscles to prevent you from getting ill. Your daily protein requirement increases with increased activity level, stress, and illness. These are the times when your body needs a lot of repair. You can get a rough estimate of your daily protein need, by using the following formula.

What is your body weight? _____ . In our example we will use 125 lb.

Now multiply your body weight by activity level. In our example, we will multiply 125 lb. by 0.5 (sedentary adult) = 62.50 or 63 grams of protein per day.

Sedentary Lifestyle	Light fitness or jogger	Sports participation or Training 3-times per/wk.	Moderate daily weight training or aerobics	Heavy weight training
0.5	0.6	0.7	0.8	0.9

Remember that protein is the last food nutrient to burn when other food nutrients are present. Protein is derived from amino acids and vital to your system's functioning. It is the building block of your body's tissues, muscles, skeletal structure, neurotransmitters, enzymes, and hormones. It is the body's primary source of amino acids. Protein is critical to your overall health and your daily functioning.

If you want to perform optimally while remaining healthy, you need to replenish your protein store daily. The daily urinary loss of protein equals the amount of protein from four quarts of milk (128 grams of protein). Also, in a strain response, proteins get broken down into sugar by your body to furnish you with energy. The rest goes to your liver where it is stored for later use. If you do not replace your daily protein store, your body cannot make the hormones that are vital to helping you manage the next stressful circumstance. This can lead to exhaustion, decreases in performance, and disease.

CARBOHYDRATES

A carbohydrate is the next food unit. This nutrient category includes fruit, vegetables, starch, grains, and legumes. **Carbohydrates** are your body's primary source of energy and can be likened to what gas does for a car. Carbon, hydrogen, and oxygen, in various configurations, make up carbohydrates. Chewing and digestion break carbohydrates down into your bloodstream. Your body can now use the byproduct of this breakdown, **glucose**, for usable energy.

Excess glucose that your body does not utilize through activity gets stored in your muscles and liver for later use. **Glycogen** is the stored form of glucose. When your body needs blood sugar, your brain biochemically tells the muscles and liver to change glycogen back to glucose where it can be used for immediate energy. Your liver also releases stored glycogen to support your body's automatic vital functions, such as breathing and thinking.

The ease with which a carbohydrate is transformed into glucose protects your body's protein reserve from being wasted in everyday activities. You just learned why an adequate protein store is vital to your performance and health. Glycogen, the stored form of glucose, spares protein from being used up as fuel. There are two kinds of carbohydrates.

The first is a **simple carbohydrate**. It is high in natural sugar. The simple sugars called glucose, fructose, and galactose are examples of a simple carbohydrate. The second is a **complex carbohydrate.** When three or more glucose molecules combine, they form a complex carbohydrate.

Both simple and complex carbohydrates break down into sugar in your system at differing rates. Simple carbohydrates break down easily into blood sugar due to a less complicated molecular structure that makes the food's natural sugar simpler to access. In contrast, complex carbohydrates do not break down easily into blood sugar. Its complex molecular structure makes these carbohydrates more difficult to digest.

But even within the simple and complex carbohydrate category, natural sugar and fiber levels vary with regard to how quickly the food converts into glucose. It is the food's natural sugar level and fiber content that determines whether it burns immediately or is time-released. The rate at which a food turns to usable energy for body fuel is called the food's **glycemic index**. A food's glycemic index influences physical, mental, emotional, and behavioral well-being. Simple and complex carbohydrates differ in sugar and fiber levels.

Simple Carbohydrates

If sugar level is high and fiber content is low, this is most likely a simple carbohydrate. In this instance, the body can quickly make glucose out of the food. Its low fiber content allows for easy access of its natural sugar into your bloodstream. The glucose raises your blood sugar level, which makes it available immediately for brain and body functioning. This quick sugar boost raises the food's glycemic index. Examples of simple carbohydrates with a high glycemic index include watermelon, bananas, kiwi, carrots, yellow squash, rice, potatoes, candy, processed cereals, and alcohol.

Complex Carbohydrates

If sugar level is low and fiber content is high, this is most likely a complex carbohydrate. These foods are more difficult to break down into usable glucose due to their high fiber and lower natural sugar content. Because of this, glucose is time-released into your bloodstream. This results in a slower and more consistent production of blood sugar, and consequently a more stable energy level, throughout your day. These foods, in general, have a low glycemic index. Examples of complex carbohydrates with a low glycemic index include most whole grains, legumes, nuts, and leafy green vegetables.

FIBER

Fiber is not a food nutrient, but it determines a carbohydrate's glycemic index. **Fiber**, a food's shell, determines the rate at which your body absorbs nutrients from food and aids in waste elimination. Fiber supplies no vitamins, minerals, or even calories. Despite this fact, fiber, commonly known as bulk or roughage, keeps things moving through your digestive tract and colon, stabilizes blood sugar, and maintains body health.

It is difficult or impossible to completely digest a carbohydrate's plant substance. It thus leaves some residue in the digestive tract. Fruit, legumes, oats, barley, and psyllium are particularly rich in fiber. The National Cancer Society and American Dietetic Association recommend 20 to 35 grams of fiber per day to prevent disease and to promote health. There are two kinds of fiber.

Soluble fiber can be broken down easily in your body. It combines with water to create softer and bulkier waste and slows down the body's absorption of glucose. The water-soluble fibers are called **pectins, gums, and mucilages**. They have a capacity to gel, which facilitates digestion and waste elimination. Soluble fiber is found mainly in citrus fruits, apples, potatoes, dried peas and beans, oatmeal, and bran. It further binds with cholesterol

compounds and body toxins in the intestine to help purify your bloodstream and lower its cholesterol level. A diet high in soluble fiber can reduce the risk of diabetes and heart disease.

Insoluble fiber, on the other hand, cannot be easily broken down by water. **Cellulose and lignin** are the insoluble fibers. This kind of fiber forms the framework of plant cell walls. This tougher roughage is also very important in helping your body to pass feces more easily through the intestines. Whole grains and wheat, cereals, and some vegetables, such as broccoli and carrots, are good sources of cellulose, while asparagus, wheat bran, and pears are good sources of lignin. High levels of insoluble fiber may decrease the likelihood of colon and rectal cancer, because it bulks up stools and speeds the passage of waste material through your intestines.

Processed foods often have their fiber removed from them. Fiber also helps with stabilizing blood sugar level. The tougher a food's fiber, the longer it takes for glucose to be released from the food and into your bloodstream. Fiber thus lowers the glycemic index of a food. It stays in your stomach longer, which allows the food's natural sugar to be time-released into your bloodstream, making it a stable form of usable energy.

FAT

Fat, your body's insulator, acts like the shock absorber of a car. It coats every nerve, vein, and artery in your body and cushions your body organs. Your body needs fat to function, especially the right kind of fat.

- It helps move blood and chemicals efficiently to every part of your body, just like the rubber that coats the electrical cord on an appliance moves, or conducts, electricity.

- In addition to conduction, fat beneath your skin insulates you from extreme temperatures.

- It also cushions vital organs by securing them in their place. This function permits you to do aerobic exercise or ride a horse without doing damage to your internal organs.

If your body doesn't have enough carbohydrates, it uses fat as an energy source for metabolism. This spares protein for its more important body-building functions. There are fats that heal, the good or unsaturated fats, and fats that kill, the bad or saturated fats. Most of us today know that unsaturated fats are better for us than saturated fats. But, probably very few people really understand why this is so.

Fats are made up from fatty acid chains of carbon, oxygen, and hydrogen atoms. The only thing that differentiates an unsaturated from a saturated fat is a small structural difference (molecular double bonds, which results in differences in melting temperatures between the two kinds of fats. This melting temperature difference is the major reason why fat is either good or bad.

Fats That Heal

Unsaturated fats have more double molecular bonds than saturated fats. And, the hydrogen atoms on these double bonds are placed in such a way that curves the molecular structure. This **cis**, or curved configuration, makes it difficult for unsaturated fatty acid chains to align and aggregate with one another, which lowers its melting temperature to 55°F. They thus stay liquid in your 98.6°F body system. In this situation, blood oxygen has little opportunity to degenerate and harden solid fat that has built up in your vascular walls. A diet high in unsaturated and low in saturated fats reduces the

potential for lifestyle diseases, such as diabetes, hypertension, and strokes. These healing fats are essential to your body's functioning and are chemically called the **essential fatty acids**. Your body requires a variety of essential nutrients (amino acids, fat, oxygen, and water) to work properly.

These essential nutrients support your body's maintenance and repair. Essential unsaturated fats help your body to maintain nerve cushioning and prevent bad fats from hardening in your vascular system. These fluid essential fatty acids also help to wash away the bad fats from your bloodstream. Examples of unsaturated fats include oil from nuts and seeds (almonds, cashews, peanuts, and walnuts), fish, and plant and vegetable oils, such as safflower, olive, corn, canola, soy, avocado, and many others.

Fats That Kill

Saturated fats, deficient in double molecular bonds, produce straight-bodied molecular chains, which tend to attract other saturated fat chains. These molecular chains are called the **trans fatty acids**. These straight-bodied, non-repelling chains create a sticky vascular environment where saturated fatty acids align, aggregate, and get stuck in your vascular walls. Manufactured saturated fatty acids require higher temperatures for melting (Erasmus, 1986; Long, 1989). This is done by adding hydrogen to the oil and heating it at a very high temperature (380° F) to raise the point at which these oils melt. This heat process straightens the molecular chains, making them more able to stick together and aggregate. The melting point of saturated, or trans, fats is 111°F. It does not melt easily in your 98.6°F bloodstream. This less fluid fat does stack up and block vascular walls, which prevents it from moving through your bloodstream.

When this bad saturated fat meets up with body oxygen, things get pretty ugly. Bloodstream oxygen mixes with saturated fat stuck in your vascular walls. Its oxidizing effect degenerates and hardens the fat, increasing your risk for cardiovascular disease. Your body needs fat to function properly. No fat to very low fat can be detrimental to your health (Des Maisons, 1997; Erasmus, 1996; Sears, 1995; Steward, et. al., 1995). It is not that you should cut fat out of your diet, but rather you should limit your daily intake of the bad fats. It is true that excessive eating of saturated fats can increase the risk of cancer, heart disease, and obesity, because these abnormal, hydrogenated fatty acid chains no longer fit the natural chemistry of our cells. The essential, unsaturated fatty acids found in some fish and plants (**omega-3**), however, have been found to decrease the risk of disease and increase well-being. It is best, in general, to limit saturated and favor unsaturated forms of fat. Saturated fat is found naturally in animal protein and in oils from coconut, cottonseed, and palm. Manufactured fats, such as butter and margarine, are also saturated.

Cholesterol And Blood Triglycerides

Cholesterol comes from food intake and the liver's enzyme and hormone production. Although we hear a lot of bad things about cholesterol today, you need cholesterol to live. Cholesterol also comes in its good and bad forms.

HIGH DENSITY LIPOPROTEIN

HDL's, the good form of cholesterol, strengthens the body's smooth veins and arteries. Now, blood can pump through your body without causing any structural damage. Cholesterol also makes up the body's sex and adrenal gland hormones. In addition, cholesterol helps our skin to stay moist. Because it does not bind easily to saturated fat, HDL cholesterol helps to wash away all the bad fats through your vascular walls by pushing it through your system. Your body makes 60 to 80% of the total cholesterol it needs each day.

LOW DENSITY LIPOPROTEIN

LDL's, the bad form of cholesterol, is more deleterious to your health. This kind of cholesterol binds easily to saturated fat. Thus, it builds up in your veins and arteries, causing blockage and increasing potential for heart attack and stroke.

BLOOD TRIGLYCERIDE LEVEL

This is the amount of bad fat circulating in your bloodstream that comes from carbohydrate intake (alcohol, starch, and sugar). A high blood triglyceride level can precipitate a heart attack or stroke, especially with the presence of other biological conditions.

Remember: It is the blood level proportion (ratio) of HDL to LDL cholesterol as well as blood triglyceride level, that you concern yourself with, rather than your overall cholesterol level. The greater your HDL to LDL ratio, the more likelihood that bad fat will be washed away from your system. By favoring unsaturated over saturated forms of fat, you increase your HDL cholesterol and decrease LDL cholesterol. You learn more about fat and your well-being further on in your reading. For now, remember that fat derived from fatty acid molecule chains is vital to your well-being because it:

- Helps to conduct nerve impulses throughout your body;
- Insulates skin from extreme temperatures;
- Cushions vital organs; and
- When carbohydrates are present, it is the second nutrient to be used for body fuel.

Water And Electrolytes

WATER

Your body uses water to traffic nutrients and waste products throughout your entire system. It functions like your car's motor oil and transmission fluid. Two thirds of your body weight is water. Water supports the life and pliability of your cells, tissues, and organs. It also constitutes a "water highway" that transports carbohydrates, fats, and proteins to their destinations and helps to prevent your blood from clotting. You can go for several weeks without food, but you die if you go ten days without water. Water is vital to your everyday functioning.

ELECTROLYTES

Your body uses these minerals (calcium, magnesium, phosphorus, potassium, and sodium) to produce electrochemical charges for nerve firing and consequent sympathetic nervous system activation. These electrolyte minerals control the body's ability to burn calories, a process otherwise known as **metabolism**.

Electrolytes, therefore, regulate body temperature, muscle contractions, blood thickness, nerve message sending and receiving and the regulation of your body fluids' phosphorus level. This phosphorus level, or **fluid pH**, is an estimate of your inter-

nal environment's alkalinity or acidity level. You learn more about this further on in your reading.

Minerals are like a car's carburetor; they provide the right amount of gas for the car's cylinders to work properly. Minerals also give strength to your bones and skeletal structure. Foods, especially fruits and vegetables, are the primary source for these electrolyte minerals. Bananas and green vegetables, for example, are a high potassium source.

First Hardy Nutrition Checkpoint

It is time to review with your Hardiness trainer what you learned so far and your experience completing the baseline nutrition survey. Do you understand the basics of food nutrition?

Summary Concepts And Terms

AMINO ACIDS

BAD FAT

CARBOHYDRATE: SIMPLE AND COMPLEX

CIS FATTY ACID

ELECTROLYTES

ESSENTIAL FATTY ACIDS

FAT

FLUID PH

FIBER

FOOD NUTRIENTS

GLUCOSE

GLYCEMIC INDEX

GLYCOGEN

GOOD FAT

HIGH DENSITY LIPOPROTEIN

INSOLUBLE FIBER: CELLULOSE AND LIGNIN

LOW DENSITY

LIPOPROTEIN

METABOLISM

OMEGA 3'S

PROTEIN

MINERALS

SATURATED FAT

SOLUBLE FIBER: PECTINS, GUMS AND MUCILAGES

TRANS FATTY ACID

TRIGLYCERIDE

UNSATURATED FAT

Test Your Knowledge

To test what you learned so far, see if you can correctly answer the following questions. Remember, the more information you have to think about what happens to you, the more building blocks you have to generate creative solutions to everyday living problems. This, in turn, strengthens your HardiAttitudes.

Commitment. The more information you seek to learn about yourself and the world, the more you demonstrate your belief that you are worthwhile and important enough to gather information that helps you.

Control. The more information you gather about yourself and your world, the greater your ability to influence the direction of your life.

Challenge. The effort you apply in learning the hardiness skills shows that you regard the time spent in developing yourself as a normal challenge of life.

For the answer key, See "Questionnaire and Test Your Knowledge Answer Keys" on page 259.

1. Which types of food characterize people's diets, when stressed?

    _____.

2. Because people undergoing a life transition have so many pressures on them, they are at high risk for

    _____.

3. Foods that have their fiber, vitamins, and chemicals removed are

    _____.

4. When you balance your food nutrients and eat for _____ _____, you eat in away that supports your HardiCoping, Social Support and Relaxation efforts?

5. Plants absorb the sun's energy and combine with the environment's oxygen, hydrogen, carbon, and nitrogen to form three different energy units called _____, _____, and _____.

6. The various combinations of oxygen, hydrogen, carbon, and nitrogen result in twenty different protein chemicals called _____ _____.

7. _____ makes up your muscles, internal organs, bones, teeth, tendons, and ligaments.

8. Stress, strain, illness, and increased activity level increases your need for _____.

9. Food protein sources include _____, _____, _____, _____, and _____.

10. The first food nutrient to burn for energy is a _____.

11. The last food nutrient to burn for energy is _____.

12. The second food nutrient to burn for energy is _____.

13. The food nutrient that serves as the building block for neurotransmitters, enzymes, and hormones is _____.

14. _____ is the chemical name for sugar and starch.

15. Simple sugars include _____, _____, and _____.

16. _____ is the form of carbohydrate that is readily accessible for body sugar.

17. _____ carbohydrates typically have more fiber.

18. The rate at which a carbohydrate turns to glucose in your body is a food's _____ _____.

19. There are two kinds of fiber. They are _____ and _____.

20. Your body's excess bloodstream glucose stored for later use is called _____.

21. _____ cushions your nerves, arteries, and organs.

22. The kind of fat that aggregates in your system and melts at 111°F is _____.

23. The _____ molecule determines the form of fat (saturated or unsaturated).

24. _____ refers to the amount of fat circulating in your bloodstream. It comes from sugar, alcohol, and fatty acids.

Learning Goals

- Do you understand the different food nutrients, their structure and body functions?

- Do you understand how electrolytes influence metabolism?

- Do you understand what makes a carbohydrate simple or complex?

- Do you understand glycemic differences between simple and complex carbohydrates?

- Do you understand differences in molecular structure that determines if an essential fatty acid is unsaturated or saturated?

CHAPTER 18

Blood Sugar and Metabolism

Diet Myths

Your performance, stamina, and health hinges upon your body's ability to turn the foods you eat into usable blood sugar (**metabolism**). During the twentieth century, many ideas emerged in regard to how nutrition impacts weight, performance, and health. We learned that:

- "To lose weight, you should cut out fat."

  Many people on low-fat diets find that their bodies still resist weight loss. Some people are sensitive to carbohydrates and sugar, and for them, a decrease in fat does not necessarily lead to weight loss.

- "If you restrict total daily calories, you will lose weight."

  By restricting calories, you may lose weight in the short run, but you may also end up with food nutrient imbalance. Also, because your body does not get enough to keep it going, you can actually put it into a starvation mode where you begin to store calories rather than burn them. In this condition, you need a lot of exercise and continued food deprivation in order to lose weight.

- "If you have enough willpower, you can control food cravings."

  Whether or not you have enough willpower to control craving foods that are unhealthy has more to do with balanced nutrition than behavioral control.

- "Fat people are lazy and unmotivated."

These cruel labels do not tell the story correctly. Stable blood sugar levels throughout the day can actually have a lot to do with burning rather than storing food calories.

- "The best diet for everyone is one that is high in carbohydrates, moderate to low in protein, and low in fat."

   Although the American Dietetic Standards are fine for the average person who does not have medical, emotional, and/or behavioral conditions, there are those who do not feel or perform well on this type of diet.

- "A carbohydrate is the best food nutrient for prolonged stamina."

   Although carbohydrates give you a short-term energy boost, for some, carbohydrate loading can result in dwindling blood sugar levels. This is especially true when the carbohydrate is simple rather than complex.

- "You can eat all the carbohydrates you want if they are not combined with fat."

   Again, carbohydrates store as fat. You have to use up the carbohydrates you eat if you do not want them to get stored as fat. With today's sedentary lifestyle today and a high carbohydrate diet, you have to be a marathon runner to burn the carbohydrates you eat each day.

Today, we know that people differ in terms of performance and health needs. It's important thus to learn the basics of sound food nutrition and blood sugar metabolism, so you and your health professionals can determine which nutrition lifestyle helps you to perform and feel well.

Blood Sugar

Blood sugar comes from the natural sugar content of the foods you eat. The chemical name for sugar is **glucose**. Recall that glucose primarily comes from the carbohydrates you eat and that your body burns glucose for energy and heat. While your muscles can use carbohydrates, protein, or fat for physical performance, your brain and eyes can only use glucose to run properly. Your brain, thus, is the first body system to be negatively impacted by fluctuating blood sugar levels. When your blood sugar level is low, your cells convert muscle and liver glycogen into glucose for body fuel. Proper nutrition assures that your brain and eyes get the precious glucose they need to function.

Your blood sugar has to be within a very specific range in order for you to perform efficiently. Normal blood sugar levels not only stabilize energy level and brain functioning, but as you will soon learn, they also initiate an array of physiological processes that enhance well-being and can encourage weight loss. There is a host of negative mental and physical symptoms that accompany low and high blood sugar levels. Further in your reading you will learn about many physical, emotional, and behavioral conditions that can be worsened by fluctuating blood sugar levels. Let's review for a moment the specifics of blood sugar level.

Your **blood glucose level** is determined by how many milligrams (1 milligram =0.0003) of glucose are in 100 cubic centimeters of your blood. This is approximately three 1/2 ounces, or almost 1/2 cup. A normal blood sugar level, then, is 70 to 150 milligrams of glucose in approximately 1/2 cup of blood. Anything below 70 and above 150 is regarded as an abnormal blood sugar level. This is the amount of blood sugar you need circulating throughout your brain and body in order to run efficiently.

Because blood sugar can be dangerous to your health in high levels, your body continually senses the range of your blood sugar so it can store excess amounts for later use. Once it exceeds 150 milligrams per 1/2 cup of blood, your body has difficulty storing blood sugar. This is why, at such levels, it begins to show up in your urine. This can be a very dangerous situation. A blood sugar level above 150 is a hyperglycemic (high blood sugar) state, whereas a blood sugar level below 70 is a hypoglycemic (low blood sugar) state. For you, your symptoms rather than the numbers are the real indicators of these conditions.

TABLE 1. Blood Sugar Range Levels

Low 70 and lower milligrams

Normal 70-150 milligrams

High 150-240 milligrams

Your body functions normally within a tight range of blood sugar levels. Anything above or below it distresses you physically, mentally, and behaviorally. Although low blood sugar debilitates you physically, mentally, and behaviorally, high blood sugar endangers your health. It can weaken your veins and arteries, and wear out your blood sugar organs. It can also harm eye function, as your eyes use blood sugar for nourishment. This can be a problem for people who have diabetes (insufficient insulin production leading to dangerously high blood sugar levels). Fluctuations in blood sugar level can result in a variety of symptoms and disrupt your physical, mental, and behavioral well-being. Food choice, illness, and stress can cause blood sugar levels to fluctuate.

Blood Sugar Symptom Chart

Low/Severe. *Physical:* Night sweats, excessive sweating, hand tremor, blurred vision, fainting or blacking out, exhaustion, stuttering, muscle weakness, and slurred speech. *Mental:* Word-finding problems, confusion, depression, and cloudiness. *Behavioral:* Out of control, isolative, clumsy, aggressive, nightmares, temper tantrums, and suicidal gestures.

Low/Moderate and Mild. *Physical:* Tired, headache, migraine, muscle weakness, dizziness, jittery, cold hands and feet, shortness of breath, racing heart or heart palpitations, anxiety, panic, allergies, muscle pain, sugar cravings, bad breath, gastrointestinal problems, aching eye sockets, and diarrhea or constipation. *Mental:* Forgetful, sad, depressed, fearful, decreased concentration and attention, suspicion, and worry and doubt. *Behavioral:* Irritable, oppositional, mood swings, insomnia, restless, hyperactive, impotence, low sex drive, nighttime waking, waking up tired, yawning, hyperverbal, and light and sound sensitive.

Normal. *Physical:* Normal heart, respiration, and motor rate, pain-free, good digestion, and normal bowel movements. *Mental:* Stable movement, good memory, concentration, and attention, hopeful, and sound insight and judgment. *Behavioral:* Motivated, goal-directed, socially cooperative, good performance, morale, and conduct, strong HardiAttitudes.

High. *Physical:* Excessive urination, sweating, and thirst, blurred vision, nausea, and hypertension. *Mental:* Dizziness and confusion. *Behavioral:* Irritability and unexplainable weight loss.

Low Blood Sugar Questionnaire

Before we leave this section on blood sugar, answer the following questions to see if you show any signs of fluctuating blood sugar levels.

1. Do you feel better when you eat less?

2. Do you need sugar or caffeine several times a day for pick-me-ups?

3. Do you have unexplainable mood swings during the day?

4. Do you have unexplainable anxiety that comes and goes during the day?

5. Does eating make a real difference on your mood and energy level?

6. Do you have problems with anger?

7. Do you have attention and concentration difficulties?

8. Do you crave carbohydrates?

9. Do you bloat after you eat, especially when you eat carbohydrates?

10. Do you suddenly get sad, tearful, or depressed for no apparent reason?

11. Does eating decrease anxiety and hyperactivity in you?

12. Do you feel fatigued throughout your day, although you got a good night sleep?

If you answered yes to many of these questions, you may be showing some of the signs of low blood sugar. There can be several reasons for low blood sugar, which including poor diet, insufficient food intake, illness, stress, and endocrine organ disease. There are several resources in your suggested reading list if you feel you want to explore this further. Also, further on in your reading you learn about a nutrition approach that is helpful for managing fluctuating blood sugar levels.

Carbohydrates can significantly affect your blood sugar level because they are the food nutrient highest in natural sugar. Although amino acids from protein, and **glycerol** (form of glucose) from fat, can be broken down into glucose if needed, your best immediate source of glucose is carbohydrates (sugar and starch). Recall that carbohydrates are either simple or complex. The simple carbohydrates have a shorter molecular structure, are higher in natural sugar and lower in fiber, and thus can be digested and absorbed into your bloodstream more readily. The complex carbohydrates have a longer molecular structure, are lower in natural sugar and higher in fiber, and thus cannot be digested and absorbed into your bloodstream easily.

The Endocrine System, Your Blood Sugar Manager

The **endocrine** system's primary job is nutrient metabolism. Saliva and digestive juices work together to break down from raw food material what it needs for system functioning, like antibodies, body enzymes, and hormones. Your **endocrine organs** then utilize these metabolic byproducts to make **hormones**, the chemical messengers that orchestrate hormonal, nerve, and immune system functioning. Although the endocrine system houses other organs, in this component, we concern ourselves most with the **pancreas** and the **liver**, the organs most relevant to energy production.

The Pancreas

This endocrine organ produces the two most powerful blood sugar hormones in your body: insulin and glucagon. Your pancreas manages the amount of sugar in your bloodstream at any one time with **insulin**. Insulin is derived from food products. It transforms blood sugar to fat and opens the body's cells to allow transport and storage in the muscles for later use. Thus, it is regarded as the mechanism for blood sugar storing.

Insulin's glucose-storing function helps you in two key ways. These include:

- Blood sugar, in excess, changes the natural chemistry of your cells, deteriorating and weakening your vascular walls and damaging your organs. It can cause stroke, coma, eye and foot nerve complications, and other degenerative diseases.

- Your body can only tolerate so much blood sugar floating around in your vascular system at any one time. Recall that when your blood sugar exceeds 150 milligrams, it spills into your urine. This is because the pancreas can no longer efficiently store the excess blood sugar. Your body's ability to store blood sugar as fat gives you a reserve of energy in times of stress, strain, and illness.

The Liver

Veins and arteries carry blood and food nutrients to this endocrine organ. It takes almost all these digested food products and changes them into useful body enzymes and hormones. It changes some of these hormones into glucose and fat for energy production. Your liver can produce the necessary amount of glucose you need per day to function. Your pancreas also produces **glucagon**; the hormone that is the chemical key that opens the liver's "doors" so that it can release blood sugar into your bloodstream. It also metabolizes stored fat for energy use. Glucagon comes from protein.

The pancreas' two powerful blood sugar hormones are of interest to us because they play a role in

stamina and performance. Insulin and glucagon have polar functions. One stores blood sugar, and the other burns blood sugar. Under normal conditions, these hormones function harmoniously with one another. Stress, illness, and eating habits, however, can disrupt their functioning. Today, excessive reliance on saturated fat and man-made food products overstimulates insulin production. This, in combination with stress, can wear out your pancreas, which results in **type II diabetes**. Our ancestors did not enjoy the abundance of processed foods that we have today. The pancreas is not designed to manage the amount of sugar and fat that typifies the American diet. This can lead to a condition called **hyperinsulinemia** (Sears, 1995). This is when years of carbohydrate abuse dulls our cells' responsiveness to insulin. In this condition, the pancreas must release larger amounts of insulin into the body than is needed for the cells to take notice. It is like knocking on a friend's door to let him know you are outside, but because he has the radio turned on full blast, he cannot hear you. To get a response, you must knock harder. Hyperinsulinemia is a condition in which the body resists insulin. This leads to inefficient fuel burning, greater fat storage, and frequent drops in brain and body blood sugar.

Excessive insulin circulating in your bloodstream robs your brain and body of needed blood sugar. This is a risk performance, morale, conduct, and health risk. Now, your brain is in dire need of blood sugar. Your cells' resistance to insulin confused your pancreas so much that it stores all of your blood sugar. Your liver and muscles may have the blood sugar you need to return you to normal functioning, but it cannot get out without the help of glucagon. *Remember,* insulin and glucagon have polar functions, when one is out, the other is dormant. Low brain sugar leads to a condition called **hypoglycemia**. This condition undermines your stamina, performance, mood, and health. It can also cause you to crave carbohydrates for sugar replenishment. Now, you are into a carbohydrate and insulin cycle that increases your risk for weight gain. Sugar cravings, thus, have more to do with a diet high in carbohydrates and saturated fat than they do with willpower. Excessive insulin output can also:

- Stimulate an increase in blood triglyceride (blood fat that clogs the arteries and comes from sugar, starch, and alcohol intake) level;

- Stimulate the kidneys (the organ that flushes toxins and waste from your system) to retain salt and fluid (leading to high blood pressure and hypertension);

- Stimulate the liver to produce cholesterol (a hormone that in excess can contribute to low density lipoprotein, LDL, fat; the type of cholesterol that is bad for your body);

- Promote blood clotting and vascular constriction;

- Depress the immune system;

- Stimulate cellular inflammation and pain transmission;

- Decrease body oxygen; and

- Inhibit production of eicosanoids, a super hormone that holds your body cells together.

When insulin and glucagon function normally, your body produces a superhormone called an **eicosanoid**. This hormone functions as a messenger key that maintains the integrity of your cells. Degenerative diseases begin when your cells lose their structural glue. This shifts them from normal to abnormal. Your vascular walls can become brittle, making you more vulnerable to stroke and cellular abnormalities that can result in cancer of various sorts. Further, your body organs are less able to carry out their designated functions.

Whereas insulin inhibits eicosanoid production, glucagon stimulates it.

If you want to maintain your performance and health, your daily nutrition should emphasize a balance in food nutrients so as not to induce an insulin response. There are three main ways that you can overstimulate your blood sugar level and consequently an insulin response:

1. By ingesting excessive carbohydrates in a meal, especially if they are high in natural sugar and low in fiber and if eaten without other food nutrients;

2. By eating too large of a meal at one sitting. The size of your meal, no matter how well you combine your food nutrients, can produce too much blood sugar, requiring significant amounts of insulin to manage it. Just think about the Thanksgiving holiday. After a large meal, most people nap. One reason is because large amounts of food increases the pancreas' output of insulin. Insulin, just doing its job, robs our brain of blood sugar, which can make us very sleepy and glucose deprived; and

3. By the fight or flight response in which the pancreas manages the blood sugar released through your system during sympathetic arousal. Because of this, stress and strain can actually cause you to store fat. Many who begin relaxation exercises are pleasantly surprised when they begin to lose weight but have not changed their diet.

Summary Concepts And Terms

BLOOD GLUCOSE LEVEL

BLOOD SUGAR

EICOSANOID

ENDOCRINE SYSTEM

GLUCAGON

GLYCOGEN

GLUCOSE

GLYCEROL

HYPERINSULINEMIA

HYPOGLYCEMIA

INSULIN

LIVER

METABOLISM

PANCREAS

Test Your Knowledge

To test what you learned so far, see if you can correctly answer the following questions. Remember, the more information you have to think about what happens to you, the more building blocks you have to generate creative solutions to everyday living problems. This, in turn, strengthens your HardiAttitudes.

Commitment. The more information you seek to learn about yourself and the world, the more you demonstrate your belief that you are worthwhile and important enough to gather information that helps you.

Control. The more information you gather about yourself and your world, the greater your ability to influence the direction of your life.

Challenge. The effort you apply in learning the hardiness skills shows that you regard the time spent in developing yourself as a normal challenge of life.

For the answer key, See "Questionnaire and Test Your Knowledge Answer Keys" on page 259.

1. The chemical name for blood sugar is

   _____.

2. Glucose comes from two sources of carbohydrate: they are _____ and

   _____.

3. The body organ that uses the biggest supply of blood sugar is the _____.

4. Blood sugar stored in your muscle cells and liver is called _____.

5. A normal range of blood sugar falls between _____ and _____ milligrams of glucose per 100 cubic centimeters of blood.

6. High blood sugar levels range between _____ and _____ milligrams of glucose per 100 cubic centimeters of blood.

7. A blood sugar level below 70 brings about a _____ blood sugar state.

8. Heart palpitations and anxiety symptoms are often signs of

   _____.

9. Excessive thirst and sweating, and blurred vision are often signs of

   _____.

10. Carbohydrates that have a shorter molecular chain, are higher in natural sugar and lower in fiber, and can easily break down into glucose are _____ carbohydrates.

11. Carbohydrates that are lower in natural sugar, higher in fiber, and not easily broken down into glucose in your bloodstream are called_____.

12. The endocrine system's primary job is

   _____.

13. The two endocrine organs most relevant to energy production are _____ and _____.

14. The pancreatic hormone that stores blood sugar is called _____.

15. The pancreatic hormone that releases fat into your bloodstream for energy production is called _____.

16. When your body's blood sugar is tightly controlled, you are operating at high metabolic efficiency. True or False?

17. The body hormone that stimulates eicosanoid production is _____.

18. A biological condition where your cells become resistant to insulin is _____.

19. An _____ is a super-hormone that protects the integrity of your cells.

Learning Goals

- Do you appreciate the relationship between blood sugar, energy level, and performance and health?

- Do you understand the endocrine system's role in managing blood sugar?

- Do you understand the relationship between insulin and glucagon?

- Do you understand differences between glucose, glycerol, and glycogen?

- Do you understand insulin and glucagons' different body functions?

- Do you know the biological reasons for hyperinsulinemia?

CHAPTER 19

Carbohydrates

Carbohydrates And The Glycemic Index

Your body converts solid and liquid food into usable energy. A food's sugar and fiber content determines how quickly your body can process it for bloodsugar. Carbohydrate's, for example, natural sugar level make them a quick energy source but also easily recognized by insulin. You can optimize your performance and health by knowing how your body biochemically responds to fluctuations in blood sugar level. Like food type and amount, stress and illness, and certain medications can stimulate an insulin response. You can learn to eat in a way that complements your body chemistry and shields you from developing conditions that stem from poor nutrition habits, like hyperinsulinemia.

Fact 1: A high natural sugar and low fiber carbohydrate is high glycemic (sugar easily accessed and broken down into glucose). High glycemic carbohydrates are fast acting because they easily change your blood sugar level. Although you get an immediate sugar boost, insulin also gets immediately stimulated. When this happens, your body operates at a lower metabolic rate due to an insulin dump.

Fact 2: A low natural sugar and high fiber carbohydrate is low glycemic because it is not easily broken down into glucose. This makes low glycemic carbohydrates slow acting and time-released. Insulin does not over-react in this condition so that glucagon can get the glucose you need from your liver, and stored glycogen. Your

---

metabolism raises, when your habits do not over-stimulate body insulin.

The Glycemic Index

The glycemic index is a quantitative scale that tells you how fast a food gets broken down into glucose from the point of ingestion. The index bases this comparison upon the rate at which a spoonful of glucose reaches the bloodstream. One hundred percent of pure glucose reaches your bloodstream within 15 to 20 minutes. This standard is the basis from which the glycemic index makes its comparisons.

You can choose foods that maximize metabolism and support the design of your endocrine system by knowing how carbohydrates differ from one another in regard to the glycemic index. In general:

- High glycemic carbohydrates, 80 to 100%, turn into usable sugar within 15 to 20 minutes. And if other conditions are right, they activate insulin and slow metabolism;

- Moderate glycemic carbohydrates, 50 to 80%, turn into usable sugar within 45 minutes to 2 hours. And, if other conditions are right, they inhibit insulin and raise metabolism; and

- Low glycemic carbohydrates, 30% and below, turn into usable sugar within 2 to 3 hours. And, if other conditions are right, inhibit insulin and raise metabolism.

High 80% to 100%. Glucose, Maltose, White, Wheat & French Bread, Millet, Instant White & Brown Rice, Low Fiber Rye Crisps, Instant Oatmeal Instant Rice Meal, Grapenuts, Corn Flakes, Corn Chex, Muesli, Instant Mashed Potatoes, Microwaved French Fries, Low to No Fat Ice Cream, Tofu Ice Cream, Air-Popped Pop Corn, Puffed Rice Cakes, Corn Chips, Carrots, Rutabaga, Winter Squash, Turnips and Beets, Parsnips and Corn, Banana, Raisins, Papaya, Mango, All Dried Fruit, Dates, Kiwi, Prunes, Watermelon, and Prune Juice.

Moderate 50% to 80%. Lactose, Sucrose, Pumpernickle, White Spaghetti, Wheat Spaghetti, Pasta, Pinto Beans, Canned Kidney Beans, Baked, Navy, and Garbanzo Beans, Cheerios, Crispix, Rice Crispies, Shredded Wheat, Rolled Oats, Most Candy Bars, Potato Chips w/Fat, Oranges, and Orange Juice.

Low 30% to 50%. Whole Rye, Barley, and Slow-Cooked Oatmeal, Lentil, Black Eyed Peas, Lima Beans, Chick Peas, and Dried Kidney Beans, High Fat Ice Cream, Skim and Whole Milk, Yogurt, Tomato Soup, Apple, Grapes, Figs, Applesauce, Cantaloupe, Peach, Pear, Apricot, Tangerine, Lemon, Lime, Nectarine, and Honeydew Melon.

Very Low 30% and Below. Fructose, Soy Beans, Peanuts, Broccoli, Bok Choy, Green Beans, Lettuce, Parsley, Celery, Asparagus, Cauliflower, Kale, Artichoke, Arugula, Broccoli Rape, Red/Green Peppers, Brussel Sprouts, Escarole, Leeks, Olives, Onions, Radishes, Zucchini, Water Chestnuts, Turnip Greens, Cherries, Plums, Blueberries, Grapefruit, Blackberries, and Raspberries.

This glycemic food list is by no means exhaustive. If you want a more extensive glycemic food list, refer to the suggested reading list (De Wees Allen, 1997; Eades and Eades, 1996; and Sears, 1995). For those of you who do not want to get caught up in the web of carbohydrates' glycemic values, we provide you with a red flag carbohydrate list.

Red Flag Carbohydrate List

- Exotic fruits and fruits with inedible skins: Most exotic fruits are high glycemic carbohydrates.

Also, fruits with inedible skins, like bananas, cantaloupe, guava, kiwi, oranges, papaya, pineapple, and watermelon are moderately high to very high glycemic carbohydrates.

- Light foods: These kind of carbohydrates are usually man-made and processed, as opposed to brown foods that usually have higher fiber and lower sugar. Light foods have had their fiber, minerals and vitamins removed, and chemicals added. White rice, potatoes, bread, bagels, cake, muffin, pasta, cookies, crackers, tortillas, pastry, pie, and many others light foods are usually high glycemic. Most sugary breakfast cereals also fall into this light, high glycemic food area.

- Dried fruit: Dried fruit ferments and is high in sugar. This high glycemic carbohydrate also has mold that is bad for people who have mold allergies.

- Fruit drinks and vegetable juices, such as carrot juice: This decade's upsurge of fruit and vegetable stands, as a health alternative, has its pitfalls and can be a nightmare to your pancreas. It takes, for example, 10 to 12 raw carrots to make one 8-oz. cup of carrot juice. Do you realize how much natural sugar you are drinking when you have one of these "health" drinks? Persons with migraines should especially be cautious with these kind of drinks as too much blood sugar can cause your veins and arteries to over-constrict and then expand as a way to compensate. This produces the migraine.

- Orange and yellow vegetables, as opposed to green ones, are usually higher in natural sugar: Carrots, summer squash and corn, etc., are very high glycemic carbohydrates. If eaten, eat occasionally and only in small proportions.Orange and yellow fruits, as opposed to darker red and purple ones, are usually higher in natural sugar: Again, bananas, cantaloupe, oranges and pineapple are higher glycemic fruits, while cherries,

plums, blueberries and apples are lower glycemic fruits. Again, note that in the lower glycemic fruits, the skin is edible.

- Alcohol: Beware that unlike all other nutrient sources, alcohol does not have to go to your stomach to be digested. The moment it reaches your salivary glands, it's transported into your bloodstream. It is 100% carbo-fuel, and it burns first in the presence of other food nutrients.

Other Conditions That Influence Carbohydrates' Glycemic Index

A carbohydrate's glycemic index only tells you how quickly the carbohydrate turns to usable sugar with implications for insulin and metabolism. There are additional conditions that influence the rate at which carbohydrates turn into usable energy.

- How you combine your food nutrients determines a carbohydrate's glycemic index. Although, for example, raw carrots are high glycemic carbohydrates, if you cook them with an essential fatty acid, you change the rate at which the carrot turns into usable sugar.

- Whether or not you eat a food raw or cooked can change the rate at which the food turns into usable energy. Cooking removes a food's fiber, such as in pasta. By removing its fiber, digestive juices can break a food down more easily and turn it into usable sugar. The length of cooking time determines the percentage of fiber breakdown.

Nutrition Standards

Whether or not a food nutrient performs optimally depends upon the presence of the other food nutrients. Food nutrients combine to create a metabolic impact. Metabolism slows down when you eat carbohydrates, protein, and fat independent of one another.

The American Dietetic Association

The American Dietetic Association (ADA) recently came up with new daily food nutrient guidelines. They recommend a diet that is high in carbohydrates and low in fat and protein if you want to prevent disease and maintain weight and health. Specifically, the ADA recommends that approximately 80% of your daily calories come from carbohydrates and 15% to 20% of your daily calories come from protein and fat. The ADA's food pyramid suggests that we primarily eat complex carbohydrates from fruit, vegetables, and whole grains, foods low in cholesterol and saturated fat, and foods moderate in salt. In addition, people who drink alcohol should do so in moderation. Further, they recommend that we eat a variety of foods and combine this with exercise.

Zone Nutrition Experts

Some researchers contend that the best nutrition is an approach that emphasizes metabolism. This, they say, assures performance and health, and prevents disease. In order to maximize metabolic function, you need to eat in a way that balances the insulin and glucagon hormones (Eades and Eades, 1996; Sears, 1995; and Heller and Heller, 1993).

Zone nutrition experts emphasize a nutrition approach that concerns itself more with food nutrient percentages per meal than overall daily food nutrient percentages, as in the American Dietetic Standard. To optimize hormonal balance, they suggest that each meal per day consist of 40% carbohydrate, 30% protein, and 30% fat. This specific food nutrient combination keeps insulin levels low and glucagon levels high. In this condition, you burn rather than store fat. This is why Zone experts emphasize the glycemic index of carbohydrates and concern themselves with food combinations that maximize metabolism.

What happens to metabolism when you eat carbohydrates with and without the other food nutrients?

- When you eat high glycemic carbohydrates without the other food nutrients, insulin increases and metabolism is inefficient;

- When you eat high glycemic carbohydrates with protein and fat, insulin lowers and metabolism becomes more efficient;

- When you eat low glycemic carbohydrates without the other food nutrients, insulin lowers but metabolism is less efficient than if combined with protein and fat; and

- When you eat low glycemic carbohydrates with protein and fat, metabolism is optimal.

The HardiSurvey III-R

You begin to eat well when you eat enough of each food nutrient per day to protect your health and to prevent disease. Daily wear and tear utilizes the food nutrients you eat per day. You thus need to make sure that the you replenish the nutrients used up in body processes the day before. Stress, in particular, uses up much of your daily food nutrient reserve. When you are stressed, ill, pregnant, or highly active, you need more daily protein for body repair, as your body uses it to replenish enzymes, hormones, antibodies, and neurotransmitters. You prolong stress and illness, if you do not replenish your daily food nutrient reserve.

Stress And Nutrition

If you took the HardiSurvey® as part of your training, you can review its results now. See if your level of stress vulnerability warrants extra nutrient support at this time. Then, answer the questions that follow. For the HardiSurvey questionnaire, See "Appendix H: HardiSurveyIII-R" on page 249.

1. Do you have enough hardy resources (HardiAttitudes, HardiCoping, and Hardy Social Support) to protect your performance and health at this time?

2. Do you tend to regressively cope?

3. Do you report a lot of stress in your life? If so, do you also report strain?

4. Have you been getting ill a lot? Does your illness reoccur?

5. If you answered no to questions 1 through 3, and yes to question 4, you need to make sure you get enough of the food nutrients per day to protect your stamina, performance, and health. High stress can lead to hypoglycemia, which makes you vulnerable to sugar and saturated fat cravings. This further stresses you physically, mentally, and behaviorally. To minimize sugar and fat cravings, and low blood sugar during stressful times, you want to:

- Make sure your food choices adequately satisfy your daily nutrient needs,

- Make sure you eat three meals and three snacks per day and,

- Adjust your meal size to keep bloodstream insulin levels low.

Summary Concepts And Terms

AMERICAN DIETETIC NUTRITION STANDARDS

GLYCEMIC INDEX

RED FLAG CARBOHYDRATE LIST

ZONE NUTRITION STANDARDS

Test Your Knowledge

To test what you learned so far, see if you can correctly answer the following questions. Remember, the more information you have to think about what happens to you, the more building blocks you have to generate creative solutions to everyday living problems. This, in turn, strengthens your HardiAttitudes.

Commitment. The more information you seek to learn about yourself and the world, the more you demonstrate your belief that you are worthwhile and important enough to gather information that helps you.

Control. The more information you gather about yourself and your world, the greater your ability to influence the direction of your life.

Challenge. The effort you apply in learning the hardiness skills shows that you regard the time spent in developing yourself as a normal challenge of life.

For the answer key, See "Questionnaire and Test Your Knowledge Answer Keys" on page 259.

1. The _____ is the rate at which a carbohydrate turns into sugar.

2. The food nutrient that easily stimulates insulin is a _____.

3. Saturated fat can stimulate an insulin response. True or False?

4. _____ carbohydrates are slow-acting.

5. A meal composed of _____% carbohydrate, _____% protein, and _____% fat enhances metabolic function.

6. Most sound nutrition approaches emphasize balance in the _____ _____.

Learning Goals

- Do you appreciate differences in high versus low glycemic foods?

- Do you understand the insulin relationship to a food and drinks' glycemic level?

- Can you see how food combining can heighten metabolic efficiency?

CHAPTER 20

Put Your Learning into Practice

Nutrition Case Examples

In this chapter, you learn how to develop a nutrition plan that supports your performance and health goals. Read the case examples that follow before you begin the Hardy Nutrition Exercise #2, Put Your Learning Into Practice on .

The Case Of Elizabeth

Elizabeth has low blood sugar and migraines. She knew that diet was not good for low blood sugar, but she was surprised to find out that her nutrition habits may be causing her migraines. Let us see how Elizabeth felt as a result of the changes she made in her daily nutrition.

PART A: ELIZABETH'S BASELINE NUTRITION

Elizabeth first reviews the Pre-Training Nutrition Survey she collected on herself prior to beginning this component. She then sums each food nutrient category, and finally, she summarizes her findings by calculating the total percentage of each food nutrient that comes from her total daily calorie intake.

Let's take a few minutes to look at her data collection and computations. This is the sample nutrition survey you reviewed at the beginning of this component. Let one of her data collection days represent the other two days.

TABLE **Baseline Nutrition Worksheet**

Time	Food & Drink	Qty.	Cal.	Carb.	Prot.	Fat	Fiber
6 am	Coffee	6 oz	4	1	0	0	0
	Coffee	6 oz	4	1	0	0	0
	Coffee	6 oz	4	1	0	0	0
	Chips Ahoy	3	160	21	2	8	0
11:30 am	Pretzels	1 oz	110	23	2	1	0
	Cheeseburger	1 reg	318	23	17.3	15	1
	Pepsi-Cola	8 oz	160	39.6	0	0	0
	Coffee	6 oz	4	1	0	0	0
4 pm	Baby Ruth candy-bar	1	277	37.2	5.6	13.3	1.9
	Trail Mix	6 oz	150	23	3	7	3
	Coffee	6 oz	4	1	0	0	0
7 pm	Rice, white cooked	8 oz	166	35	6.6	0.6	3
	Chicken roasted w/skin	4 oz	340	0	29.4	23.8	0
	Carrots	1 cup	70	16.4	1.8	0.2	5.2
	Dinner roll	11 oz	87	14.7	2.7	1.8	1.1
	Butter	2 TBS	200	0	0.2	22.8	0
	Coffee	6 oz	4	1	0	0	0
8:30 pm	Apple Pie	14 oz	430	51	4	23	0
Step 2	Sum Categories		2492	289.9	74.6	116.5	15.2

TABLE Baseline Strain Rating Scale

Rating: 1 = mild; 2 = moderate; 3 = strong

Physical	RATE	MENTAL	RATE	BEHAVIORAL	RATE
Headache	1 _2_ 3	Clouded mind	1 _2_ 3	Insecure	1 2 3
Migraine	1 2 _3_	Worry	1 2 3	Phobic or fear-	1 2 3
Rapid heart rate	1 2 3	Ideas of threat	1 2 3	Self-conscious	1 2 3
Anxiety	1 2 _3_	Intrusive ideas	1 2 3	Angry	1 2 3
Rapid breathing	1 _2_ 3	Lose line of idea	1 2 3	Impulsive	1 _2_ 3
Light headed	1 2 3	Racing thoughts	1 2 3	Hyperactive	1 2 _3_
Dizzy	_1_ 2 3	Cannot focus	1 2 _3_	Talk a lot/fast	1 2 _3_
Short of breath	1 _2_ 3	Hopeless ideas	1 2 3	Argumentative	1 2 _3_
Shallow breath	1 _2_ 3	Grim thoughts	1 _2_ 3	Rude or loud	1 2 3
Nausea	1 _2_ 3	Sad thoughts	1 _2_ 3	Confrontational	1 2 3
Constipation	1 _2_ 3	Confused ideas	1 _2_ 3	Clumsy	1 2 _3_
Diarrhea	1 _2_ 3	Negative ideas	1 2 3	Inhibited	1 2 3
Indigestion	1 _2_ 3	Literal thinking	1 2 3	Unmotivated	1 2 3
Sweating	1 _2_ 3	Angry thoughts	1 2 3	Impatient	1 _2_ 3
Cold hands/feet	1 _2_ 3	Uncreative ideas	1 2 3	Rigid	_1_ 2 3
Tingling	1 2 3	Forgetful	1 _2_ 3	Aggressive	1 2 3
Swelling	1 2 3	Inattentive	1 2 _3_	Excited	1 2 3
Aches and pains	1 2 3	Can't find word	1 2 3	Withdrawn	1 _2_ 3
Tension	1 2 _3_	Mind goes blank	1 2 _3_	Irritable	1 _2_ 3
Jittery	1 2 _3_	Can't find name	1 _2_ 3	Short temper	1 _2_ 3
Tired/fatigued	1 2 3	Indecisive	1 2 3	Moody	1 2 3
Other:	1 2 3	Other:	1 2 3	Other:	1 2 3
Total Score	**33**		**21**		**23**

		TABLE	Elizabeth's Baseline Nutrition Calculations	Product
Step 3	A	Multiply Total Carbohydrate Calories (289.9) X 4 =		1159.6
	B	Divide by Total Daily Calories (2492) =		0.46
	C	Multiply by 100 to change the number in 3 B into a percentage		46%
	A	Multiply Total Protein Calories (74.6) X 4 =		298.4
	B	Divide by Total Daily Calories (2492) =		0.12
	C	Multiply by 100 to change the number in 4 B into a percentage		12%
	A	Multiply Total Fat Calories (116.5) X 9 =		1048.5
	B	Divide by Total Daily Calories (2492) =		0.42
	C	Multiply by 100 to change the number in 5 B into a percentage		42%

1. Based on your learning to date, do you think you eat in a way that enhances your well-being and performance level? Do you eat in a way that stimulates a lot of insulin?

I have too many symptoms which most likely means I am not eating in a way that maximizes my health and well-being.

2. Do you show symptoms that might be related to your nutrition habits? If so, do you show symptoms physically, mentally, or behaviorally, or in all three forms?

Yes, my nutrition habits cause some of my symptoms. They are all involved, although physical symptoms exceed the other two categories.

3. Based upon your learning thus far, what is it about your daily nutrition that leads to these symptoms?

I do not start out the day with a balanced meal, which sets me up for low blood sugar, and caffeine and carbohydrate craving all day long (this can stimulate nausea). I also do not eat every 2 to 3 hours, which is very important for a low blood sugar condition. I drink way too much coffee during the day, which makes me tired, jittery, hyperactive, clumsy, and anxious. It also leads to poor circulation (cold hands and feet). The protein I do eat is concentrated in one or two meals and is high in saturated fat, which is difficult to digest and stimulates too much insulin. This too is not good for a low blood sugar condition. I also eat too many high glycemic carbohydrates and not enough fresh fruits and vegetables that are high in fiber and nutrition. All of these nutrition habits can worsen a low blood sugar problem, causing constipation and migraines.

4. Which nutrition change(s) seems necessary to your well-being?

Eat less saturated fat X Eat more protein ___ Eat more protein from nuts and legumes X Eat more fresh fruit X Eat more fresh vegetables X Eat more fat ___ Eat more often X_ Eat less sugar X Eat lower glycemic carbohydrates X Eat fewer fast foods (high in saturated fat that stimulates insulin) X Drink more water X Eat a more balanced diet X Eat more nutritious foods X Eat breakfast X Eat less fried foods ___ Eat 6 meals per day X Eat healthy snacks X Other: Drink less coffee

5. Nutrition Objective: People differ in their reasons for changing their nutrition habits. There are those who change their eating habits because they are not feeling well (symptoms) and want to feel better. Others change their nutrition hab-

its in order to lose a few pounds. And, there are those who change their nutrition habits because they want to live a long, healthy life. Do you have a nutrition objective?

I want to feel physically better. I want to decrease low blood sugar symptoms, which should also decrease my migraines.

6. Now, choose nutrition changes that support the nutrition objective you identified in Question 5.

Change 1: I will decrease caffeine and increase water intake.

Change 2: I will eat 3 meals and 2 snacks per day.

Change 3: I will eat fresh foods that are balanced in all the food nutrients and higher in fiber. I will also eat lower glycemic carbohydrates.

Change 4: I will get protein from unsaturated fat sources.

7. Take a few moments to jot down reasons for these nutrition changes. Support these nutrition changes with your learning thus far.

Caffeine stimulates insulin, which robs me of blood sugar, and contributes to my daily blood sugar slump. Blood sugar fluctuations most likely also contribute to my anxiety and heart palpitations. This can also give me migraines. I also learned that I crave sugar and caffeine to boost my concentration and energy.

In addition, eating protein at each meal can reduce my blood sugar symptoms, because it produces glucagon, which keeps my insulin levels low. Protein will also help my body to renew itself from the stress of working full-time while I go to school. Although my HardiSurvey III-R indicates that I have adequate coping buffers, I need to eat in such a way that supports my overall hardiness. I also learned that too much coffee can actually rob me of energy. I will drink water as a replacement for coffee.

After remaining on this new nutrition program for three days, Elizabeth evaluates if the four nutrition changes she selected were instrumental in bringing about a decrease in her strain symptoms. If after the three days she thinks her program needs a little more fine tuning, she can return to Part A to find other changes that may help her to fulfill her nutrition objective.

PART B: ELIZABETH'S NEW MEAL PLAN

Elizabeth begins her new nutrition program by collecting data on what she eats and drinks for three consecutive days. In addition, she rates herself daily in terms of strain. The following post-nutrition survey shows changes in Elizabeth's daily nutrition that support her nutrition objective. We will regard Day One as prototypical of her daily nutrition.

TABLE New Meal Plan Worksheet

Time	Food & Drink	Qty.	Calorie	Carbs.	Protein	Fat	Fiber
6 am	Orrowheat whole wheat bread	1	60	11	3	1	2
	Alta Dena Plain Non-fat yogurt	8 oz	100	13	13	.8	0
	Peanut Butter Super-chunk	2 TBS	190	4	9	17	0.6

TABLE **New Meal Plan Worksheet**

Time	Food & Drink	Qty.	Calorie	Carbs.	Protein	Fat	Fiber
	Coffee	6 oz	4	1	0	0	0
9 am	Apple with skin	1 med	81	21	0.3	0.5	3.7
	Almonds whole	4 oz	418	14.5	14.5	37.05	7.75
	Water	16 oz	0	0	0	0	0
11 am	Health Valley Fat-free Lentil soup	10 oz	160	24	18	0	20.6
	Iceberg lettuce shredded	1 cup	10	2	0.9	0.2	1.06
	Olive oil	1 TBS	120	0	0	14	0
	Cherries, Fresh w/ pit	1 cup	104	24	1.7	1.4	3.3
	Water	16 oz	0	0	0	0	0
	Coffee	6 oz	4	1	0	0	0
3 pm	Zone Protein Bar	1	190	20	14	6	2
	Coffee	6 oz	4	1	0	0	0
6 pm	Chicken breast skinless	4 oz	181	0	35.2	4	0
	Green beans fresh, cooked	8 oz	80	17.8	4.2	0.6	4
	Wild rice	4 oz	115	24.2	4.5	0.4	2.1
	Romaine lettuce shredded	1 cup	8	1.4	0.4	0.1	0.4
	Cucumber sliced	4 oz	7	1.4	0.4	0.1	0.4
	Tomato	1 med	26	5	2	0.5	1
	Olive oil	1 TBS	120	0	0	14	0
	Apple w/skin	1 med	81	21	0.3	0.5	3.7
	Water	16 oz	0	0	0	0	0
8:30 pm	Fat-free Louis Rich thinly sliced turkey-breast	4 oz	100	0.9	5.20	0	2.6
	Wasa Hearty Rye cracker	1	45	9	2	0	2.6
	Apricot whole	1 sm	17	4	0.33	0	0

TABLE New Meal Plan Worksheet

Time	Food & Drink	Qty.	Calorie	Carbs.	Protein	Fat	Fiber
	Water	16 oz	0	0	0	0	0
Step 2	Sum Categories		2225	221.2	128.93	98.15	57.81

TABLE Elizabeth's New Meal Plan Calculations

			Product
Step 3	A	Multiply Total Carbohydrate Calories (221.2) X 4 =	884.8
	B	Divide by Total Daily Calories (2225) =	0.39
	C	Multiply by 100 to change the number in 3 B into a percentage	39%
	A	Multiply Total Protein Calories (128.93) X 4 =	515.72
	B	Divide by Total Daily Calories (2225) =	0.23
	C	Multiply by 100 to change the number in 4 B into a percentage	23%
	A	Multiply Total Fat Calories (98.15) X 9 =	883.35
	B	Divide by Total Daily Calories (2225) =	0.38
	C	Multiply by 100 to change the number in 5 B into a percentage	38%

TABLE Strain Rating Scale

Rating: 1 = mild; 2 = moderate; 3 = strong

Physical	RATE	MENTAL	RATE	BEHAVIORAL	RATE
Headache	1 2 3	Clouded mind	1 2 3	Insecure	1 2 3
Migraine	1 2 3	Worry	1 2 3	Phobic or fear-	1 2 3
Rapid heart rate	1 2 3	Ideas of threat	1 2 3	Self-conscious	1 2 3
Anxiety	1 2 3	Intrusive ideas	1 2 3	Angry	1 2 3
Rapid breathing	1 2 3	Lose line of idea	1 2 3	Impulsive	1 2 3
Light headed	1 2 3	Racing thoughts	1 2 3	Hyperactive	1 2 3
Dizzy	1 2 3	Cannot focus	1 2 3	Talk a lot/fast	1 2 3
Short of breath	1 2 3	Hopeless ideas	1 2 3	Argumentative	1 2 3
Shallow breath	1 2 3	Grim thoughts	1 2 3	Rude or loud	1 2 3

TABLE Strain Rating Scale

Rating: 1 = mild; 2 = moderate; 3 = strong

Physical	RATE	MENTAL	RATE	BEHAVIORAL	RATE
Nausea	1 2 3	Sad thoughts	1 2 3	Confrontational	1 2 3
Constipation	1 2 3	Confused ideas	1 2 3	Clumsy	1 2 3
Diarrhea	1 2 3	Negative ideas	1 2 3	Inhibited	1 2 3
Indigestion	1 2 3	Literal thinking	1 2 3	Unmotivated	1 2 3
Sweating	1 2 3	Angry thoughts	1 2 3	Impatient	1 2 3
Cold hands/feet	1 2 3	Uncreative ideas	1 2 3	Rigid	1 2 3
Tingling	1 2 3	Forgetful	1 2 3	Aggressive	1 2 3
Swelling	1 2 3	Inattentive	1 2 3	Excited	1 2 3
Aches and pains	1 2 3	Can't find word	1 2 3	Withdrawn	1 2 3
Tension	1 2 3	Mind goes blank	1 2 3	Irritable	1 2 3
Jittery	1 2 3	Can't find name	1 2 3	Short temper	1 2 3
Tired/fatigued	1̲ 2 3	Indecisive	1 2 3	Moody	1 2 3
Other:	1 2 3	Other:	1 2 3	Other:	1 2 3
Total Score	**1**		**0**		**0**

ELIZABETH'S NUTRITION CHANGE RESULTS

Baseline Daily Food Nutrient Intake and Symptoms of Strain

Carbohydrate 46.5%, Protein 11%, Fat 42%, Fiber 15.2 grams

Physical 33%, Mental 21%, Behavioral 23%

New Meal Plan Daily Food Nutrient Intake and Symptoms of Strain

Carbohydrate 23%, Protein 23%, Fat 38%, Fiber 57.81 grams

Physical 1%, Mental 0%, Behavioral 0%

Did your food choices support your nutrition objective and changes?

Yes, I started out each day with a balanced combination of food nutrients per meal. My daily protein intake increased significantly adding more balance to my total daily nutrient intake as well. Further, my protein sources now come less from saturated animal fat and more from unsaturated (essential fatty acids) grains, nuts, and legumes. Although this switch in food source did not decrease significantly my fat percentage per total daily calories, it did help to really increase my daily fiber grams. I also decreased the percentage of my daily calories that come from carbohydrates. And, most importantly, for my low blood sugar condition, I avoided high glycemic carbohydrates. Finally, I drank 8 8-oz cups of water per day and decreased my caffeine intake from 6 to 3 cups of coffee per day. These nutrition changes seemed to have significantly decreased my physical, mental, and behavioral symptoms. It seems like my symptoms were 100% diet-related.

The Case Of Tom

Tom has performance anxiety, both socially and professionally. Relaxation exercises has helped Tom to reduce his anxiety to some degree. He wants to see if he can reduce his anxiety symptoms further by changing his diet.

Like Elizabeth, Tom first reviews the Pre-Training Nutrition Survey he collected on himself prior to beginning this component. He then sums each food nutrient category, and finally, he summarizes his findings by calculating the total percentage of each food nutrient that comes from his total daily calorie intake.

We will assume that the sample nutrition day represents Tom's nutrition for the other two days.

TABLE Baseline Nutrition Worksheet

Time	Food & Drink	Qty.	Cal.	Carb.	Protein	Fat	Fiber
7 am	Kellogg's All-Bran 100%	4 oz	284	82	4	0	8
	Milk Whole	8 oz	150	12	8	1	0
	Honeydew Melon	4 oz	28.5	7	0.75	0	0.51
	Orange Juice freshly squeezed	8 oz	112	26	1.7	0	0.5
11 am	Dried apple rings	4 oz	280	72	0	0	5.41
	Pepsi-Cola Caffeine Free	12 oz	160	39	0	0	0
2 pm	Spaghetti w/marinara sauce	8 oz	240	72	13	10	0.26
	French bread	2 slice	140	30	2	2	2
	Water	8 oz	0	0	0	0	0
4 pm	Cashews roasted fresh w/oil	2 oz	340	6	8.8	9	1.23
	Water	8 oz	0	0	0	0	0

TABLE Baseline Nutrition Worksheet

Time	Food & Drink	Qty.	Cal.	Carb.	Protein	Fat	Fiber
6:30 pm	Bean burrito w/ sauce	10 oz	540	70	26	22	7
	Spanish rice	6 oz	363	19	0	27	0
	Butter	1 TBS	100	0	0.1	11.40	0
	Pepsi-Cola Caffeine Free	12 oz	160	39	0	0	0
8:30 pm	Watermelon	1 cup	51	11	1	0	0.6
	Pretzels	2 oz	210	44	1	2	0
10 pm	Oreo cookies	3	140	24	1	6	0
Step 2	Sum Categories		3298.5	553	67.35	90.4	25.51

TABLE Tom's Baseline Nutrition Calculations

			Product
Step 3 A		Multiply Total Carbohydrate Calories (553) X 4 =	2212
	B	Divide by Total Daily Calories (3298.5) =	0.67
	C	Multiply by 100 to change the number in 3 B into a percentage	67%
	A	Multiply Total Protein Calories (67.35) X 4 =	269.4
	B	Divide by Total Daily Calories (3298.5) =	0.08
	C	Multiply by 100 to change the number in 4 B into a percentage	8%
	A	Multiply Total Fat Calories (90.4) X 9 =	813.6
	B	Divide by Total Daily Calories (3298.5) =	0.25
	C	Multiply by 100 to change the number in 5 B into a percentage	25%

TABLE Baseline Strain Rating Scale

Rating: 1 = mild; 2 = moderate; 3 = strong

Physical	RATE	MENTAL	RATE	BEHAVIORAL	RATE
Headache	1 2 3	Clouded mind	1 2 3	Insecure	1 2 3
Migraine	1 2 3	Worry	1 2 3	Phobic, panic,	1 2 3
Rapid heart rate	1 2 3	Ideas of threat	1 2 3	Self-conscious	1 2 3

TABLE Baseline Strain Rating Scale

Rating: 1 = mild; 2 = moderate; 3 = strong

Physical	RATE	MENTAL	RATE	BEHAVIORAL	RATE
Anxiety	1 2 <u>3</u>	Intrusive ideas	1 2 <u>3</u>	Angry	1 2 3
Rapid breathing	1 2 <u>3</u>	Lose line of idea	1 2 <u>3</u>	Impulsive	1 2 3
Light headed	1 2 3	Racing thoughts	1 2 3	Hyperactive	1 2 <u>3</u>
Dizzy	1 2 <u>3</u>	Cannot focus	1 2 <u>3</u>	Talk a lot/fast	1 2 <u>3</u>
Short of breath	1 <u>2</u> 3	Hopeless ideas	1 2 3	Argumentative	1 2 3
Shallow breath	1 2 <u>3</u>	Grim thoughts	1 2 3	Rude or loud	1 2 3
Nausea	1 2 3	Sad thoughts	1 2 3	Confrontational	1 2 3
Constipation	1 2 3	Confused ideas	1 <u>2</u> 3	Clumsy	1 2 3
Diarrhea	1 2 3	Negative ideas	1 2 3	Inhibited	1 <u>2</u> 3
Indigestion	1 2 3	Literal thinking	1 2 3	Unmotivated	1 2 3
Sweating	1 2 3	Angry thoughts	1 <u>2</u> 3	Impatient	1 2 3
Cold hands/feet	1 <u>2</u> 3	Uncreative ideas	1 2 3	Rigid	1 2 3
Tingling	1 2 3	Forgetful	<u>1</u> 2 3	Aggressive	1 2 3
Swelling	1 2 3	Inattentive	1 2 3	Excited	1 2 <u>3</u>
Aches and pains	1 2 3	Can't find word	1 2 3	Withdrawn	1 <u>2</u> 3
Tension	1 2 <u>3</u>	Mind goes blank	1 2 3	Irritable	1 <u>2</u> 3
Jittery	1 2 3	Can't find name	1 2 3	Short temper	1 2 3
Tired/fatigued	1 2 3	Indecisive	1 <u>2</u> 3	Moody	1 2 3
Other:	1 2 3	Other:	1 2 3	Other:	1 2 3
Total Score	23		22		16

1. Based on your learning to date, do you think you eat in a way that enhances your well-being and performance level? Do you eat in a way that stimulates a lot of insulin?

Although I eat nutritious foods, I have too many symptoms, which most likely means I am not eating in a way that supports my biology.

2. Do you show symptoms that might be related to your nutrition habits? If so, do you show symptoms physically, mentally, or behaviorally?

Yes, I show symptoms related to the way eat. I also have symptoms in all of the strain categories.

3. Based upon your learning thus far, what is it about your daily nutrition that leads to these symptoms?

As mentioned, in general my daily food and liquid choices are nutritious, and I eat something every 2-3 hours. My primary food nutrient, however, seems to come from simple carbohydrates (fresh fruit and fruit juices), which may be too high in sugar for me. And, although my percentage of daily carbohydrate, protein, and fat intake satisfies the American Dietetic Standards, I might actually feel better increasing my protein intake somewhat.

4. Which nutrition change(s) seems necessary to your well-being?

Eat less saturated fat ___ Eat more protein X Eat more protein from nuts and legumes ____ Eat more fresh fruit ___ Eat more fresh vegetables ___ Eat more fat ___ Eat more often __ Eat less sugar X Eat lower glycemic carbohydrates X_ Eat fewer fast foods (high in saturated fat that stimulates insulin)___ Drink more water X Eat a more balanced diet ____ Eat more nutritious foods ___ Eat breakfast ____ Eat less fried foods ___ Eat 6 meals per day ___ Eat healthy snacks ___ Other: Drink less high sugar fruit and cola drinks

5. Nutrition Objective: People differ in their reasons for changing their nutrition habits. There are those who change their eating habits because they are not feeling well (symptoms) and want to feel better. Others change their nutrition habits in order to lose a few pounds. And, there are those who change their nutrition habits because they want to live a long, healthy life. Do you have a nutrition objective?

I want to find out which percentage of carbohydrates, protein, and fat make up my total daily calories. I will monitor my anxiety and panic to see which percentage of food nutrients per day helps to decrease my symptoms.

6. Now, choose nutrition changes that support the nutrition objective you identified in question five.

Change 1: I will increase the percentage of protein I eat per meal.

Change 2: I will decrease the amount of carbohydrates I eat daily and also eat lower glycemic carbohydrates.

Change 3: I will drink less high sugar colas and drinks.

Change 4: I will drink more water per day.

7. Take a few moments to jot down reasons for these nutrition changes. Support these nutrition changes with your learning thus far.

I know my symptoms are signs of excessive sympathetic nervous system arousal, which places me in a chronic fight or flight response. I do not know whether psychological fear or the way I eat underlies my problems. Regardless, sympathetic nervous system activity can stimulate a lot of blood sugar, which simultaneously activates insulin production. It also stimulates adrenaline. All the high-sugar fresh fruits, juices, and colas that I drink, are probably not the best for a person who has high anxiety. Although I initially resisted this idea, I now think that perhaps I might feel better if I lower my daily carbohydrate intake. And, I may also decrease strain symptoms by not over taxing my body by eating too much. I thus might also lower the amount of calories I eat per day.

After remaining on this new nutrition program for three days, Tom evaluates if the four nutrition changes he selected were instrumental in bringing about a decrease in his strain symptoms. If after the three days, he thinks his program needs a little more fine tuning, he can return to Part A to find other changes that may help him to fulfill his nutrition objective.

TOM'S NEW MEAL PLAN

Tom begins his new nutrition program. He will collect data on what he eats and drinks for three consecutive days, and also rate himself daily in terms of strain. Review the following nutrition worksheet to see how the food and drink he chose to eat applied to his nutrition objective and changes. We will regard Day One as prototypical of his daily nutrition.

TABLE New Meal Plan Worksheet

Time	Food & Drink	Qty.	Calorie	Carbs.	Protein	Fat	Fiber
6 am	Dannon Non-fat Blueberry yogurt	8 oz	100	16	8	0	0
	Apple with skin	1 med	81	21	0.3	0	3.7
	Peanut Butter Super-chunk	2 TBS	190	4	9	17	0.6
	Water	16 oz	0	0	0	0	0
9 am	Alpine Lace American Cheese	2	100	2	10	6	0
	Wasa Crispbread, Hearty-rye	2	100	20	4	0	2
	Water	16 oz	0	0	0	0	0
12 pm	Health Valley Fat-free Lentil Soup	10 oz	160	24	20	0	20.6
	Pear	1 med	100	25	0	1	4
	Romaine lettuce	1 cup	8	1.4	0.4	0.1	0.4
	Tomato	1 med	26	5	2	0.5	1
	Italian Creamy Dressing Lt.	2 TBS	52	4	0	4	0
	Avocado	1/2	153	7.5	2	15	0
3 pm	Almonds whole	1 oz	104.5	5	6	8	0
	Apricot	1	17	4	0.33	0	0
	Ocean Spray Reduced Cran-berry Apple Drink	8 oz	40	13	0	0	0
7 pm	Swordfish sauteed	3 oz	170	0	24	4	0
	Olive oil	2 TBS	240	0	0	26	0
	Spinach cooked	8 oz	52	6	6	0	0
	Hain's Rice Oriental 3 Grain Goodness	4 oz	120	15	4	5	0

TABLE New Meal Plan Worksheet

Time	Food & Drink	Qty.	Calorie	Carbs.	Protein	Fat	Fiber
10 pm	Blueberries fresh	1 cup	82	20	1	0	0
	Borden's Hi Protein Fat-free Milk	8 oz	100	13	8	0	0
	Frookie Brand Animal Crackers	12	130	18	2	4	0
Step 2	Sum Categories		2125.5	223.9	107.03	90.6	32.3

TABLE Tom's New Meal Plan Calculations

			Product
Step 3	A	Multiply Total Carbohydrate Calories (223.9) X 4 =	895.60
	B	Divide by Total Daily Calories (2125.5) =	0.42
	C	Multiply by 100 to change the number in 3 B into a percentage	42%
	A	Multiply Total Protein Calories (107.03) X 4 =	428.12
	B	Divide by Total Daily Calories (2125.5) =	0.20
	C	Multiply by 100 to change the number in 4 B into a percentage	20%
	A	Multiply Total Fat Calories (90.6) X 9 =	815.4
	B	Divide by Total Daily Calories (2125.5) =	0.38
	C	Multiply by 100 to change the number in 5 B into a percentage	38%

TABLE Strain Rating Scale

Rating: 1 = mild; 2 = moderate; 3 = strong

Physical	RATE	MENTAL	RATE	BEHAVIORAL	RATE
Headache	1 2 3	Clouded mind	1 2 3	Insecure	1 2 3
Migraine	1 2 3	Worry	1 2 3	Phobic, panic, or fearful	1 2 3
Rapid heart rate	1 2 3	Ideas of threat	1 2 3	Self-conscious	1 2 3
Anxiety	1 2 3	Intrusive ideas	1 2 3	Angry	1 2 3

TABLE Strain Rating Scale

Rating: 1 = mild; 2 = moderate; 3 = strong

Physical	RATE	MENTAL	RATE	BEHAVIORAL	RATE
Rapid breathing	1 2 3	Lose line of idea	1 2 3	Impulsive	1 2 3
Light headed	1 2 3	Racing thoughts	1 2 3	Hyperactive	1 2 3
Dizzy	1 2 3	Cannot focus	1 2 3	Talk a lot/fast	1 2 3
Short of breath	1 2 3	Hopeless ideas	1 2 3	Argumentative	1 2 3
Shallow breath	1 2 3	Grim thoughts	1 2 3	Rude or loud	1 2 3
Nausea	1 2 3	Sad thoughts	1 2 3	Confrontational	1 2 3
Constipation	1 2 3	Confused ideas	1 2 3	Clumsy	1 2 3
Diarrhea	1 2 3	Negative ideas	1 2 3	Inhibited	1 2 3
Indigestion	1 2 3	Literal thinking	1 2 3	Unmotivated	1 2 3
Sweating	1 2 3	Angry thoughts	1 2 3	Impatient	1 2 3
Cold hands/feet	1 2 3	Uncreative ideas	1 2 3	Rigid	1 2 3
Tingling	1 2 3	Forgetful	1 2 3	Aggressive	1 2 3
Swelling	1 2 3	Inattentive	1 2 3	Excited	1 2 3
Aches and pains	1 2 3	Can't find word	1 2 3	Withdrawn	1 2 3
Tension	1 2 3	Mind goes blank	1 2 3	Irritable	1 2 3
Jittery	1 2 3	Can't find name	1 2 3	Short temper	1 2 3

TABLE Strain Rating Scale

Rating: 1 = mild; 2 = moderate; 3 = strong

Physical	RATE	MENTAL	RATE	BEHAVIORAL	RATE
Tired/fatigued	1 2 3	Indecisive	1 2 3	Moody	1 2 3
Other:	1 2 3	Other:	1 2 3	Other:	1 2 3
Total Score	0		0		0

TOM'S NUTRITION CHANGE RESULTS

Baseline Daily Food Nutrient Intake and Symptoms of Strain

Carbohydrate 67%, Protein 8%, Fat 25%, Fiber 25.51 grams

Physical 23%, Mental 22%, Behavioral 16%

New Meal Plan Daily Food Nutrient Intake and Symptoms of Strain

Carbohydrate 42%, Protein 20%, Fat 38%, Fiber 32.3 grams

Physical 0%, Mental 0%, Behavioral 0%

Did your food choices support your nutrition objective and changes?

Yes, I increased my daily protein intake by 12% and decreased my daily carbohydrate intake by 25%. Also, I chose lower glycemic carbohydrates. I further ate a better balance of all the food nutrients per meal. And, I also drank sugar-free fruit drinks and completely stopped drinking Pepsi-Cola. In addition, I continued to make nutritious food choices (nuts, whole grains, legumes, fresh fruits and vegetables, and unsaturated fat). I could still increase my daily water intake. And, despite these changes, my fiber intake is still within the upper limit of the recommended range. Finally, I had to chair a meeting at work, and I barely noticed any anxiety symptoms. It seems like my past nutrition choices were related to my anxiety condition.

Nutrition Wrap-Up

Hardy Nutrition Exercise 2: Put Your Learning Into Practice

For Hardy Nutrition Exercise 2 you first review your baseline nutrition data, See "Appendix B: Hardy Nutrition Exercise 1, Baseline Nutrition Worksheet" on page 223. See if you want to change some of your nutrition habits to enhance your performance and health. Next, See "Appendix C: Hardy Nutrition Exercise 2, Put Your Learning Into Practice" on page 227. Develop a nutrition program that will help you achieve your nutrition goals. Then, you carry it out. If you need further help in understanding how to complete this exercise, you may want to review again Elizabeth and Toms' nutrition worksheets. There are also helpful meal planning suggestions in Appendices D and E. See "Appendix D: Plan Your Meal With Ease" on page 233. See "Appendix E: American Dietetic Association Food Standards and the Zone's Approach to Nutrition" on page 234.

Test Your Nutrition Knowledge

At this point, you may want to Test Your Knowledge about Nutrition. To take the test, See "Appendix G: Test Your Nutrition Knowledge" on page 239. For this test's answer key See "Questionnaire and Test Your Knowledge Answer Keys" on page 259.

We hope you have learned something new about your body and how it reacts to the food you eat. Eating in a way that supports your body chemistry furthers your health and performance and life goals. Your teacher has this questionnaire's answer key.

Final Hardy Nutrition Checkpoint

Take a moment to review your learning with your Hardiness trainer. Any questions or concerns you have at this time should be raised before you complete this HardiTraining component.

Summary Concepts And Terms

CASE OF ELIZABETH

CASE OF TOM

Learning Goals

- Can you calculate food nutrient percentages from your daily food and drink?

- Do you appreciate the relationship between daily food nutrient percentages and strain symptoms?

CHAPTER 21

Physical Activity

Introduction

Regular physical activity is an important component of a hardy lifestyle. Personal habits have a critical influence on a person's level of health and longevity. There is general agreement that one's health is complex, continually changing, and can be undermined by our hectic environment. Today's high tech world makes it possible for people to sit around more. Cars, computers, and labor-saving devices have dramatically reduced the energy we have to use to live and work. Paradoxically, this generally lowered level of physical activity can undermine health and needs to be offset by your personal resolve.

During the last twenty years, medical evidence shows that our health can be substantially influenced by our behaviors. Those who have an inherited predisposition for a disease may be able to reduce their chances of getting it, or at least minimize its effect, by modifying unhealthy actions and developing healthy behaviors. Having a hardy lifestyle can get you physically fit and happy, strengthen your immune system, and provide strong resistance to premature development of disease. For example, if you are a couch potato, modest increases in physical activity will enhance your health, keep you physically fit, and give you an active, longer life. People can take charge of their behaviors for lifelong health by increasing their physical activity. You can change your lifestyle, which will help you perform, feel, and look better.

The HardiTraining® program described in the introduction to this workbook is based on scientific research, which looks at the individual as a complete person. There is a sense of unity between mind and body. But these days, while some pay considerable attention to their mind or spirit, they ignore their body. This may be explained in part by the daunting perception that it takes very hard, continuous exercise to gain any health benefits. Others do not pay attention to mind or body, really risking poor performance, degenerative diseases, obesity and early death. The case for being physically active has always made sense. And now, medical research on physical activity has shown that even moderate levels of activity, if regular, help you maintain or regain your health and vitality.

On the average, physically active people outlive inactive ones, even if they start their activity later in life. Exercise can be life-long medicine, but in order to receive the benefits it must be done regularly. People can reduce their risk of heart disease, cancer, stroke, obesity, diabetes and osteoporosis by improving their lifestyle behaviors of physical activity, eating habits, coping strategies, social support patterns and relaxation efforts (see the Introduction to this Workbook). Regular exercise is one of the best ways to reduce the risk of chronic, degenerative disease.

What this means is that the risk of being undermined by disease can be at least partially reduced by something that is well within your own control—your level of physical activity (and other lifestyle aspects). So take action! The more healthful the behaviors you acquire, the greater your likelihood of living a vigorous life with better performance and health.

Behavior modification is the key to becoming healthier by substituting beneficial habits for under-mining ones. A physical activity plan should include the following components:

1. Knowledge about health, yourself, and how to change problem behaviors to healthier life choices.

2. Establishing both short and long term goals. Goals should be reasonable and attainable.

3. Setting up a personal and social system that rewards you for your accomplishments.

4. Developing the motivating belief that you are in charge of your health and will succeed.

Note: To do these things, it makes sense to combine this physical activity component with the other lifestyle components of HardiTraining®.

Hardy Physical Fitness

Physical Fitness

Your bodys' ability to function well at work and at home is your **physical fitness**. The four components of fitness are associated with increasing energy and enthusiasm for living, resisting serious and chronic disease, and maintaining a desirable weight. Physical activity helps people generate more energy, manage stress and boost their immune system. It also provides many psychological benefits, such as those feelings of commitment, control, and challenge that make up the HardiAttitudes (see the Introduction to this Workbook). The four components of physical fitness endorsed by the American College of Sports Medicine are:

Body Composition. The amount of lean (muscle, bone and water) versus fat tissue in your body is your body composition. Healthy body composition is a great deal of lean tissue (about 80 to 90%) and very little fat (no more than 10 to 20%). An aspect of aging, the proportion of fat increases slowly in our 30s and more rapidly thereafter. Physical activity and other lifestyle behaviors, however, can minimize this natural rate of fat increase.

Cardiorespiratory Capacity. Cardiorespiratory capacity is the ability of the heart, lungs and circulatory system to deliver fuel and oxygen to the tissues. It is the most important component of fitness and is a major sign of whether the heart is healthy. It also plays a role in stamina, metabolism and body weight.

Flexibility. Flexibility is the ability of joints to move through their full range of motion. Poor flexibility leads to stiffness, discomfort and sprains. Poor flexibility is also a complicating factor in osteoporosis.

Muscular Strength. Muscular strength is the amount of force a muscle can exert with a single maximum effort. Adequate muscular strength is important to performance of daily tasks and body alignment, and a preventive factor in osteoporosis. An increase in muscular strength means increased lean body mass and therefore a higher rate of metabolism, which is likely to reduce body weight and body fat.

Principles Of Physical Conditioning

Which standard is best for the development of your personal fitness program? There are a variety of approaches to customizing programs to individual needs. For programs to be effective, however, they must all include the following principles:

Principle Of Progression

To develop a successful conditioning program, progression, specificity and reversal must be taken into account. The idea here is that as the amount of exercise is progressively increased, the body continues to adapt to the changing demands, and that increases fitness. So, to be beneficial, the amount of physical activity in your program must exceed the current level of your activity. There are three dimensions of the amount of physical activity:

Frequency. Frequency refers to how often you perform the activity. If a person is reasonably active, it probably requires 3 to 5 days per week of physical exercise to gain some benefits. But if a person is a couch potato, much less physical activity than this will help.

Intensity. Intensity refers to the activity's degree of difficulty. Substantial benefits occur when exercise is more intense than routine daily activity.

Duration. Duration refers to time spent performing the activity. Cardiorespiratory conditioning requires at least 20 minutes of high-intensity exercise, while being physically active requires 30 to 45 minutes of low intensity exercise.

Principle Of Specificity

The idea here is that your particular fitness goal will determine the specifics of your physical activity program. Developing a particular fitness goal requires performance of exercises specifically designed to bring it about. For example, if your goal is muscular strength, a productive physical activity plan may include exercises targeted to various muscle groups of the body.

Principle Of Reversal

The benefits of fitness can be reversed. Just as the body can adapt to higher levels of activity and become healthier, it adapts to lower levels of activity and becomes less efficient. Conditioning must be consistent in frequency, intensity and duration to maintain your goals of physical fitness and health.

The Ten Commandments Of Physical Training

Train The Way You Want Your Body To Change

Exercise according to what you want to accomplish. For greater strength, lift weights; for more flexibility, stretch; for a strong heart or weight reduction, engage in sustained activity that makes you out of breath and your heart beat fast.

Train Regularly. The optimal conditioning schedule is 3-5 days per week. A period of rest is essential for your body to adapt to and recover from the impact of vigorous exercise. Training less than 3-5 days increases risk of some injuries and loss of fitness benefits. Training more than 3-5 days increases risk of other injuries and burnout.

Getting Fit Takes Patience. Slowly increase duration and frequency before increasing intensity of the activity. Progressing gradually will help you avoid injury, overstraining and boredom. Periodic general assessments of your progress will help you appreciate the gradual changes that you are making.

Warm Up Before, and Cool Down After, the Exercise Session. Warm-up and stretching helps the body adjust to exercise and decreases the likeli-

hood of injury. Cool-down restores circulation to its normal level and reduces strain on the cardiovascular system. Cool-downs and warm-ups are both important.

Choose Activities According to Your Fitness Goals. It is important to establish not only long-term goals, but also the short-term goals that will help you get there. A generic exercise program that is useful for most people should center on cardio-respiratory endurance and body composition followed by flexibility and muscular strength. Select activities appropriate to your fitness level, goals, personality, accessibility and convenience.

Listen to Your Body. While you should maintain a structured, consistent workout program, don't exercise when you have a virus or cold. It is okay to skip the session.

Do Physical Activity with a Partner. Friends can motivate and encourage you to continue your efforts when you are bored. A pet can be a good substitute for a human companion.

Be Patient and Positive about Yourself and Your Goals. Getting fit and being fit takes time. Don't expect miracles overnight and be sure to reward yourself for each accomplishment. Rewards should be something you like, such as going to the movies, or buying an article of clothing, but should not be things that can undermine fitness and health, such as eating fatty or sweet foods.

Schedule Your Exercise as Part of Your Regular Daily Activities. Doing this is only hard at first. See if you can bring family and friends into your exercise routine.

Keep Your Exercise Program in Perspective. It should not consume all of your time, attention and energy. A healthy balance of activities will bring you a happy state of life.

Setting Goals And Assessing Progress

Think carefully about the exercise goals you can easily reach (short term goals), and how these beginnings can lead you to your eventual long-term fitness goals. It is best if you get into the habit of regularly assessing progress you are making in reaching both short- term and long-term goals. Your Hardiness trainer can help you with assessment procedures. Whenever you make progress in reaching short-term or long-term goals, you should not only reward yourself but also reflect on how the success makes you feel. We bet you will feel greater commitment, control, and challenge—the three Cs of HardiAttitudes.

Note: Before starting an exercise program, make sure to get a physical examination. If you have a physical health problem (such as heart disease or obesity), you and your physician will have to take that into account in planning and reaching your physical activity goals.

Frequently Asked Questions

1. Is there a limit to how physically fit I can become?

Yes, the body has limits of adaptability (such as lung capacity) and many factors are hereditary. Physical conditioning can improve fitness regardless of hereditary limits. It can also slow down the aging process.

2. How can I fit my exercise program into my busy day?

Choose a regular, scheduled time and make it a priority. If you are on a trip, take a walk, or select a hotel, which has an exercise facility.

3. Where can I work out?

Find accessible, convenient, and enjoyable places that you'll be likely to use regularly

Summary Concepts And Terms

BODY COMPOSITION

CARDIORESPIRATORY CAPACITY

FLEXIBILITY

MUSCLE STRENGTH

PHYSICAL FITNESS

PRINCIPLE OF PROGRESSION

PRINCIPLE OF SPECIFICITY

PRINCIPLE OF REVERSAL

CHAPTER 22

Improving Your Body Composition

What Is Body Composition?

The medical profession and general public are recognizing the fact that obesity significantly contributes to chronic diseases and shortens the life span. The amount and location of fat deposits also puts some people at significant health risk for heart disease and diabetes. The benefits of maintaining a desirable fat and weight level are important for being healthy. Body composition is made up of two types of tissue:

Lean body mass includes all nonfat tissues, such as bone, connective tissue, organs, muscle, and water. About 60% of lean body mass is water.

Body fat includes both essential and nonessential fats. As is elaborated in the HardiTraining® nutrition component, essential fat is necessary for normal body growth, functioning and repair. Essential fat makes up only about 3 percent of total body weight in men and 12 percent in women. Nonessential (or unnecessary) fat is stored in fat cells. The amount of storage fat depends on gender, age, heredity, metabolism, diet, activity level and cultural practices. The more fat is stored in your fat cells, the heavier and less trim looking you will be.

Body Composition Health Standards

There are several technical ways of measuring the ratio of body fat to lean body mass. These include height-weight tables, which assume that weight should be proportional to height. The **waist-hip ratio** is the best available index for determining disease risk associated with fat distribution. Specifically, people with more fat in the abdomen than the hips tend to be at greater risk for cardiovascular disease and diabetes. Skinfold measurements are done with calipers at specific sites (e.g., the waist) to estimate percentage of body fat. Especially useful is the **body mass index** (BMI), which assumes that weight should be proportional to height, but is more accurate than Height-Weight Tables. BMI is calculated by dividing your body weight (in kilograms) by the square of your height (in millimeters), and comparing this figure to an index.

Although a professional exercise physiologist will use these approaches, you probably do not have access to them on a daily basis. You are best off monitoring your total weight, clothing size and fit, and physical performance ability, as follows:

Morbid Obesity. Being more than 100 pounds overweight greatly increases the risk of serious illnesses, such as diabetes, heart disease and cancer, and shortens the life span. There may be a genetic (metabolic or hormonal) tendency to morbid obesity. But medical attention and a comprehensive lifestyle approach, like HardiTraining®, can make a difference in weight reduction and improved health.

Obesity. People who are less than 100 pounds overweight are obese. Most of them do not have a genetic predisposition to gain weight. They slowly gather excess body fat by eating more calories than they expend in physical activity. The urge to eat so much is often motivated by poor coping, social sup-

port, and relaxation. When body fat exceeds 35% for males and 40% for females, the risk of serious degenerative diseases (e.g., cancer, cardiovascular disease, and diabetes) goes way up.

Fat Distribution. Fat distribution is also an important factor in health because people who tend to gain weight in the abdominal area are at higher risk for coronary heart disease, high blood pressure, diabetes and stroke than are people who gain weight in the hips. You can get a sense of your fat distribution by how your clothes fit. In clothing, if the size you must wear in order to have enough waist room is loose on the hips and elsewhere, especially if needing to be taken in, you probably tend to gain weight in the abdominal area.

Insufficient Body Fat. Too little body fat—less than 8% for women and 5% for men is also dangerous. It can lead to muscle wasting and fatigue, and may be linked to an eating disorder. In women, an extremely low percentage of body fat is associated with amenorrhea and a loss of bone mass that hastens osteoporosis. Once again, you can get a sense if you have insufficient body fat by how your clothes fit. If the size you need for your height just hangs limp on you, you probably have insufficient body fat.

Age Related Fat. For many people, chronological age involves a natural increase in body fat beginning somewhere between 30 to 40 years of age. As muscles become weaker, bone density decreases and physical activity is reduced, percentage of body fat increases. Has your weight and clothing size increased with age?

Daily Activity Performance. Obese people tend to be less fit and lack muscular strength, endurance and flexibility, making everyday activities extremely difficult and less rewarding. Do you have difficulty doing the daily activities that others take for granted?

Appearance And Self-Image. The ideal body composition for appearance depends on individual preference and cultural standards. The ability to change your body depends not only on how you exercise, eat, cope, relate to others, and relax, but also on your heredity. Everyone should strive for a healthy body, but unrealistic ideals can lead to a negative self-image, low self-esteem, and eating disorders.

Hardy Physical Activity Exercise 1, Assessing And Setting Goals For Your Body Composition

Please answer the following questions:

1. How many pounds overweight are you? 0____ 1-30 ____ 31-50 ____ 51-100 ____ 101+____

2. What level of obesity is this? Normal _____ Obese _____ Morbid Obese ____

3. Do you have trouble with how clothing fits around your hips? Yes No

4. Do you have trouble with how clothing fits around your waist? Yes No

5. Have you been gaining weight steadily as you get older? Yes No

6. Does your clothing fit tighter or less well as you get older? Yes No

7. Is it hard to perform the daily activities that are routine for others? Yes No

If you are heavier than you should be, your clothes don't fit well, your clothes size is bigger than you would like and you have trouble performing daily activities, you need to be involved in weight reduction and loss of body fat. Please set the following goals for yourself, but be sure they agree with the goals you were asked for in the Hardy Nutrition component, and that you consult your Hardiness trainer, if necessary:

> The number of pounds I want to lose is:
> _____ pounds.
>
> The clothing size I would like to fit into is size:_____.

My Goal: I assert that by coordinating the physical activity I do with the weight reduction menu, I will go on in this coordinated HardiTraining® approach. I will continue to expend more calories through my physical activity program than I take in through eating until I reach the desired weight and clothing size I established above, and thereafter, I will balance physical activity and menu to maintain my new weight and clothing size:

Your Signature: _____ Date:_____

If doing this exercise shows you that you are not heavier than you should be, then you need not sign the assertion above. Instead, just complete the following quiz and session goals, and go on to the next section on cardiorespiratory fitness.

EXERCISE END

Hardy Physical Activity Exercise 2, My Aerobic Physical Activity Contract

It is time now to commit yourself to carrying out an aerobic physical activity program. This program will be helpful to you not only in improving cardiorespiratory fitness, but also in reaching weight reduction goals you may have established in the first Hardy Physical Activity exercise.

1. Commit yourself to a form of physical activity (walking, jogging, cycling, swimming). If you have been sedentary, we recommend walking to start with. For my first exercise plan I will:

   _____
   _____
   _____
   _____

2. Will you stay with that form of physical activity throughout your exercise plan, or would you like to change after a while? If you wish to change, to what other physical activities?

   _____
   _____
   _____
   _____

3. Determine your conditioning heart rate and write it down here:

   My conditioning heart rate is:

   _____.

4. Are you willing to work slowly toward a time when you are exercising within your conditioning heart rate? Yes _____ No _____ Maybe _____

5. Are you willing to work slowly toward a time when you are doing moderate exercise for between 20 and 40 minutes a day, on the days when you are exercising? Yes _____ No _____ Maybe _____

6. Will you commit yourself to warming up before and cooling down after an exercise session? Yes _____ No _____ Maybe _____

7. Will you commit yourself to generally increasing the energy expenditure in your daily living? Yes _____ No _____ Maybe _____

8. Will you commit yourself to regular exercise sessions in a set place at a set time? Yes _____ No _____ Maybe _____

9. Will you commit yourself to trying to enlist friends, family, or pets to exercise with you? Yes _____ No _____ Maybe _____

10. List here the ways in which yourself or others will reward you for fulfilling these commitments you have made.

    _____
    _____
    _____
    _____

11. Are you having problems with this exercise contract?

    _____
    _____
    _____
    _____

EXERCISE END

How To Lose Weight Through Exercise And Nutrition

Most people interested in losing body weight don't realize that this hinges on decreasing body fat. Excess weight is largely due to excess fat stored in the body. In order to decrease body weight, the energy balance needs to change so that the calories expended in physical activity are more than the calories consumed in food. Here's how you expend more calories than you consume:

Choose A Healthy Target Weight. This goal should be suitable to your age, body type and present weight. If you have not done so already, consult your Hardiness trainer on a reasonable target weight. Physical activity and weight loss dieting decrease your weight by cutting down on excess fat stored in your body. So, as you decrease in weight, you will also notice that your clothing size decreases and the clothes fit you better. As you begin to lose weight, you should reward yourself immediately with something you like (such as going to the movies, or buying a CD, but not by eating sweet or fatty foods, or by exercising less). Remember, after the rapid initial weight loss due to excreting water and other body fluids, you will reach a plateau after which your weight decrease will be much slower but more permanent. Don't give up when you reach the plateau.

Weight Control Through Physical Activity. To lose weight, a negative calorie balance must be achieved by either consuming fewer or burning more calories. To lose one half to one pound per week, you must have a negative balance of 1,750 to 3,500 calories per week or 250 to 500 calories per day. In trying to lose weight, it's easiest to start by increasing big muscle activity rather than decreasing calorie consumption. This is because exercise raises, whereas dieting lowers, metabolism, and raising metabolism uses up calories. Moderate endurance exercise of the cardiorespiratory sort described in the next section is the best way to burn fat. As you will see in the next section, you need to work up to a schedule of cardiorespiratory activity that involves 30 to 45 minutes, 3 times a week.

Weight Control Through How You Eat. The best policy is to eat three small, balanced meals a day plus a healthy snack in between each meal and in the evening. Practice moderation in your diet and substitute nonfat foods rather than denying yourself all food. Carbohydrates and proteins should replace excess fats in the diet. The body digests fats easily, but digesting complex carbohydrates actually burns calories and makes you feel full. Thus, increasing

your consumption of complex carbohydrates while decreasing fats can help you lose weight. Consume no more than 22% of your calories from fat. A diet that does not primarily consist of red meats and processed foods can greatly reduce fat intake (See the Hardy Nutrition component for details).

You should not reduce calorie intake below 1,500 for men or 1,200 for women. Emphasize dietary cuts in fat calories. Remember to drink 8 or more glasses of water daily (not including coffee, soft drinks or juices).

Frequently Asked Questions

1. Is spot reducing effective?

   No, you cannot lose fat in a specific part of the body by exercising that part, though you may increase its muscular tone. You only reduce overall fat by creating a negative energy balance, using more energy than you take in.

2. How does exercise affect body composition?

   Cardiorespiratory or aerobic exercise burns calories, so it helps create a negative energy balance by raising the metabolic rate. Weight training does not use as many calories, but it does increase lean body mass, improving body composition and slowly raising metabolism.

3. How do I develop a healthy-looking body?

   A healthy body depends on regular exercise, healthy eating, and self control. Heredity, age and gender influence appearance as we gain or lose weight. A hardy lifestyle is the best thing you can do to improve body appearance.

4. Can I lose weight on my own?

   The key to losing weight on your own is to be persistent and focus on gradual loss. Most people give up after the initial loss of water weight.

Summary Concepts And Terms

AGE-RELATED FAT

BODY COMPOSITION

BODY FAT

BODY MASS INDEX

FAT DISTRIBUTION

LEAN BODY MASS

OBESITY

WAIST-HIP RATIO

Test Your Knowledge

To test what you learned so far, see if you can correctly answer the following questions. Remember, the more information you have to think about what happens to you, the more building blocks you have to generate creative solutions to everyday living problems. This, in turn, strengthens your HardiAttitudes.

Commitment. The more information you seek to learn about yourself and the world, the more you demonstrate your belief that you are worthwhile and important enough to gather information that helps you.

Control. The more information you gather about yourself and your world, the greater your ability to influence the direction of your life.

Challenge. The effort you apply in learning the hardiness skills shows that you regard the time spent in developing yourself as a normal challenge of life.

For the answer key, See "Questionnaire and Test Your Knowledge Answer Keys" on page 259.

Challenge. The effort you apply in learning the hardiness skills show that you regard the time spent in developing yourself as a normal challenge of life.

1. As to living longer, _____ _____ people generally have the advantage.

2. _____ physical activity will help you maintain or regain your health.

3. The four components of physical fitness are: _____ ; _____ ; _____ ; _____ .

4. The most important component of physical fitness is _____ .

5. The three principles that define a successful physical conditioning program are: _____ , _____ , _____ .

6. The conditioning program principle of progression involves _____ , _____ , and _____ .

7. Listening to your body is one of the _____ _____ of physical training.

8. Body composition is made up of _____ _____ _____ and _____ _____ .

9. Morbid obesity involves being more than ____ pounds overweight.

10. Obesity involves being up to _____ pounds overweight.

11. An important factor in health is the _____ of fat.

12. Beginning somewhere between 30 and 40 years of age, there is a natural increase in body _____ .

13. Too little body fat is less than ___% for women, and ___% for men.

Learning Goals

- Did you read the two chapters? Yes No
- Do you know the degenerative diseases that are decreased in likelihood by physical fitness?
- Do you know the difference in longevity physical fitness can make?
- Do you know the four components of physical fitness?
- Do you know which of the four components of physical fitness is the most important? Do you know the three principles that define a successful physical conditioning program?
- Do you know the Ten Commandments of physical training?
- Do you know the health standards of body composition?
- Did you complete Physical Activity Exercise 1?
- Did you take the two chapter quizzes?

CHAPTER 23

Improving Cardiorespiratory Fitness

Aerobic Exercise

Cardiorespiratory exercise has been documented as a valuable treatment for many physical and mental problems. Aerobic exercise improves personal health, reduces the risk factors for chronic disease, and improves how you feel about yourself. To be aerobic, exercise need not be strenuous, but must continue long enough to use up the body's available glucose so that more has to be produced by breaking down the fat stored in the body. Moderate physical activity of 30 minutes or more will do it. So, just doing enough aerobic exercise not to be sedentary can make a world of difference in improving cardiorespiratory capacity, which is the most important component of physical fitness. The positive effects of aerobic exercise are:

Improved Cardiovascular Functioning. This is the most important component of physical fitness, and the benefits are numerous because it effects the whole person. Aerobic exercise improves the ability of the heart, lungs and circulatory system to deliver basic fuels to the tissues and remove waste products. Regular aerobic exercise makes the cardiovascular system stronger, more efficient and able to more effectively recover from stressful situations.

Better Control Of Blood Fats. Aerobic exercise combined with a low fat diet helps lower levels of **low-density lipoproteins** (LDL). Elevated LDL levels can bring too much cholesterol to the blood vessels, allowing fatty deposits to adhere on vascular walls, beginning the process of calcification that can end in heart disease. Also, aerobic exercise is the only activity that increases **high-density lipoproteins** (HDL). HDLs remove cholesterol from the vascular system for excretion and in that way protects against heart disease. Finally, aerobic exercise also reduces triglycerides, the level of which is a major fat risk factor in some chronic diseases.

Improved Metabolism. Aerobic exercise increases **metabolism**, the process by which food calories are burned off as energy. Also, it increases the size of muscular tissue. Further, aerobic exercise increases the number of capillaries in the muscles, supplies them with more oxygen and fuel, and trains the muscles to use these resources more efficiently over a longer period of time.

Better Control Of Body Weight. Aerobic exercise influences body chemistry through increasing metabolism. This is how such exercise can decrease body fat while increasing muscle size. Combined with a healthy, low fat diet, regular aerobic exercise ensures that enough calories are burned for weight loss, if needed, or to maintain proper body weight.

Improved Mood. Over the long term, aerobic exercise decreases the secretion of hormones triggered by the fight or flight reaction to stressful situations and may facilitate the secretion of endorphins, which can moderate pain levels, reduce fatigue, and produce heightened levels of consciousness and comfort.

Decreased Risk Of Degenerative Diseases. Regular aerobic exercise helps maintain bone density, protects against development of diabetes, and lowers high blood pressure and the risk of heart disease.

Planning An Aerobic Conditioning Program

Aerobic Conditioning

Aerobic conditioning is the major basis in physical activity for improving cardiorespiratory fitness and weight reduction. Factors to consider before beginning your program is your current level of fitness. If you are sedentary or have been inactive for some time, or are overweight, you should begin with a less vigorous activity. As you improve your level of endurance, the duration and intensity of your program can be increased. Regularity is more important than time of day.

At the outset, you should assess your cardiorespiratory fitness, so that you can make an informed judgment as to how vigorous your initial physical activity program should be. Cardiorespiratory fitness is determined by the body's ability to take up, distribute, and use oxygen during physical activity. There are two easy tests that provide estimates of cardiorespiratory fitness. They are:

THE 1-MILE WALK

This test measures the level of oxygen consumption based on the amount of time it takes to complete one mile of walking and the heart rate at the end of the mile. The faster the time and the lower the heart rate, the higher the level of cardiorespiratory fitness.

THE 3-MINUTE STEP

This test measures how long it takes the pulse to return to resting rate after three minutes of jogging or stepping in place. The faster the rate of recovery, the higher the level of cardiorespiratory fitness.

Note: Assessment of cardiorespiratory fitness before beginning on an exercise program is probably not even required for healthy people. But, if there is any medical problem that might complicate the assessment and/or influence the strenuousness of the exercise program, a physician should be consulted before doing anything. Let's turn to the specifics of your aerobic conditioning program.

Select A Type Of Physical Activity

The activities that use large muscle groups continually, and are therefore aerobic, include walking, jogging, cycling, swimming and dancing. Select activities that are enjoyable, you have time to perform, and will not cause you physical injury. If you have been sedentary, it's best to start with walking. Remember that the ancient Greek physician, Hippocrates, promoted walking as the best medicine.

Plan The Frequency Of Your Exercise. Beginners should probably start with 3 non-consecutive days per week and work up to 5. Even when you've reached 5 days a week, take a day of rest following every 2 to 3 days of exercise.

Determine The Intensity Of Your Exercise. The heart rate at which you exercise to experience cardiorespiratory benefits is what we call your **target heart rate**. It is 50% to 85% of your **maximum heart rate reserve**. Choose one of the following three methods to determine the level of intensity necessary to improve your fitness:

1. As you exercise, you should feel your heart beating faster and you should be sweating. If you can carry on a conversation without being too short of breath, continue that level of physi-

cal activity. But if you can't talk easily, slow down.

2. If you want to be more precise, find your maximum heart rate by subtracting your age from 220. Find your resting heart rate by taking your pulse at the wrist after at least 10 minutes of rest. Then find your heart rate reserve by subtracting your resting heart rate from your maximum heart rate. Finally, to find your conditioning heart rate range in which exercise will benefit you, subtract your age from 220 and then apply the result within a range of 60 to 85% of your heart rate reserve to your resting heart rate. If you have been sedentary, begin exercising at the lower (50%) end of your conditioning heart rate range.

3. Evaluate your accomplishments: At the beginning, especially if you have been sedentary, don't even worry about whether you are exercising in your conditioning heart rate range. The only thing of importance is to make a start. As you become fit, then try to exercise within that conditioning heart rate range. Check yourself out again every 8 to 10 weeks as you adjust to your exercise intensity level. As you adjust, you may want to raise the intensity level until you reach your final exercise goal.

Plan The Duration Of Your Exercise Sessions

To improve cardiorespiratory capacity, or to lose weight, your goal should be to exercise regularly in your conditioning heart rate zone. This may require about 20 to 40 minutes of low to moderate intensity exercise, or 20 minutes of high intensity exercise. You can separate the time into blocks during the day. As your body adapts to a particular exercise routine, the intensity, duration and frequency may be increased. Adaptation may take from 30 to 90 days. When you have reached your desired exercise goal, you need not change the routine further, but keep doing it.

Warming Up And Cooling Down. Muscles work better when stretched beyond resting level. Doing some stretching before your aerobic exercise also decreases the chance of injury. Warm up with low-intensity movements similar to those of your aerobic activity (so, if your exercise involves jogging, warm up by walking). Similarly, the cool-down period should consist of 5-10 minutes of reduced activity. Cool down is valuable because it returns heart rate to its natural level gradually, rather than all at once, which is risky.

Expend More Energy Daily. By using daily activities, like walking to burn more physical energy, you support your overall exercise goals. Try climbing the stairs more often at home or work and parking your car some distance from where you are going. Also, take a friend or a pet for walks. This increased physical activity will help in weight loss.

Make A Regular And Rewarding Exercise Plan.

You already know that you need to do your exercise plan several times a week. It is also helpful to set aside a permanent time and place to exercise that fit into your daily living. When you have finished your exercise for the day, reward yourself or get a reward from others (but not by eating sweet or fatty foods). All this helps in sticking to your plan. If you are having trouble keeping on the plan, the coping component of HardiTraining® may be useful to you. If your family and friends do not help you, the social support component of HardiTraining® may be useful.

First Hardy Physical Activity Checkpoint

Please contact your Hardiness trainer and share your plan for aerobic conditioning, including your goals and procedures. If you need assistance, get it from your trainer.

Summary Concepts And Terms

AEROBIC CONDITIONING

LOW DENSITY LIPOPROTEINS

HIGH DENSITY LIPOPROTEINS

MAXIMUM HEART RATE RESERVE

ONE-MILE WALK

TARGET HEART RATE

THREE-MINUTE STEP

Test Your Knowledge

To test what you learned so far, see if you can correctly answer the following questions. Remember, the more information you have to think about what happens to you, the more building blocks you have to generate creative solutions to everyday living problems. This, in turn, strengthens your HardiAttitudes.

Commitment. The more information you seek to learn about yourself and the world, the more you demonstrate your belief that you are worthwhile and important enough to gather information that helps you.

Control. The more information you gather about yourself and your world, the more able you are to influence the direction of your life.

Challenge. The effort you apply in learning the hardiness skills show that you regard the time spent in developing yourself as a normal challenge of life.

For the answer key, See "Questionnaire and Test Your Knowledge Answer Keys" on page 259.

1. _____ is the major basis in physical activity for improving cardiorespiratory fitness and weight reduction.

2. The _____ measures the level of oxygen consumption based on the amount of time it takes to complete one mile of walking and the heart rate at the end of the mile.

3. The _____ measures how long it takes the pulse to return to resting rate after three minutes of jogging or stepping in place.

The faster the rate of recovery, the higher the level of cardiorespiratory fitness.

4. The heart rate at which you exercise to experience cardiorespiratory benefits is called the

_____.

5. The target heart rate is 50% to 85% of a person's _____.

Learning Goals

- Know the positive effects of doing aerobic exercise

- Know how to plan an aerobic conditioning program, and

- Understand how to evaluate your target heart rate and maximum heart rate reserve.

CHAPTER 24

Improving Your Flexibility

The Benefits of Flexibility and Stretching

Flexibility has not received as much recognition as other physical fitness factors. Nonetheless, flexibility has considerable value. It delays the osteoporosis process, reduces hardening of tendons and ligaments, and decreases the likelihood of postural problems caused by shortened soft tissue. Flexibility is the range of motion that bones go through at various joints and it is limited by the structure of the joint. A muscle's stretching capacity equals the stretching capacity of the joint to which it is attached. Like other fitness components, flexibility improves with specific physical activity and decreases with inactivity.

Good flexibility is essential to joint health. Joints surrounded by tight muscles, tendons and ligaments are subject to deterioration and injury. Poor flexibility and weak muscles in the back, hips, and thighs can cause spinal misalignment, pressure on spinal nerves, and back pain. Further, improved flexibility may enhance relaxation by decreasing muscular tension and improving tendon viscosity. People with flexible bodies often have flexible minds.

What Determines Flexibility?

The three determinants of flexibility are:

The Joint Structure. This is the type of joint, the flexibility of the joint capsule that supports the joint, and the amount of fat and muscle tissue encompassing the joint. Joint structure cannot be changed.

Muscle Elasticity and Length. In the muscle, collagen fibers provide mass and support, whereas elastin fibers are flexible and pull a stretched muscle back to the resting position. Through regular muscle stretching, elastin and other muscle fibers can be lengthened, thereby improving the range of motion.

Nervous System Activity. If a muscle is stretched suddenly, the nerve receptors notify the spinal cord, which sends a message to the muscle to contract. The larger the movement, the greater the muscle contraction. Thus, quick and jerky movements can make a muscle stretch and contract at the same time, increasing the risk of injury. Further, if a muscle is contracted, nerve receptors can trigger a relaxation reaction. Thus, contracting a muscle before stretching it can cause it to relax and then be able to stretch further. Practicing this on purpose is called proprioceptive neuromuscular facilitation. It is possible to "reset" the sensitivity of stretch receptors by stretching, relaxing, and stretching again.

Planning and Using Your Flexibility Program

Types of Stretching Exercises

Like aerobic exercise programs, flexibility programs have the characteristics of activity type, intensity, duration and frequency.

STATIC STRETCHING

This involves slow and gradual stretching of a muscle and holding it for 10 to 60 seconds. An example (the toe-touch exercise) is sitting on the floor with legs apart, and slowly stretching to try to touch first one foot and then the other with your hands. Another example (the leg-stretch exercise) is placing your hands on a table with one foot closer to the table than the other, while you slowly lean toward the table by bending the knee closest to it while keeping the other knee straight. In this exercise, you alternate which leg is closest to the table. The slow movement provokes less reaction from stretch nerve receptors, so you can safely stretch farther than usual.

BALLISTIC STRETCHING

This involves stretching the muscles suddenly in a bouncing movement. You vigorously and repeatedly stretch the muscles to the limit of their flexibility. So-called aerobic dancing involves a lot of ballistic stretching. The heightened reaction of stretch nerve receptors can cause injury. For this reason, the trend is away from ballistic stretching toward static stretching exercises.

PROPRIOCEPTIVE NEUROMUSCULAR FACILITATION

(PNF) techniques use the nerve receptor's relaxation reflex to stretch muscles farther by having contracted them first. While PNF may involve more effective stretching, it also tends to cause greater muscle soreness than do other stretching techniques. PNF is about as effective as static stretching.

All things considered, you are best off, when beginning your attempt to improve flexibility, to emphasize static stretching exercises. Good examples include head turns and tilts, towel stretches, across-the-body stretches, upper back stretches, step stretches, side lunges, sole stretches, trunk rotation and, of course, the two examples listed earlier under static stretching.

Intensity and Duration

For each exercise, slowly stretch to the point of slight discomfort and hold that position for 15 to 60 seconds. As the discomfort fades, stretch a bit farther. Rest for 30 to 60 seconds between each stretch and do 3 to 5 repetitions of each. Continue with this progression principle. A complete flexibility workout will take 15 to 30 minutes.

Frequency. Do stretching exercises 3 to 5 days a week. They can be done at any time during the day. As to their content, time and place, you are only limited by your imagination.

Avoiding and Managing Lower Back Pain. Poor posture when standing, sitting, lying, or lifting is responsible for many back injuries. Also playing a role in back injuries are imbalances in muscular strength among various muscle groups and poor flexibility. Exercises to improve the flexibility of the back include the wall stretch, step stretch, leg stretch, doubling knee-to-chest, trunk twist, back bridge, pelvic tilt, modified sit-up, press-up and wall squat. If you have back pain problems, don't perform exercises that involve increasing forward curvature in the lower back area.

Frequently Asked Questions

1. Are there stretching exercises I shouldn't do? Yes. You should avoid any exercises that put excessive pressure on the joints, especially the spine and knees.

2. Can I stretch too far? Yes. Muscle tissue can be stretched too far and rupture or become otherwise damaged, especially during static stretching with a partner.

3. Can jogging impair flexibility? Because of the limited motion of the running stride, jogging tends to decrease flexibility. Walkers and runners should perform leg and arm stretches before they begin their aerobic activity.

Hardy Physical Activity Exercise 4, Planning and Carrying Out Your Flexibility Program

NAME: _____

DATE: _____

TRAINER NAME:
_____
_____

1. Write down the specifics of the flexibility program that you will be doing:

TYPE (S) OF ACTIVITY:
_____.

FREQUENCY:
_____.

DURATION:
_____.

2. When you are satisfied with the specifics of your program, begin carrying it out. After a week of doing so, put down here what your experiences have been:

_____

_____

_____

_____

Also write down how carrying through on your program leads you to feel concerning commitment, control, and challenge (those indicators of HardiAttitudes):

_____
_____
_____
_____
_____
_____
_____
_____
_____
_____

END OF HARDY PHYSICAL ACTIVITY EXERCISE

Third Hardy Physical Activity Checkpoint

Take a moment to review your learning with your Hardiness trainer. Any questions or concerns you have at this time should be raised before you complete this HardiTraining component.

Test Your Knowledge

To test what you learned so far, see if you can correctly answer the following questions. Remember, the more information you have to think about what happens to you, the more building blocks you have to generate creative solutions to everyday living problems. This, in turn, strengthens your HardiAttitudes.

Commitment. The more information you seek to learn about yourself and the world, the more you demonstrate your belief that you are worthwhile and important enough to gather information that helps you.

Control. The more information you gather about yourself and your world, the more able you are to influence the direction of your life.

Challenge. The effort you apply in learning the hardiness skills show that you regard the time spent in developing yourself as a normal challenge of life.

For the answer key, See "Questionnaire and Test Your Knowledge Answer Keys" on page 259.

1. A muscle's _____ equals the stretching capacity of the joint to which it is attached.

2. Joint structure, muscle elasticity and length, and _____ are the three determinants of flexibility.

3. _____ techniques use the nerve receptor's relaxation reflex to stretch muscles farther by having contracted them first.

4. _____ involves stretching the muscles in a bouncing movement.

5. Slow and gradual stretching of a muscle and holding it for 10 to 60 seconds is called _____ stretching.

Learning Goals

- Do you know the benefits of flexibility?
- Do you know what determines flexibility?
- Do you know the three types of flexibility exercises?

Summary Concepts and Terms

FLEXIBILITY

STATIC STRETCHING

BALLISTIC STRETCHING

PROPRIOCEPTIVE NEUROMUSCULAR FACILITA-
TION

CHAPTER 25

Weight Training

Improving Your Strength And Endurance

Muscular strength and endurance is most directly increased through weight training. When a greater load than is on them at rest stresses muscles, they adapt and
thereby improve their capabilities. Weight training has been shown to be beneficial
in preventing some skeletal injuries, reducing osteoporosis (in combination with
flexibility exercises), and decreasing the stress of daily muscular tasks. Also,
weight training can improve physical appearance and reduce body fat. Here are
some guidelines for establishing a weight training program.

Muscular Strength And Endurance Exercise Benefits

As the muscles become stronger, performance of everyday work is easier. Stronger
muscles also mean better body alignment, less chance of lower back pain, and
stronger joint tendons and ligaments. Also, engaging in muscular strength and
endurance exercises increases lean body mass, which raises metabolism and
depletes fat tissue.

Assessment

Muscular strength is the maximum amount of force a muscle can produce in a single effort. It can be assessed by measuring the maximum weight that can be lifted at one time. **Muscular endurance** is the ability of a muscle to exert sub-maximum force continuously. It can be assessed by counting the maximum number of repetitions of muscular activity (such as sit-ups or push-ups).

Physiological Effects Of Weight Training

Movement occurs when muscles contract and pull on the tendons, which in turn move the bones. Strong muscles cause better movement, keep postural alignment, increase bone density, and reduce joint degeneration.

Weight training increases muscular strength by increasing the number and size of muscle fibers and improving the body's ability to call upon motor units to exert force. The process of increasing the size of muscle fibers is called **hypertrophy**. Losing muscle fibers through disuse is called **atrophy**.

A **motor unit** is made up of a nerve connected to a number of muscle fibers. Weight training requires one or more motor units to contract, and all of the fibers to contract to their maximum capacity in order to exert force. The number of motor units initially recruited depends on the perceived amount of force required to move the object.

Weight Training Exercise Types

Isometric Exercise. This involves applying force without movement. These exercises can be per-formed with an immobile object (such as a wall) for resistance, or simply by tightening a muscle. Iso-metric exercises tend to develop strength only at or near the joints.

Isotonic Exercise. This involves applying force with movement, using either weights or your own body weight (as in push-ups and sit-ups). Such exercise involves two types of muscle contraction: A concentric contraction occurs when the muscle applies force as it shortens and an eccentric contrac-tion occurs when the muscle applies force as it lengthens. The two most common isotonic tech-niques are **constant resistance exercise**, which uses a constant weight throughout a joint's entire range of motion, and **variable resistance exercise**, on which the load is changed in order to maintain maximum load throughout the range of motion.

Isokinetic Exercise. This involves exerting force at a constant speed against an equal force exerted by a special strength-training machine.

Weight Training Exercise Type Comparisons

Isometric exercises require no equipment, build strength rapidly, and are useful for rehabilitating joints. But, they have a short, specific range of motion and, hence, have to be performed at several different angles for each joint. Isotonic exercises can be performed with or without equipment. They are excellent at building endurance and strength throughout a joint's range of motion, but are not suitable for rehabilitation. Isokinetic exercises are excellent in building strength and endurance, but require expensive equipment that is not as com-monly available as other kinds of weight machines.

Planning And Carrying Out A Weight Training Program

Your weight-training program should be designed for specific needs and with minimum risk of injury.

Choosing Equipment. Weight machines are safe, convenient and easy to use. They make it easy to isolate and work on specific muscles. Free weights require more skill and neuromotor coordination, but they strengthen the body in ways that are more specific to daily living.

Selecting Exercises. A comprehensive weight-training program works all the major muscle groups, including the neck, upper back, shoulders, arms, chest, abdomen, lower back, thighs, buttocks and calves. A specific weight-training program targets the specific region of the body to be improved. Which type of program will you choose? When in doubt, use a comprehensive program.

Resistance. The amount of weight lifted determines the manner and speed with which the body will adapt to the stress. To build strength rapidly, lift weights as heavy as 80% of your maximum capacity. To build endurance or joint mobility, choose 20% to 60% of your maximum capacity and lift more times.

Repetitions And Sets. A repetition is one lift. A set is a group of repetitions of an exercise followed by a short rest period. To improve strength, you must perform enough repetitions to progressively fatigue your muscles. Specifically:

1. A heavy weight and a low number of repetitions (1 to 5) builds strength.

2. A light weight and high number of repetitions (20 to 25) builds endurance.

3. For comprehensive strength, do 8 to 12 repetitions of each exercise.

4. As muscle strength increases, slowly increase the amount of resistance (weight).

You need to consider both workout and rest procedures. Specifically, a rest period allows the muscles to work at high enough intensity in the next set to increase fitness. You should perform 3 sets of each exercise for optimal development. Allow 2 to 3 minutes between sets if you are doing the same exercise again. Exercise the larger muscles first and the smaller ones later in the session.

Warm Up And Cool Down. You should do both a general warm up (such as walking) and a specific warm up using the muscles involved in the weight lifting exercise you will perform. For a cool down, relax 5 to 15 minutes after exercising and stretch to prevent muscle soreness.

Exercise Frequency. You should weight-train 2 to 4 days per week (3 times is optimal). Rotate the specific muscle groups that you exercise over the days (e.g., upper body one day, lower body the next). This allows time for muscle tissue to repair itself by not being exercised on consecutive days.

Program Design

To begin training, choose a weight that you can easily move through a set involving 8 to 10 repetitions. Gradually add weight and sets until you can perform 3 sets of 10 repetitions for each muscle group. If you can do more than 12 repetitions, add weight until you can do only 7 or 8.

Weight-Training Safety

Proper lifting technique involves performing the exercises smoothly, with control and good form, through the full range of motion. Use spotters (observers) when performing a potentially dangerous exercise. Weight machines are noted for their safety, but are not risk free, so follow the guidelines for use that come with them. Do not continue to train an injured joint or muscle and report any injury to your physician. Also consult your physician if you have unusual symptoms, such as fainting or blackouts, during exercise.

Frequently Asked Questions

1. How long must I lift weights before I begin to see changes in my body? Both strength and soreness often increase quickly in the early stages of training. Changes in the muscle size begin after about 6 to 10 weeks of training. Soreness disappears with rest and proper warm ups.

2. If I stop weight training, will my muscles turn to fat? No. Fat and muscle are two different kinds of tissue. One cannot turn into the other.

3. What causes muscle soreness in the day or two following a weight training workout? Injury to muscle fibers causes the release of excess lactic acid into muscles, which breaks down part of the muscle tissue and causes soreness. If you exercise regularly, your muscles will produce protective proteins to prevent discomfort. It will not cost you anything in body functioning for this pain to be removed.

Hardy Physical Activity Exercise 4: Planning And

Carrying Out Your Muscular Strength And Endurance Program

Write down here the specifics of what you will be doing in your muscular strength and endurance program.

1. Muscle Groups Involved and Type of Activity

   Hint: Don't feel that you have to involve all muscle groups at the beginning of your program. Also, recognize that some exercises involve more than one muscle group, such as push-ups (which include arms, shoulders and chest) and sit-ups (which include abdomen, lower back, chest and buttocks).

NECK:

_____
_____

UPPER BACK:

_____
_____

SHOULDERS:

_____
_____

ARMS:

_____
_____

CHEST:

_____
_____

ABDOMEN:

_____
_____

LOWER BACK:

_____
_____
_____

THIGHS:

_____
_____
_____

BUTTOCKS:

_____
_____
_____

CALVES:

_____
_____
_____

2. Planned Repetitions, Sets, and Rests (Intensity)

   Hint: Include information on how heavy the weights will be, along with what will constitute one repetition and one set, and how long a rest there will be between sets.

   _____
   _____
   _____
   _____

3. Planned Frequency of Exercises

   Hint: Include here not only how many times a week you will exercise, but also the specifics of alternating the muscle groups worked on.

   _____
   _____
   _____
   _____

When you are satisfied with the specifics of your muscular strength and endurance program, begin carrying it out. After the first week of exercising, write down here what your experiences have been:

_____
_____
_____
_____

In addition to recording bodily changes you may have experienced, write down whether carrying out your program has increased your sense of

commitment, control, and challenge (the three Cs of HardiAttitudes):

_____
_____
_____
_____

EXERCISE END

Summary Concepts And Terms

ATROPHY

CONSTANT RESISTANCE EXERCISE

HYPERTROPHY

ISOKINETIC

ISOMETRIC

ISOTONIC

MOTOR UNIT

MUSCULAR ENDURANCE

MUSCULAR STRENGTH

VARIABLE RESISTANT EXERCISE

Test Your Knowledge

To test what you learned so far, see if you can correctly answer the following questions. Remember, the more information you have to think about what happens to you, the more building blocks you have to generate creative solutions to everyday living problems. This, in turn, strengthens your HardiAttitudes.

Commitment. The more information you seek to learn about yourself and the world, the more you demonstrate your belief that you are worthwhile and important enough to gather information that helps you.

Control. The more information you gather about yourself and your world, the more able you are to influence the direction of your life.

Challenge. The effort you apply in learning the hardiness skills show that you regard the time spent in developing yourself as a normal challenge of life.

For the answer key, See "Questionnaire and Test Your Knowledge Answer Keys" on page 259.

1. In preventing some skeletal injuries, _____ has been shown to be useful.

2. Muscular strength is the maximum amount of _____ a muscle can produce in a single effort.

3. The amount of continuous submaximum force a muscle can deliver is muscular_____.

4. The three types of weight training exercises are:

5. _____ exercises require expensive equipment.

6. _____exercise involves applying force without movement.

7. _____ exercise involves applying force with movement using weights or your own body.

8. In a weight training program, _____,_____, and _____ are indicative of intensity.

Learning Goals

- Do you know how to avoid and manage lower back pain?

- Have you planned and carried out a flexibility program?

- Do you know the benefits of muscular strength and endurance?

- Do you know the physiological effects of weight training?

- Do you know the three types of weight training exercises?

- Have you planned and carried out a weight training program?

- Did you take the three chapter quizzes?

CHAPTER 26

Additional Physical Activity Programs

Mild Physical Activity Program

Keep up your light aerobic and other exercise programs until you have adapted to them. Then it is time to move on to more strenuous programs, until you have reached your long-term goal. Listed below are some examples of programs going from mild to vigorous. Involving fast walking, jogging, running, cycling, or swimming, these more strenuous programs improve not only cardiorespiratory fitness, but also body composition and muscular endurance. As you will see, some of the more vigorous programs even contribute to muscular strength and flexibility. Once you get to these programs, you will be able to lower your other exercise programs that are solely for muscular strength, endurance and flexibility.

Even when you reach your long-term goal, however, you must keep exercising at that level in order to maintain the fitness you have achieved. If your goal was weight reduction, you should continue at the exercise level that worked, and you can probably shift from a weight reduction diet to one that maintains your weight.

Advanced Walking

1. Purpose: To improve lean body composition (lose weight), and improve cardio-respiratory fitness.
2. Intensity, Duration, and Frequency

a. Begin at the lower end of your heart target zone, increase your pace, and vary your speed.

b. Walk 30 minutes (about 2 miles) and work up to 60 minutes (about 4 miles).

c. Walk at least every other day.

3. Calorie Cost: Work toward using 150-300 calories per session.

4. At the Beginning: You walk somewhat faster than in the light physical activity program. Monitor your pulse to keep your heart in the target zone. Slow down when necessary.

5. As You Progress

a. Increase your pace and duration, gradually lengthening the periods of fast walking.

b. If you reach your weight reduction goal, maintain the same activity program but go on a weight maintenance diet.

Medium Physical Activity Program

Pre-Jogging

1. Purpose: To prepare for the jogging program that improves cardiorespiratory endurance and can accelerate weight loss (if that is your goal).

2. Intensity, Duration and Frequency

Start walking at a moderate pace (3 to 4 miles per hour) and add intervals of slow jogging (5 or 6 miles per hour).

Increase gradually to 4 minutes of jogging per 1 minute of walking.

Exercise for 15 to 30 minutes, every other day.

3. Calorie Cost: Work up to using 200 to 350 calories per session.

4. At the Beginning: Expect to do 2 to 4 times more walking than jogging at first. You may have to exercise at less than your heart target rate.

5. As You Progress

When you are doing mostly jogging in your 30-minute session, consider changing to the next difficulty program.

Increase intensity and duration to reach target heart rate and accelerate weight reduction (if that is your aim).

Vigorous Physical Activity Program

Jogging

1. Equipment: Buy comfortable jogging shoes with good heel support. Consult with an athletic shoe specialist for suggestions.

2. Purpose: To develop and maintain a high level of cardiorespiratory fitness, a lean body, and muscular endurance.

3. Intensity, Duration and Frequency

Intensity should depend on your target heart rate zone; your speed will probably be 5.5 to 7.5 miles per hour.

Begin by jogging for 15 minutes and work up to 30-60 minutes.

Exercise every other day.

4. Calorie Cost: Use about 300-750 calories per session.

5. At the Beginning: Start with 15 minutes of jogging. Because this program burns more calories per minute than the other three programs, it is less time-consuming.

6. As You Progress

Stay within your target heart rate zone by increasing pace and distance.

Vary your program to keep it interesting.

Vigorous Physical Activity Program

Bicycling. Bicycling can greatly increase your fitness, and it's a fun, economical alternative to driving.

1. Equipment and Technique

   Rent or borrow a bike until you know you'll use one regularly.

   A good 3 or 10-speed bike is all you need for general fitness.

2. Choose a soft saddle and make sure it's at the right height.

   Clothing should be comfortable but snug enough not to get caught in the chain or the wind.

   If you ride on the road, always wear a helmet and, if needed, protective glasses and gloves.

   If you've never ridden before, consider taking a course to learn braking, shifting, handling emergencies, and maintaining your bike.

3. Purpose: To develop and maintain healthy body composition, cardiorespiratory endurance, muscular strength, and flexibility of the legs.

4. Intensity, Duration and Frequency

   If you've been sedentary, begin cycling at 10-20 percent below your target heart rate zone.

   Increase your speed gradually until you can cycle at 12-15 miles per hour (4-5 minutes per mile).

   Cycle for at least 20 minutes, 3 times per week.

5. Calorie Cost: Use a calorie-cost table to determine how many calories you're burning. You can burn more by increasing speed or duration (distance); the latter is preferable.

6. At the Beginning: Begin with a 10-minute warm-up, including stretching your hamstrings, back and neck. Choose safe routes without traffic or use a stationary bike in front of the television.

7. As You Progress

   Use intervals to improve your fitness, such as increasing speed for 4-8 minutes or 1-2 miles, and then coasting. Hills are also good interval training.

   Cycle for 20-60 minutes.

Swimming. Swimming is one of the best activities for developing all-around fitness. Water supports body weight, so much less stress is placed on joints, ligaments and tendons than in walking or jogging.

1. Equipment: You need access to a swimming pool, a swimsuit and goggles.

2. Purpose: To develop and maintain cardiorespiratory endurance, muscular strength and endurance and flexibility.

3. Intensity, Duration and Frequency

   Because swimming is not weight bearing and is not done in an upright position, it raises heart rate less than other activities do, so you need to recalculate your target heart rate zone.

   Base duration on intensity and calorie costs.

   Swim at least 3 times per week.

4. Calorie Cost: Work up to at least 300 calories per session.

5. At the Beginning

   If you aren't experienced, invest in instruction.

If you've been sedentary, begin 10-20 percent below target heart rate, 3 times per week for 2-3 weeks.

Take rest intervals as needed, working on decreasing rest time.

6. As You Progress

Gradually increase either duration or intensity or both to reach target heart rate zone. Continue swim-rest intervals for 20 minutes, with rest intervals of 30-45 seconds.

Increase number of continuous laps and total duration of your session until you reach target calorie cost and fitness level.

Alternate strokes to rest muscles and prolong swimming time.

Hardy Physical Activity Exercise 5, Planning And Carrying Out Your Advanced Physical Activity Program

It is time to phase out your introductory cardiorespiratory fitness program in favor of the mild, medium, and vigorous, physical activity programs. The vigorous, and to some degree the mild and medium physical activity programs, include within them activities that build muscular strength, endurance, and flexibility, as well as cardiorespiratory fitness. As your progress to the vigorous physical activity program, you can cut down on your flexibility and muscular strength and endurance programs. Just remember, however, that it is still important to engage in both warm up and cool down activities before and after your physical activity program.

1 Identify below the specifics of the physical activity program you will carry out:

_____
_____
_____
_____

2. Type of Activity (e.g., fast walking, pre-jogging, bicycling and swimming):

_____
_____
_____

Intensity of Sessions (i.e., pace at which you will carry out the activity):

_____
_____
_____
_____

3. Duration of Sessions:

_____
_____
_____

4. Frequency of Sessions (i.e., how often per week):

_____
_____
_____

5. When will you exercise (day and time of week):

_____
_____
_____

6. After you have tried your advanced physical activity program for a week, write down your experiences here:

Was it hard, are you satisfied with your progress? Do you feel good about what you have done? Did you sense of commitment, control, and challenge increase by carrying out the advanced physical activity program? Answer these questions below:

EXERCISE END

Fourth And Final Hardy Physical Activity Checkpoint

Share with your Hardiness trainer how you are doing on your program and feeling about it. What progress have you made toward cardiorespiratory fitness, lean body composition, muscular strength and endurance, and flexibility? Does making progress in physical fitness increase your HardiAttitudes of commitment, control, and challenge?

Summary Concepts And Terms

ACTIVITY LEVELS: MILD, MEDIUM, AND VIGOROUS

APPENDICES

Appendix A: Strain Rating Scale

TABLE Strain Rating Scale

Rating: 1 = mild; 2 = moderate; 3 = strong

Physical	Rate	Mental	Rate	Behavioral	Rate
Headache	1 2 3	Clouded mind	1 2 3	Insecure	1 2 3
Migraine	1 2 3	Worry	1 2 3	Phobic or fearful	1 2 3
Rapid heart rate	1 2 3	Ideas of threat	1 2 3	Self-conscious	1 2 3
Anxiety	1 2 3	Intrusive ideas	1 2 3	Angry	1 2 3
Rapid breathing	1 2 3	Easily distracted	1 2 3	Impulsive	1 2 3
Light headed	1 2 3	Racing thoughts	1 2 3	Hyperactive	1 2 3
Dizzy	1 2 3	Cannot focus	1 2 3	Talk a lot/fast	1 2 3
Short of breath	1 2 3	Indecisive	1 2 3	Argumentative	1 2 3
Shallow breath	1 2 3	Grim thoughts	1 2 3	Rude or loud	1 2 3
Nausea	1 2 3	Sad thoughts	1 2 3	Confrontational	1 2 3
Constipation	1 2 3	Confused ideas	1 2 3	Clumsy	1 2 3
Diarrhea	1 2 3	Negative ideas	1 2 3	Inhibited	1 2 3
Indigestion	1 2 3	Hopeless ideas	1 2 3	Unmotivated	1 2 3
Sweating	1 2 3	Angry thoughts	1 2 3	Impatient	1 2 3
Cold hands/feet	1 2 3	Uncreative ideas	1 2 3	Aggressive	1 2 3
Tingling	1 2 3	Forgetful	1 2 3	Rigid	1 2 3
Swelling	1 2 3	Inattentive	1 2 3	Excited	1 2 3
Aches and pains	1 2 3	Can't recall words	1 2 3	Withdrawn	1 2 3
Tension	1 2 3	Mind goes blank	1 2 3	Irritable	1 2 3
Jittery	1 2 3	Can't recall names	1 2 3	Temper	1 2 3
Tired/fatigued	1 2 3	Indecisive	1 2 3	Moody	1 2 3
Other:	1 2 3	Other:	1 2 3	Other:	1 2 3
Total Score					

Appendix B: Hardy Nutrition Exercise 1, Baseline Nutrition Worksheet

TABLE 1. **Baseline Nutrition Worksheet**

Time	Food & Drink	Qty.	Calorie	Carbs.	Protein	Fat	Fiber
Step 2	Sum Categories						

		Baseline Nutrition Calculations	Product
Step 3	A	Multiply Total Carbohydrate Calories _____ X 4 =	
	B	Divide by Total Daily Calories _____ =	
	C	Multiply by 100 to change the number in 3 B into a percentage	
	A	Multiply Total Protein Calories _____ X 4 =	
	B	Divide by Total Daily Calories _____ =	
	C	Multiply by 100 to change the number in 4 B into a percentage	
	A	Multiply Total Fat Calories _____ X 9 =	
	B	Divide by Total Daily Calories _____ =	
	C	Multiply by 100 to change the number in 5 B into a percentage	

TABLE 2. Baseline Strain Rating Scale

Rating: 1 = mild; 2 = moderate; 3 = strong

Physical	Rate	Mental	Rate	Behavioral	Rate
Headache	1 2 3	Clouded mind	1 2 3	Insecure	1 2 3
Migraine	1 2 3	Worry	1 2 3	Phobic or fearful	1 2 3
Rapid heart rate	1 2 3	Ideas of threat	1 2 3	Self-conscious	1 2 3
Anxiety	1 2 3	Intrusive ideas	1 2 3	Angry	1 2 3
Rapid breathing	1 2 3	Lose line of idea	1 2 3	Impulsive	1 2 3
Light Headed	1 2 3	Racing thoughts	1 2 3	Hyperactive	1 2 3
Dizzy	1 2 3	Cannot focus	1 2 3	Talk a lot/fast	1 2 3
Short of breath	1 2 3	Hopeless ideas	1 2 3	Argumentative	1 2 3
Shallow breath	1 2 3	Grim thoughts	1 2 3	Rude or loud	1 2 3

TABLE 2. Baseline Strain Rating Scale

Rating: 1 = mild; 2 = moderate; 3 = strong

Physical	Rate	Mental	Rate	Behavioral	Rate
Nausea	1 2 3	Sad thoughts	1 2 3	Confrontational	1 2 3
Constipation	1 2 3	Confused ideas	1 2 3	Clumsy	1 2 3
Diarrhea	1 2 3	Negative ideas	1 2 3	Inhibited	1 2 3
Indigestion	1 2 3	Literal thinking	1 2 3	Unmotivated	1 2 3
Sweating	1 2 3	Angry thoughts	1 2 3	Impatient	1 2 3
Cold hands/feet	1 2 3	Forgetful	1 2 3	Rigid	1 2 3
Tingling	1 2 3	Forgetful	1 2 3	Aggressive	1 2 3
Swelling	1 2 3	Inattentive	1 2 3	Excited	1 2 3
Aches and pains	1 2 3	Can't find word	1 2 3	Withdrawn	1 2 3
Tension	1 2 3	Mind goes blank	1 2 3	Irritable	1 2 3
Jittery	1 2 3	Can't find name	1 2 3	Short temper	1 2 3
Tired/fatigued	1 2 3	Indecisive	1 2 3	Moody	1 2 3
Other:	1 2 3	Other:	1 2 3	Other:	1 2 3
Total Score					

Appendix C: Hardy Nutrition Exercise 2, Put Your Learning Into Practice

Based on your learning to date, do you think you eat in a way that enhances your well-being and performance level? Do you eat in a way that stimulates a lot of insulin?

_____
_____
_____
_____

Do you show symptoms that might be related to your nutrition habits? If so, do you show symptoms physically, mentally, or behaviorally, or in all three forms?

_____
_____
_____
_____

Based upon your learning thus far, what is it about your daily nutrition that leads to these symptoms?

_____
_____
_____
_____

Which nutrition change(s) seems necessary to your well-being? Place an X next to the change that you wish to make.

Eat More	X	Eat	X	Eat Less	X
Protein from nuts and legumes		More Often		Saturated fat	
Fresh fruit		Foods balanced in all the food nutrients		Sugar	
Fresh vegetables		Six meals per day		Fewer fast foods	
Lower glycemic carbohydrates		Breakfast		Processed foods	
Protein		Healthy snacks		Overall fat	
Water		More nutritious foods		Fried foods	

Eat More	X	Eat	X	Eat Less	X
Essential fatty acids		Other:		Other:	
Other:					

Nutrition Objective: People differ in their reasons for changing their nutrition habits. There are those who change their eating habits because they are not feeling well (symptoms) and want to feel better. Others change their nutrition habits in order to lose a few pounds. And there are those who change their nutrition habits because they want to live a long, healthy lifestyle. Do you have a nutrition objective?

_____
_____
_____
_____

Which nutrition changes support the nutrition objective that you identified in question five?

Change 1: _____

Change 2: _____

Change 3: _____

Change 4: _____

Take a few moments to jot down reasons for these nutrition changes. Support these nutrition changes with your learning thus far.

_____
_____
_____
_____

After remaining on this new nutrition program for three days, you evaluate if the four nutrition changes that you selected were instrumental in bringing about a decrease in your strain symptoms. If after the three days, you think your program needs a little more fine tuning, you can return to Part A to find other changes that may help you to fulfill your nutrition objective.

TABLE 3. New Meal Plan Nutrition Worksheet

Time	Food & Drink	Qty.	Calorie	Carbs.	Protein	Fat	Fiber
Step 2	Sum Categories						

TABLE 4. New Meal Plan Food Nutrient Calculations

			Product
Step 3	A	Multiply Total Carbohydrate Calories _____ X 4 =	
	B	Divide by Total Daily Calories _____ =	
	C	Multiply by 100 to change the number in 3 B into a percentage	
	A	Multiply Total Protein Calories _____ X 4 =	
	B	Divide by Total Daily Calories _____ =	
	C	Multiply by 100 to change the number in 4 B into a percentage	
	A	Multiply Total Fat Calories _____ X 9 =	
	B	Divide by Total Daily Calories _____ =	
	C	Multiply by 100 to change the number in 5 B into a percentage	

TABLE 5. New Meal Plan Strain Rating Scale

Rating: 1 = mild; 2 = moderate; 3 = strong

Physical	Rate	Mental	Rate	Behavioral	Rate
Headache	1 2 3	Clouded mind	1 2 3	Insecure	1 2
Migraine	1 2 3	Worry	1 2 3	Phobic, panic, or fearful	1 2
Rapid heart rate	1 2 3	Ideas of threat	1 2 3	Self-conscious	1 2
Anxiety	1 2 3	Intrusive ideas	1 2 3	Angry	1 2
Rapid breathing	1 2 3	Lose line of idea	1 2 3	Impulsive	1 2
Light headed	1 2 3	Racing thoughts	1 2 3	Hyperactive	1 2
Dizzy	1 2 3	Cannot focus	1 2 3	Talk a lot/fast	1 2
Short of breath	1 2 3	Hopeless ideas	1 2 3	Argumentative	1 2
Shallow breath	1 2 3	Grim thoughts	1 2 3	Rude or loud	1 2
Nausea	1 2 3	Sad thoughts	1 2 3	Confrontational	1 2
Constipation	1 2 3	Confused ideas	1 2 3	Clumsy	1 2

TABLE 5. New Meal Plan Strain Rating Scale

Rating: 1 = mild; 2 = moderate; 3 = strong

Physical	Rate	Mental	Rate	Behavioral	Rate
Diarrhea	1 2 3	Negative ideas	1 2 3	Inhibited	1 2
Indigestion	1 2 3	Literal thinking	1 2 3	Unmotivated	1 2
Sweating	1 2 3	Angry thoughts	1 2 3	Impatient	1 2
Cold hands/feet	1 2 3	Forgetful	1 2 3	Rigid	1 2
Tingling	1 2 3	Forgetful	1 2 3	Aggressive	1 2
Swelling	1 2 3	Inattentive	1 2 3	Excited	1 2
Aches and pains	1 2 3	Can't find word	1 2 3	Withdrawn	1 2
Tension	1 2 3	Mind goes blank	1 2 3	Irritable	1 2
Jittery	1 2 3	Can't find name	1 2 3	Short temper	1 2
Tired/fatigued	1 2 3	Indecisive	1 2 3	Moody	1 2
Other:	1 2 3	Other:	1 2 3	Other:	1 2
Total Score					

Part B: Once you have completed the post nutrition worksheet, you compare and contrast your baseline food nutrient daily intake and strain symptoms with your new nutrition plan's daily food nutrient intake and strain symptoms when eating in this new way.

Baseline Daily Food Nutrient Intake and Symptoms of Strain Ratings

Carbohydrate _____%, Protein _____%, Fat _____%, Fiber _____ grams

Physical _____%, Mental _____%, Behavioral _____%

New Meal Plan Daily Food Nutrient Intake and Symptoms of Strain Ratings

Carbohydrate _____%, Protein _____%, Fat _____%, Fiber _____ grams

Physical _____%, Mental _____%, Behavioral _____%

Did your food choices support your nutrition objective and changes?

_____

_____

_____

EXERCISE END

Appendix D: Plan Your Meal With Ease

CHOOSE Lower glycemic carbohydrates, complex carbohydrates, unsaturated fat, a diet high in essential fatty acids, foods high in soluble and insoluble fiber, and in potassium, magnesium, and calcium.

CARBOHYDRATES Carbohydrates should come primarily from fruits and complex vegetables, grains, and legumes that are high in fiber and low in natural and added sugar. They should also be high in minerals and vitamins.

PROTEIN Animal protein should be lean and low in saturated fat and from fish, legumes, nuts and low fat dairy products, seafood that is high in omega 3's like salmon, halibut, and swordfish.

FAT Fat should come from nuts and vegetable oils. Nuts can include peanuts, cashews, walnuts, and almonds. Vegetable oils can include olive, soy, peanut, walnut, canola, flaxseed, safflower and corn oil. You should store it so it stays fresh. It should also consist of essential fatty acids that vary in mono and poly unsaturated forms.

Appendix E: American Dietetic Association Food Standards and the Zone's Approach to Nutrition

1. Which is the right nutrition approach for you? You have an opportunity to plan a nutrition program that supports your performance, leadership, and health. Through trial and error, symptom evaluation, and recommendations from medical, nutrition, and health professionals, you find out which kind of nutrition approach is best for you. The American Dietetic Association now recommends a personalized approach to healthy eating and physical activity. A healthy diet, they maintain, is one in which people eat in a way that reduces their risk for degenerative diseases. They further encourage eating a wide variety of foods that includes vegetables, whole grains, fruits, non-fat dairy products, legumes, and lean meats, like poultry and fish. Food choices from each food group should be high in vitamins, minerals and fibers. The following outlines the ADA's key recommendations for the general population.

ADEQUATE NUTRIENTS WITHIN CALORIE NEEDS

- Consume a variety of nutrient-dense foods and beverages within and among the basic food groups while choosing foods that limit the intake of saturated and trans fats, cholesterol, added sugars, salt, and alcohol.

- Meet recommended intakes within energy needs by adopting a balanced eating pattern, such as the U.S. Department of Agriculture (USDA) Food Guide or the Dietary Approaches to Stop Hypertension (DASH) Eating Plan.

WEIGHT MANAGEMENT

- To maintain body weight in a healthy range, balance calories from foods and beverages with calories expended.

- To prevent gradual weight gain over time, make small decreases in food and beverage calories and increase physical activity.

PHYSICAL ACTIVITY

- Engage in regular physical activity and reduce sedentary activities to promote health, psychological well-being, and a healthy body weight.

- To reduce the risk of chronic disease in adulthood: Engage in at least 30 minutes of moderate-intensity physical activity, above usual activity, at work or home on most days of the week.

- For most people, greater health benefits can be obtained by engaging in physical activity of more vigorous intensity or longer duration.

- To help manage body weight and prevent gradual, unhealthy body weight gain in adulthood: Engage in approximately 60 minutes of moderate- to vigorous-intensity activity on most days of the week while not exceeding caloric intake requirements.

- To sustain weight loss in adulthood: Participate in at least 60 to 90 minutes of daily moderate-intensity physical activity while not exceeding caloric intake requirements. Some people may need to consult with a healthcare provider before participating in this level of activity.

- Achieve physical fitness by including cardiovascular conditioning, stretching exercises for flexibility, and resistance exercises or calisthenics for muscle strength and endurance.

FOOD GROUPS TO ENCOURAGE

- Consume a sufficient amount of fruits and vegetables while staying within energy needs. Two cups of fruit and 2½ cups of vegetables per day are recommended for a reference 2,000-calorie intake, with higher or lower amounts depending on the calorie level.

- Choose a variety of fruits and vegetables each day. In particular, select from all five vegetable subgroups (dark green, orange, legumes, starchy vegetables, and other vegetables) several times a week.

- Consume 3 or more ounce-equivalents of whole-grain products per day, with the rest of the recommended grains coming from enriched or whole-grain products. In general, at least half the grains should come from whole grains.

- Consume 3 cups per day of fat-free or low-fat milk or equivalent milk products.

FATS

- Consume less than 10 percent of calories from saturated fatty acids and less than 300 mg/day of cholesterol, and keep trans fatty acid consumption as low as possible.

- Keep total fat intake between 20 to 35 percent of calories, with most fats coming from sources of polyunsaturated and monounsaturated fatty acids, such as fish, nuts, and vegetable oils.

- When selecting and preparing meat, poultry, dry beans, and milk or milk products, make choices that are lean, low-fat, or fat-free.

- Limit intake of fats and oils high in saturated and/or trans fatty acids, and choose products low in such fats and oils.

CARBOHYDRATES

- Choose fiber-rich fruits, vegetables, and whole grains often.

- Choose and prepare foods and beverages with little added sugars or caloric sweeteners, such as amounts suggested by the USDA Food Guide and the DASH Eating Plan.

- Reduce the incidence of dental caries by practicing good oral hygiene and consuming sugar- and starch-containing foods and beverages less frequently.

SODIUM AND POTASSIUM

- Consume less than 2,300 mg (approximately 1 teaspoon of salt) of sodium per day.

- Choose and prepare foods with little salt. At the same time, consume potassium-rich foods, such as fruits and vegetables.

ALCOHOLIC BEVERAGES

- Those who choose to drink alcoholic beverages should do so sensibly and in moderation—defined as the consumption of up to one drink per day for women and up to two drinks per day for men.

- Alcoholic beverages should not be consumed by some individuals, including those who cannot restrict their alcohol intake, women of childbearing age who may become pregnant, pregnant and lactating women, children and adolescents, individuals taking medications that can interact with alcohol, and those with specific medical conditions.

- Alcoholic beverages should be avoided by individuals engaging in activities that require attention, skill, or coordination, such as driving or operating machinery.

FOOD SAFETY

To avoid microbial food borne illness:

- Clean hands, food contact surfaces, and fruits and vegetables. Meat and poultry should not be washed or rinsed.
- Separate raw, cooked, and ready-to-eat foods while shopping, preparing, or storing foods.
- Cook foods to a safe temperature to kill microorganisms.
- Chill (refrigerate) perishable food promptly and defrost foods properly.
- Avoid raw (unpasteurized) milk or any products made from unpasteurized milk, raw or partially cooked eggs or foods containing raw eggs, raw or undercooked meat and poultry, unpasteurized juices, and raw sprouts.

Note: The Dietary Guidelines for Americans 2005 contains additional recommendations for specific populations. The full document is available at www.healthierus.gov/dietaryguidelines.

TABLE American Dietetic Nutrition Standards

Percentage of Daily Food Nutrient Calories

Carbohydrates 60 to 80%

Protein 10 to 15%

Fat 20 to 15%

Fiber Per Day 25 to 30 grams

The Zone experts recommend eating a specific percent of each food nutrient per meal to assure performance and health, and to prevent disease.

TABLE Zone Nutrition Standards

Percentage of Daily Food Nutrient Calories

Carbohydrates 40%

Protein 30%

Fat 30%

Fiber per day 25 to 30 grams

2. How often? This depends upon the size of your meal and how rich the meal is in food nutrients. In other words, how long will that meal take to digest, metabolize and be used for fuel burning. In general, The American Dietetic Association as well as the nutrition experts who advocate the Zone, recommend trying to eat small to moderate sized meals, high in the food nutrients and fiber, and low in saturated fat, 6 times per day, every 3 to 4 hours.

3. If you have low blood sugar problems, you may want to eat every 2 to 3 hours rather than every 3 to 4 hours, and make sure that your food choices are nutritious enough to sustain your performance, morale, conduct and health. Lower glycemic, high fiber carbohydrates are very important for you because they take a longer time to digest.

4. If you are ill, stressed, or engaged in high activity, which food nutrients help you to repair? Recall that protein aids body repair and is the basis for your body's enzymes, neurotransmitters, hormones, and antibodies. When you are stressed, ill, or engaged in high activity, you need, thus, to make sure you are getting enough daily protein.

5. How do you know if you are eating well? Performing and feeling well indirectly informs you about your overall health.

We all have different nutrition needs that depend upon our health, activity level and biological tendency. It is important, thus, that you get medical advice for special nutrition needs.

Appendix F: Nutrition Websites

The following websites contain nutrition, weight and body mass index, and other health calculators and food and drink calorie and food nutrient counters.

1. American Dietetic Association Site. This is the official website of the American Dietetic Association (ADA): http://www.eatright.org/Public/

2. Diet and Cancer Prevention is a site that helps people to put together a diet plan to reduce cancer risk and reoccurrences of cancer (www.dianadyermsrd.com).

3. Gatorade Sports Science Institute is a great site covering sports and sports nutrition (www.gssi.com).

4. Government Nutrition Site: http://www.nutrition.gov/home/index.php3

5. Food and Drug Administration Site: http://www.fda.gov/

6. Fast Food Finders Site. This food site provides the consumer with calorie and food nutrient breakdowns for various fast food products (http://www.olen.com/food/).

7. Food Zone Website: http://www.drsears.com/

8. Official Agriculture Network Information Center Web Site: This is an excellent web site that supplies a wealth of information on the Food Guide Pyramid: http://www.nal.usda.gov/fnic/

9. Weight Loss for Resources Site. This is an excellent website that helps people to evaluate their weight relative to what they eat and drink. For a fee, people can evaluate their diet for the percentage of food nutrients that makeup their total daily calories (http://www.weightlossresources.co.uk/lostart.htm).

10. United States Department of Agriculture Center for Nutrition Policy and Promotion (MyPyramid.gov)

Appendix G: Test Your Nutrition Knowledge

Evaluate your training thus far by completing this pre-training nutrition questionnaire. There are sixty questions on this questionnaire. See "Appendix G: Test Your Nutrition Knowledge" on page 239.

1. A high carbohydrate diet is helps you to lose weight.

   a. true

   b. false

2. A diet low in saturated fat is best for you.

   a. true

   b. false

3. A diet balanced in all the food nutrients is best for you.

   a. true

   b. false

4. All saturated fats are processed.

   a. true

   b. false

5. If you want to manage low blood sugar, you should eat less _____.

   a. protein

   b. sugar

6. How many meals per day are best for you?

   a. 3 large

   b. 8 small

   c. 6 small to moderate

7. Food nutrients are made up of:

   a. carbon, hydrogen, oxygen, and nitrogen

   b. carbohydrate, fat, protein

   c. both a and b

8. The process that turns an unsaturated fat into a saturated fat is:

    a. hydrogenation

    b. fatty acid degeneration

    c. regeneration

9. A CIS fatty acid is:

    a. saturated fat

    b. hydrogenated fat

    c. unsaturated fat

10. A Trans fatty acid is:

    a. hydrogenated fat

    b. unsaturated fat

    c. saturated fat

    d. both a and c

11. Unsaturated fat melts at:

    a. 30°F

    b. 55°F

    c. 98.6°F

    d. 111°F

12. Saturated fat melts at:

    a. 30°F

    b. 55°F

    c. 98.6°F

    d. 111°F

13. _____ degenerates saturated fat:

    a. carbon

    b. hydrogen

    c. oxygen

    d. sodium

14. The _____ makes glucose for brain and body fuel.

    a. pancreas

    b. kidney

    c. liver

    d. small intestine

15. If other food nutrients are present, a _____ burns first in your system.

    a. protein

    b. fat

    c. carbohydrate

    d. oxygen

16. If other food nutrients are present, _____ burns second in your system.

    a. protein

    b. fat

    c. carbohydrate

    d. oxygen

17. If other food nutrients are present, _____ burns last in your system.

    a. protein

    b. fat

    c. carbohydrate

    d. oxygen

18. The rate at which a food turns to sugar in your body is called:

  a. the burning index

  b. the glycemic index

  c. the metabolism index

19. The food nutrient most responsible for nerve conduction is:

  a. carbohydrate

  b. fat

  c. protein

  d. oxygen

20. The organ most responsible for producing cholesterol and sugar is:

  a. kidney

  b. stomach

  c. liver

  d. pancreas

21. The food nutrient that produces hormones, enzymes, and antibodies is:

  a. carbohydrate

  b. fat

  c. protein

  d. oxygen

22. Processed foods are ones in which:

  a. food nutrients have been removed

  b. molecular structure has been changed

  c. chemicals added

  d. All of the above

23. Stress, strain, and activity level increases your need for:

    a. protein

    b. fat

    c. carbohydrate

    d. fiber

24. Varying combinations of oxygen, hydrogen, carbon, and nitrogen produce different protein structures called:

    a. protein variants

    b. free radicals

    c. amino acids

25. The stored form of blood sugar is called:

    a. acetylcholine

    b. glycogen

    c. lactic acid

26. Glucose, fructose, and galactose are all examples of:

    a. simple sugars

    b. complex carbohydrates

    c. soluble fiber

    d. None of the above

27. Broccoli, legumes, and whole grains are examples of:

    a. simple carbohydrates

    b. complex carbohydrates

    c. protein

    d. acetylcholine

28. When a food's fiber content is low and its natural sugar content high, the rate at which it can be turned into blood sugar is:

    a. average

    b. high

    c. low

29. _____ slows down the absorption of glucose in your bloodstream and aids in waste elimination.

    a. glycogen

    b. lactic acid

    c. fiber

    d. protein

30. An unsaturated fat is also called a/an:

    a. nonessential fatty acid

    b. essential fatty acid

    c. imbalanced fat

    d. hydrogenated fat

31. Abnormal fatty acid chains that no longer fit the natural chemistry of our cells have been:

    a. glycogenated

    b. pathologized

    c. hydrogenated

    d. weakened

32. _____ is a form of blood sugar derived from fat.

    a. water

    b. lactic acid

    c. glycerol

    d. serotonin

33. The body hormone that stores blood sugar into our muscles for later use is called:

    a. lactic acid

    b. insulin

    c. glycogen

    d. glucagon

34. Sugar stored in your muscles for later use is called:

    a. norepinephrine

    b. insulin

    c. glycogen

    d. serotonin

35. Too much _____ can cause a low blood sugar reaction.

    a. norepinephrine

    b. insulin

    c. glucagon

    d. serotonin

36. Your body stores excess blood sugar as:

    a. carbohydrate

    b. protein

    c. fat

    d. carbon

37. The food nutrient that does not stimulate a release of insulin is:

    a. carbohydrate

    b. protein

    c. fat

    d. oxygen

38. You get twice as much energy from burning _____ than from burning _____:

    a. protein, fat

    b. fat, carbohydrate

    c. carbohydrate, fat

    d. fat, protein

39. If you want to maximize physical performance, you should load up on sugary foods prior to exercising.

    a. true

    b. false

40. Circulating bloodstream insulin inhibits the release of the other pancreatic hormone called _____.

    a. lactic acid

    b. acetylcholine

    c. glucagon

    d. cholesterol

41. Caffeine can stimulate insulin.

    a. true

    b. false

42. Exercise can stimulate insulin.

    a. true

    b. false

43. Meal _____ and _____ can increase insulin levels.

    a. size, carbohydrate level

    b. time, carbohydrate level

    c. size, protein level

    d. time, fat level

44. Carbohydrates do not influence mood.

      a. true

      b. false

45. Excess bloodstream insulin can stimulate:

      a. migraines

      b. premenstrual syndrome

      c. allergies

      d. weight gain

      e. all of the above

46. _____ can make you sleepy after a large meal:

      a. glucagon

      b. norepinephrine

      c. hydrochloric acid

      d. insulin

47. Low blood sugar can raise the body's:

      a. serotonin

      b.adrenaline

      c. fatty acid levels

      d. both b and c

48. High blood sugar increases your body's need for:

      a. hydrochloric acid

      b. glucagon

      c. insulin

      d. cholesterol

49. Cholesterol comes from the food you eat and is not naturally made in your body.

      a. true

      b. false

50. The body organ that gets its energy primarily from glucose is the:

　　a. heart

　　b. liver

　　c. small intestine

　　d. brain

51. To stay trim, I can eat sugar if it isn't combined with fat.

　　a. true

　　b. false

52. Insulin and glucagon are _____:

　　a. nutrients

　　b. neurotransmitters

　　c. hormones

53. The body system that regulates metabolism is the:

　　a. sympathetic nervous system

　　b. lymphatic system

　　c. endocrine system

54. _____ can cause water retention.

　　a. excess carbohydrate

　　b. insufficient protein

　　c. insulin

　　d. All of the above

55. Your pancreas produces the hormone(s):

　　a.　glucagon

　　b.　eicosanoid

　　c.　insulin

　　d.　both a and c

Appendix H: HardiSurveyIII-R

In order to score the HardiSurveyIII-R report, you need to complete the general information table below and respond to all 65 questions in order to get a report that accurately represents you. There are no right or wrong answers so please answer in an open manner. Where relevant, fill in the general information blanks or place a checkmark next to information that applies to you.

Name:_____.

Address: _____.

City: _____ : *State*: _____; *Zip Code*: _____.

Telephone Number: (_____) - _____ _____. *Age*: _____. *Gender*: _____Male; _____Female

Education: _____Less than high school; _____High School; _____Associate Degree; _____Bachelor Degree; _____Master Degree; _____Ph,.D.; _____M.D.; _____RN; _____DDS.

Culture or Race: _____Caucasian; _____Hispanic; _____African American; _____Native American; _____Asian; _____Middle Eastern; _____Other.

Number of times you have taken this test: ___1; ___2; ___3; ___4: ___Greater than 4.

Religion: _____.

Circle the number that best expresses your attitude or situation. *In general..........................*	Not at all true	A little true	Mostly true	True
1. By working hard, you can always achieve your goal.	0	1	2	3
2. I don't like to make changes in my everyday schedule.	0	1	2	3
3. I really look forward to my work.	0	1	2	3
4. I am not equipped to handle the unexpected problems of life.	0	1	2	3
5. Most of what happens in life is just meant to be.	0	1	2	3

Circle the number that best expresses your attitude or situation.	Not at all true	A little true	Mostly true	True
6. When I make plans, I'm certain I can make them work.	0	1	2	3
7. No matter how hard I try, my efforts usually accomplish little.	0	1	2	3
8. I like a lot of variety in my work.	0	1	2	3
9. Most of the time, people listen carefully to what I have to say.	0	1	2	3
10. Thinking of yourself as a free person just leads to frustration.	0	1	2	3
11. Trying your best at what you do usually pays off in the end.	0	1	2	3
12. My mistakes are usually very difficult to correct.	0	1	2	3
13. It bothers me when my daily routine gets interrupted.	0	1	2	3
14. I often wake up eager to take up life wherever it left off.	0	1	2	3
15. Lots of times, I really don't know my own mind.	0	1	2	3
16. Changes in routine provoke me to learn.	0	1	2	3
17. Most days, life is really interesting and exciting for me.	0	1	2	3
18. Its hard to imagine anyone getting excited about working.	0	1	2	3

Usually when I experience a stressful event

or problem...................

19. I admit to myself that I can't deal with it and just quit trying.	0	1	2	3
20. I discuss my feelings with someone.	0	1	2	3
21. I daydream about other things.	0	1	2	3
22. I just give up trying to reach my goal.	0	1	2	3

Circle the number that best expresses your attitude or situation.	Not at all true	A little true	Mostly true	True
23. I talk to someone who could do something concrete to help.	0	1	2	3
24. I sleep more than usual.	0	1	2	3
25. I try to come up with a strategy about what to do.	0	1	2	3
26. I pretend it hasn't really happened.	0	1	2	3
27. I go to the movies or watch TV in order to think about it less.	0	1	2	3
28. I take action to deal with the problem.	0	1	2	3
29. I think hard about what steps to take.	0	1	2	3
30. I try to learn something from the experience.	0	1	2	3
Often I have..........................				
31. General aches and pains.	0	1	2	3
32. Rapid heart beat (not from exercising).	0	1	2	3
33. Shortness of breath (not from exercising).	0	1	2	3
34. Upset stomach and/or nausea.	0	1	2	3
35. Depressed mood.	0	1	2	3
36. Difficulty concentrating and/or remembering things.	0	1	2	3
37. Nervousness or tension.	0	1	2	3
38. Tiredness, a lack of energy.	0	1	2	3
39. A feeling that life is pointless, meaningless	0	1	2	3
40. Troubling dreams.	0	1	2	3
41. Constipation and/or diarrhea.	0	1	2	3
42. I feel like I am really part of a team.	0	1	2	3
At work (or at school)................				
43. I have to be careful what I say.	0	1	2	3
44. My peers really back each other.	0	1	2	3
45. People subtly compete with each other.	0	1	2	3

Circle the number that best expresses your attitude or situation.	Not at all true	A little true	Mostly true	True
46. I am satisfied with the support I get from my colleagues.	0	1	2	3
47. People have confidence in me.	0	1	2	3
In my life...................				
48. My family gives me help in finding solutions to my problems.	0	1	2	3
49. Most people make me feel worthwhile.	0	1	2	3
50. I have to be careful what I say at home.	0	1	2	3
51. Interacting with my family brings out the best in me.	0	1	2	3
52. I don't have friends with whom I can just be myself.	0	1	2	3
53. I am satisfied with the support I get from family and friends.	0	1	2	3
54. Unexpected things keep happening.	0	1	2	3
55. There is a mismatch between what I want and what I get.	0	1	2	3
56. Things tend to happen as planned.	0	1	2	3
57. There's an orderliness that I can count on.	0	1	2	3
58. My schedule is always getting disrupted.	0	1	2	3
59. My talents and values get expressed in what I do.	0	1	2	3
Recently...........................				
60. I've had a personal life change to which I must adjust.	0	1	2	3
61. I don't have money problems that trouble me.	0	1	2	3
62. I've had a career or job change.	0	1	2	3
63. I don't have relationship difficulties that undermine me.	0	1	2	3

Circle the number that best expresses your attitude or situation.	Not at all true	A little true	Mostly true	True
64. I've been troubled by the death of a family member or friend.	0	1	2	3
65. I have not experienced an illness in a family member or friend.	0	1	2	3

HARDISURVEY® END

Appendix I: Suggested Reading List

Appleton, N., 1996. <u>Lick the Sugar Habit</u>. Avery Publishing Group, Garden City Park, New York.

Beckleman, L.& Beckleman, L. (1995). <u>Stress (Hotline).</u> Silver Burdett Publications.

Berg, F.M., 1995. <u>Health Risks of Weight Loss</u>. Published by Healthy Weight Journal, Hettinger, North Dakota.

Boroshek, A., 1997. <u>The Doctor's Pocket Calorie and Fat Counter and 70 Fast Food Chain and Restaurant Analysis</u>. Family Health Publications, Costa Mesa, California.

Bricklin, M., 1993. <u>Prevention Magazine's Nutrition Advisor</u>. Rodale Press, Emmaus, Pennsylvania.

Burchfield, S.R. (1984). <u>Stress: Psychological and Physiological Interactions</u>. Hemisphere Publications.

Chopra, D. (1995). <u>Twenty Spiritual Lessons for Creating the Life You Want</u>. Harmony Books. New York, New York.

Coleman, P. (1993). <u>Life's Parachutes.</u> Dell Publishing Company, New York, New York.

Cowart, J.D., Kominek, L.A. <u>Guided Instruction for Coping with Anxiety and Stress</u>. Audio Cassette. J & L Mental Health Associates.

Crayhon, R., 1994. <u>Nutrition Made Simple</u>. M. Evans and Company, Inc. New York, New York.

Crum, F.T. (1987). <u>The Magic of Conflict, Turning a Life of Work Into a Life of Art.</u> A Touchstone Book by Simon and Schuster, New York, New York.

Daoust, J., and Daoust, G. 1996. <u>40/30/30 Fat Burning Nutrition</u>. Wharton Publishing Company, Del Mar, California.

De Wees Allen, A., 1997. <u>Acceptable and Unacceptable Glycemic Food List</u>. Glycemic Research Institute, Washington D.C., email:drallen@www.iocafe.net.

DesMaisons, K., 1998. <u>Potatoes Not Prozac</u>. Simon and Schuster. New York, New York.

Eades, M., and Eades M., 1996. <u>Protein Power</u>. Bantam Books. New York, New York.

Erasmus, U., 1993. <u>Fats that Heal, Fats that Kill</u>. Alive Books, Burnaby British Columbia.

Eshelman, D.M., E.R., & McKay, M. (1995). <u>The Relaxation and Stress Reduction Workbook</u>. 4ᵗʰ. Ed. New Harbinger Publications, Inc. Oakland, CA

Everly, G.S. (1989). <u>A Clinical Guide to the Treatment of the Human Stress Response</u> (Plenum Series on Stress and Coping). Plenum Publications Corp.

Fezler, W. (1989). <u>Creative Imagery: How to Visualize in All Five Senses</u>. Fireside Publications.

Goldberg, Stephen, 1997. <u>Clinical Physiology Made Ridiculously Simple.</u> MedMaster, Inc., Miami.

Goodman, G. (1988). <u>The Talk Book.</u> Ballentine Books, New York, New York.

Hanh, T.N. (1998). <u>Mindful Living: A Collection of Teachings on Love, Mindfulness, a Meditation</u>. Audio Cassette. Sounds True Corp.

Heller, R.F., and Heller, R.F. 1993. <u>The Carbohydrate Addict's Diet</u>. A Signet Book, New York, New York.

Hoffer, A., & Walker, M., 1996. <u>Putting It All Together: The New Ortho-Molecular Nutrition</u>. Keats Publishing, New Canaan, Connecticut.

Joyce, M., 1995. <u>Five Minutes to Health</u>. Publishers: Five Minutes to Health, West Los Angeles, California.

Kabat-Zinn, J. (1994). <u>Wherever You Go, There You Are: Mindfulness Meditation In Everyday Life</u>. Hyperion Press.

Kirschmann, G., J., and Kirschmann, J.D., 1996. <u>Nutrition Almanac</u>. McGraw-Hill, NY, NY.

Kobasa, S.C., Maddi, S.R., Puccetti, M. and Zola, M. (1986). Relative effectiveness of Hardiness, exercise and social support as resources against illness. <u>Journal of Personality and Social Psychology,</u> 52, 525-533.

Kushner, H.S. (1981). <u>When Bad Things Happen to Good People.</u> Avon Books, New York, New York.

Maddi, S.R. (1990). Issues and interventions in stress mastery. In H.S. Friedman (Ed.), <u>Personality and Disease.</u> New York, New York.

Maddi, S.R. and Hess, M. (1992). Hardiness and Basketball Performance. <u>International Journal of Sports Psychology,</u> 1992, 21, 153-161.

Maddi, S.R. and Khoshaba, D.M. (1994) Hardiness and Mental Health. Journal of Personality Assessment, 63, 265-274

Maddi, S.R. and Khoshaba, D.M. (2005). Resiliency at Work. Amacom Press, New York, New York.

Maddi, S.R., Bartone, B.T. and Puccetti, M.C. (1987). Stressful events are indeed a factor in physical illness. Journal of Personality in Social Psychology, 52, 833-843.

McGraw, P.C. (1999). Life Strategies: Doing What Works, Doing What Matters. Hyperion Books. New York. New York.

McKay, M., Davis M. and Fanning, P. (1983). How to Communicate: The Ultimate Guide to Improving Your Personal and Professional Relationships. MJF Books, New York, New York.

Osho (2004). Pharmacy for the Soul: A Comprehensive Collection of Meditations, Relaxation and Awareness Exercises, and Other Practices for Physical and Emotional Well-Being. St. Martin's Griffin Press.

Richo, D. (1991). How To Be An Adult. Paulist Press, New York, New York.

Salpolsky, R.M. (1978). Why Zebras Don't Get Ulcers. McGraw-Hill Publications. N.Y.

Seaward, B. L. (1997). Stand Like Mountain Flow Like Water. Health Communications Publications.

Tannen, D. (1986). That's Not What I Meant. Ballentine Books, New York, New York

Viscott, D. (1977). Risking. Pocket Books, New York, New York.

Weeks, D. (1992). The Eight Essential Steps to Conflict Resolution. Tarcher/Putnam Books, New York.

QUESTIONNAIRE AND TEST YOUR KNOWLEDGE ANSWER KEYS

HardiCoping

Chapter 2, Test Your Knowledge Answer Key, HardiCoping

1. HardiCoping
2. Attitudes
3. Commitment
4. Challenge
5. Control
6. Perspective and Understanding
7. Action Plan
8. Taking Action
9. Acute
10. Chronic

Chapter 3 Test Your Knowledge Answer Key, Perspective and Understanding

1. Five
2. Commonplace
3. Manageability
4. Improvement
5. Time
6. Five
7. Personal Limitation
8. Clash of Wills
9. Misunderstanding
10. Victimization
11. External Forces
12. Situational Reconstruction
13. Focusing
14. Compensatory Self-Improvement
15. Given

16. Unpredictability

Chapter 4, Test Your Knowledge Answer Key, Planning Action

1. Planning Action
2. Goal Setting
3. Steps
4. Time Line
5. Control
6. Commitment
7. Challenge

Chapter 5, Test Your Knowledge Answer Key, Carrying Out the Plan

1. Direct Reaction
2. Observations of Self
3. Commitment
4. Control
5. Challenge

Social Support

Chapter 6, Test Your Knowledge Answer Key, Hardy Social Support

1. Hardy Social Support
2. Social Conflict
3. Assured
4. Activity Friendship
5. Mentor Friendship
6. Conflicted

Ineffective Conflict Management Questionnaire Exercise 2

1. Withdrawer
2. Withdrawer
3. Withdrawer
4. Trivializer
5. Trivializer

6. Mask Hider
7. Level Playing Field
8. Level Playing Field
9. Mask Hider
10. Level Playing Field
11. Level Playing Field
12. Mask Hider
13. Withdrawer
14. Emotional Bully
15. Emotional Bully
16. Emotional Bully
17. Withdrawer
18. Emotional Bully
19. Trivializer
20. Mask Hider
21. Trivializer
22. Trivializer
23. Withdrawer
24. Level Playing Field
25. Level Playing Field
26. Mask Hider
27. Emotional Bully
28. Mask Hider
29. Emotional Bully
30. Withdrawer

Chapter 7, Test Your Knowledge Answer Key, Stressful Social Interactions

1. High Emotional Arousal, Inadequate Skill Set, and Fear
2. Withdrawer, Bully, Leveler, Mask Hider, Trivializer
3. Bully and Mask Hider
4. Trivializer
5. In the Service of the Relationship
6. Situational Reconstruction and Focusing

7. Withdrawing

8. Leveling the Playing Field

Chapter 8, Test Your Knowledge Answer Key, Hardy Communication

1. To convey observations, thoughts, needs, and feelings, and to bring about intimacy in relationship

2. Intent

3. IRA

4. Thought

5. Learned Idea

6. Cut and Pasting

7. Psychic Interpretation

8. Pigeonholing

9. Emotional trigger warning signs

10. Right

Chapter 9, Test Your Knowledge Answer Key, Assistance and Encouragement

1. Empathy, Acceptance, and Admiration

2. Take up the slack

3. Being a sounding board

4. Giving Space

5. Overprotection and Pampering, and Subtle or Not-So-Subtle Competition

Relaxation

Chapter 10, Test Your Knowledge Answer Key, Hardy Relaxation

1. Relaxation

2. Acute, positive

3. Strain

4. Chronic

Chapter 11, Test Your Knowledge Answer Key, Physiology of Stress

1. Neuron

2. Action potential

3. Minerals

4. Neurotransmitter

5. Catecholamines

6. Central Nervous System

7. Reticular activating system

8. Limbic system

9. Frontal lobe/Neocortex

10. Somatic

11. Central Nervous System

12. Somatic

13. Autonomic

14. Sympathetic

15. Autonomic

16. Sympathetic and parasympathetic

17. Parasympathetic

18. Sympathetic

19. Parasympathetic

20. Sympathetic

21. Parasympathetic

22. Sympathetic

23. Parasympathetic

24. Parasympathetic

25. Parasympathetic

26. Excessive

27. Sympathetic

Chapter 12, Test Your Knowledge Answer Key, Body Awareness

1. Relaxation

2. Body

3. Baseline

4. Strain

5. Challenge

6. Control

7. Commitment

Chapter 13, Test Your Knowledge Answer Key, Science of Breathing

1. Inhalation

2. Exhalation

3. Trachea

4. Bronchi

5. Bronchioles

6. Alveoli

7. Energy

8. Carbon dioxide

9. Thoracically

10. Diaphragmatically

11. Diaphragmatically

12. Lower third

13. Diaphragmatically

14. Alkaline

15. Rate, Rhythm, Depth

16. Diaphragm

17. Alkaline

18. Alkaline

19. Oxygen

20. pH

21. 7.4

22. Sulphur and phosphorus

23. Calcium, potassium, and sodium

24. Parasympathetic

25. Lungs

26. Rate

27. Normal

28. Vigorous

29. Relaxed

30. Breathing

31. Control

32. Commitment

33. Challenge

Chapter 14, Test Your Knowledge Answer Key, Progressive Muscle Relaxation

1. Muscle tension
2. Tension, relaxation
3. Control
4. Commitment
5. Challenge

Chapter 15, Test Your Knowledge Answer Key, Meditation

1. Stress reduction
2. Mindfulness
3. Association
4. Nature of thinking
5. Mantra
6. Self-involved
7. Mindful meditation
8. Attaching
9. Perspective, understanding

Chapter 16, Test Your Knowledge Answer Key, Imagery

1. Imagery
2. Relaxation
3. Sensory
4. Alpha

Nutrition

Chapter 17, Test Your Knowledge Answer Key, Nutrition Basics

1. Imbalanced food nutrients
2. Chemical dependency
3. Processed
4. Life enhancement
5. Food nutrients

6. Amino acids
7. Protein
8. Protein
9. Dairy, meat, fish, nuts, legumes
10. Carbohydrate
11. Protein
12. Fat
13. Protein
14. Glucose
15. Glucose, fructose, galactose
16. Glucose
17. Complex
18. Glycemic index
19. Soluble, insoluble
20. Glycogen
21. Fat
22. Saturated
23. Hydrogen
24. Triglycerides

Chapter 18, Test Your Knowledge Answer Key, Blood Sugar and Metabolism

1. Glucose
2. Simple, complex
3. Brain
4. Glycogen
5. 70 to 150
6. 150 to 240
7. Hypoglycemic
8. Low blood sugar
9. High blood sugar
10. Simple
11. Complex
12. Metabolism

13. Pancreas, liver
14. Insulin
15. Glucagon
16. True
17. Glucagon
18. Hyperinsulinemia
19. Eicosanoid

Chapter 19, Test Your Knowledge Answer Key, Carbohydrates

1. Glycemic index
2. Carbohydrate
3. True
4. Complex
5. 40, 30, 30
6. Food nutrients

Chapter 20, Test Your Nutrition Knowledge Answer Key (From Appendix G), Put Your Learning Into Practice

1. b
2. a
3. a
4. b
5. b.
6. c.
7. c
8. a
9. c
10. d
11. b
12. d
13. c
14. c

15. c

16. b

17. a

18. b

19. b

20. c

21. c

22. d

23. a

24. c

25. b

26. a

27. b

28. b

29. c

30. b

31. c

32. c

33. b

34. c

35. b

36. c

37. b

38. b

39. b

40. c

41. a

42. a

43. a

44. b

45. e

46. d

47. d

48. c

49. b

50. d

51. b

52. c

53. c

54. d

55. d

Exercise

Chapter 22, Test Your Knowledge Answer Key, Improving Your Body Composition

1. Physically active

2. Hardy

3. Body composition, cardiorespiratory capacity, flexibility and muscular strength

4. Cardio-respiratory capacity

5. Progression, specificity, reversal

6. Frequency, intensity, duration

7. Ten commandments

8. Lean body mass, body fat

9. 100 pounds

10. 99 pounds

11. Fat distribution

12. Fat

13. 8%, 5%

Chapter 23, Test Your Knowledge Answer Key, Improving Cardiorespiratory Fitness

1. Aerobic conditioning

2. One-mile walk

3. Three-minute step

4. Heart rate reserve

5. Maximum heart rate reserve

Chapter 24, Test Your Knowledge Answer Key, Improving Flexibility

1. Stretching capacity

2. Nervous system activity

3. Proprioceptive neuromuscular facilitation

4. Ballistic stretching

5. Static stretching

Chapter 25, Test Your Knowledge Answer Key, Weight Training

1. Weight training

2. Force

3. Endurance

4. Isometric, isotonic, isokinetic

5. Isokinetic

6. Isometric

7. Isotonic

8. Resistance, repetition, and frequency

GLOSSARY

A

ACTIVITY FRIENDSHIP

In this social support function, people share mutually satisfying activities. 56

ACUTE STRESS

This is a change that disrupts our usual routine and requires that we make a physical, mental, and behavioral adjustment to it. 98

This refers to disruptive changes that people must adapt to daily. They are time-limited but can be minor or major in intensity. 4

AEROBIC CONDITIONING

Aerobic conditioning is the major basis in physical activity for improving cardiorespiratory fitness and weight reduction. 200

ALVEOLI

The air sacs of the lungs. 117

AMERICAN DIETETIC STANDARDS

The ADA recommends that 80% of your daily calories come from carbohydrates, and 15% of your daily calories come from protein and fat. 164

AMINO ACIDS

Various combinations of oxygen, hydrogen, carbon, and nitrogen produce these twenty different protein chemical structures. 144

ASSISTANCE

This hardiness concept emphasizes how human beings use their resources and capabilities to help others reach what they need or want. 9

ATROPHY

Losing muscle fibers through disuse. 204

B

BASELINE DATA COLLECTION

Whenever you want to increase or decrease some behavior or experience, it is wise to begin by measuring the behavior or experience before you try to change it. 112

BLOOD SUGAR

Sugar that comes from the sugar content of the foods you eat. 154

BODY COMPOSITION

The amount of lean versus fat muscle tissue, water, and bone in your body. 186

BODY FAT

Body fat is the percentage of fat in the body that is made up of essential and nonessential fatty acids. 191

BODY MASS INDEX

This index assumes weight to be proportional to height. 192

BRONCHI

These are the windpipe branches to that are attached to each lung. 117

BRONCHIOLES

These are thousands of tubes attached to each bronchi. 117

C

CARBOHYDRATES

This food nutrient is your body's primary energy source and comes from sugar and starch. 145

CARBON DIOXIDE

The gas byproduct of the metabolic interaction between oxygen and food nutrients. 117

CARDIORESPIRATORY CAPACITY

The ability of the heart, lungs and circulatory system to deliver fuel and oxygen to the tissues. 187

CHALLENGE

People strong in challenge believe that what makes their lives worthwhile is to continue to grow in knowledge and wisdom through what they learn from experience, whether positive or negative. 8

CHRONIC STRESS

This is when stressful problems have less to do with ongoing changes happening to you than the ongoing mismatch or conflict between you and your world. 98

CLASH OF WILLS

This form of understanding stems from strong disagreements between people that underly or add to the stressfulness of a situation. 19

COMMITMENT

This refers to the HardiAttitude that shows people value and involve themselves deeply in whatever they do. 8

COMMONPLACE PERSPECTIVE

This is the perspective that a stressful circumstance is the kind of thing that happens regularly in people's lives. 17

COMPLEX CARBOHYDRATE

This form of a carbohydrate comes from starch and generally is low in natural sugar and high in fiber. 145

CONSTANT RESISTANCE

An isotonic technique that uses a constant weight throughout a joint's entire range of motion. 204

CONTROL

People strong in control believe that if they struggle and try, they may well be able to influence the direction and outcome of things going on around them. 8

COUNTERFEIT REACTIONS

These are inauthentic ways that people can react to others problems. They subtly and not so subtly make themselves feel good by putting other people down when they need us most. 91

D

DIAPHRAGMATIC BREATHING

The lungs attach to this muscle and helps your lungs to inflate sufficiently for adequate inhalation. 118

DIRECT REACTIONS TO YOUR PLANNED ACTIONS

This form of feedback strengthens people's HardiAttitudes when others comment about the effects of their action plan. 44

E

EICOSANOID

This hormone functions as a messenger key that maintains the integrity of your cells. 158

EMOTIONAL SUPPORT FRIENDSHIP

This refers to emotional behaviors where people give or get friendship through understanding, empathy, or love. 55

ENCOURAGEMENT

This is when people assist others by empathizing with them and believing in their ability to cope in a hardy fashion. 9

ESSENTIAL FATTY ACIDS

These healing, unsaturated, Cis fatty acids are essential to your body's functioning and coat every nerve, fiber, and organ in your body. 147

EXTERNAL FORCES

This form of understanding views powerful outside forces as underlying or adding to the stressfulness of a situation. 19

F

FAT

This food nutrient is the second food nutrient to burn. It acts as a body cushion, insulator, and stabilizer of blood sugar. 146

FIBER

The food's shell made up of a molecular structure that resists digestive break-down. 146

FIBER, INSOLUBLE

This kind of fiber is the cellulose and lignin in food that does not easily combine with water and thus cannot be broken down easily. 146

FIBER, SOLUBLE

This water-soluble fiber comes from pectins, gums, and mucilage in fruits, vegetables, grains, legumes, and nuts. 146

FIGHT OR FLIGHT RESPONSE

This is the body's arousal response to danger posed by acute and chronic stresses. 5

FIVE USEFUL FORMS OF PERSPECTIVE

These are forms of perspective people use to adjust their perception of a stressful circumstance that helps them to begin to solve it. 17

FIVE USEFUL FORMS OF UNDERSTANDING

These commonly-shared understandings help people to appreciate the roots of the problem so that they can begin to solve it. 18

FLEXIBILITY

The ability of joints to move through their full range of motion. 187

FOCUSING

This HardiCoping technique helps people to uncover emotional information that keeps them from solving stressful problems. 27

FOOD NUTRIENTS

A food nutrient is a molecular energy unit that comes from the foods you eat and assists your body in maintenance, repair, and enzyme, neurotransmitter, hormone, and antibody production. 143

FREQUENCY

This refers to how often you perform an activity. 187

FUNCTIONS OF SOCIAL SUPPORT

These support functions help people to give and get various types of social support that strengthens their social support network. 55

G

GABA-AMINOBUTRYIC ACID

This neurotransmitter is an inhibitory nerve chemical that induces body relaxation. 103

GLUCAGON

This is the hormone that is the chemical key that opens the liver's cells so that it can release blood sugar into your blood stream 157

GLUCOSE

The chemical name for blood sugar. 145

GLUTAMATE

This hormone is a neuromodulator that stimulates brain activity involved in learning, recall, and problem-solving. 103

GLYCEMIC INDEX

This is a quantitative scale that tells you how fast a food gets broken down into glucose from the point of ingestion. 162

GLYCOGEN

The form of glucose that gets stored in your muscles. 145

H

HARDIATTITUDE OF CHALLENGE

This HardiAttitude is the belief that what ever happens to people in life is grist for the mill for new learning and development. 8

HARDIATTITUDE OF COMMITMENT

This is the hardiness attitude that people are important and worthwhile enough to involve themselves fully in whatever they do. 8

HARDIATTITUDE OF CONTROL

This is the HardiAttitude that no matter how hard people struggle and try, they can positively influence much of what happens to them in life. 8

HARDICOPING

This concept refers to the problem solving technique in which people fix stressful situations by thinking them through and by taking needed actions. 13

HARDY MESSENGER SKILLS

These skills help people to send and receive effective communications that adequately conveys message intent. 54

HARDY SOCIAL SUPPORT

This is when people assist and encourage others to actively solve their problems through HardiCoping. 53

HEALTH PRACTICES

This refers to preventive health behaviors that people do to decrease their body's strain reactions. 8

HEART RATE RESERVE

The heart rate at which you exercise to experience cardiorespiratory benefits is what we call your target heart rate. 201

HIGH DENSITY LIPO-PROTEIN

The good cholesterol helps to build a strong, durable, and flexible smooth vein and artery lining so that blood can rush through it without causing any structural damage. 148

HYPERINSULINEMIA, CELL'S SENSITIVITY TO INSULIN

This is when years of carbohydrate abuse dulls our cells capacity for knowing how insulin is needed to manage varying amounts of blood sugar. 157

HYPERTROPHY

The process of increasing the size of muscle fibers. 204

HYPOGLYCEMIA

Low brain sugar. 157

I

IMPROVEMENT PERSPECTIVE

This form of perspective views a stressful situations as changeable. 18

INHERITED PHYSICAL VULNERABILITIES

These are individual differences in response to prolonged strain that stems from our genetic inheritances. 6

INSULIN

It transforms blood sugar to fat, and opens the body's cells to allow transport and storage in the muscles for later use. 156

ISOKINETIC EXERCISE

This involves exerting force at a constant speed against an equal force exerted by a special strength-training machine. 204

ISOTONIC EXERCISE

This involves applying force with movement by using either weights or your own body weight (as in push-ups and sit-ups). 204
This involves applying force without move-

ment. 204

L

LEAN BODY MASS

This kind of body mass includes all nonfat tissues, such as bone, muscle, water, organs and connective tissues. 191

LIVER

This endocrine organ receives blood and its food nutrients from your veins and arteries, and takes these digested products and changes them into useful body enzymes and hormones (proteins from amino acids). 157

LOW DENSITY LIPO-PROTEIN

This kind of cholesterol binds easily to saturated fat. It builds up, thus, in your vein and artery system causing blockage and potential for heart attack and stroke. 148

M

MANAGEABILITY PERSPECTIVE

This form of perspective views stressful situations as neither good nor bad. 18

MATERIAL FRIENDSHIP

This social support function is the provision of goods or services to aid one's coping efforts. 55

MAXIMUM HEART RATE RESERVE

To get the benefits from cardiorespiratory activity, you exercise at a target heart rate that is 50 to 85% of your maximum heart rate reserve. 201

MEDITATION MINDFULNESS BENEFIT

This type of meditation activity advances one's ability to control which thoughts to respond to by observing how the mind works. 133

MEDITATION STRESS-REDUCTION BENEFIT

This type of meditation activity relaxes the body by focusing attention, which reduces the mind's activity. 132

MENTOR FRIENDSHIP

This social support function emphasizes friendship-based upon people's knowledge or expertise. 55

METABOLISM

This is the process by which food calories get burned for body energy. 200

MINERALS

Minerals come from the earth's elements and aid nerve firing. 149

MISUNDERSTANDING

This form of understanding stems from misunderstandings between people that underly or add to the stressfulness of a situation. 18

MORBID OBESITY

This is when you are more than 100 pounds overweight 192

MOTOR UNIT

A motor unit is made up of a nerve connected to a number of muscle fibers. 204

MUSCULAR ENDURANCE

This is the ability of a muscle to exert sub-maximum force continuously. 204

MUSCULAR STRENGTH

The amount of force a muscle can exert with a single maximum effort. 187

N

NEURON

The smallest unit of our nervous system is the nerve cell. Internal and external cellular fluids (potassium, sodium, chloride) bathe our cells. 104

NORMAL BREATH RATE

Your breathing rate is between 12 to 15 breaths per minute in normal activities. 120

NOURISHMENT DEFINITION

The act or process of nourishing or being nourished. 143

O

OBESITY

People who are less than 100 pounds overweight are obese. 192

OBSERVATIONS MADE OF YOU BY OTHERS

This form of feedback strengthens people's HardiAttitudes by having others observing them when taking steps to solve stressful situations. 44

OBSERVATIONS OF YOURSELF IN ACTION

This form of feedback strengthens people's HardiAttitudes because they see themselves acting constructively when carrying out their action plans. 44

P

PERIPHERAL NERVOUS SYSTEM, THE AUTONOMIC BRANCH

This branch regulates the balance of the body's internal environment, and controls respiration, heart rate, blood circulation, and some motor activities. 102

PERIPHERAL NERVOUS SYSTEM, THE SOMATIC BRANCH

This branch carries sensory and motor impulses to and from the central nervous system. 102

PERSONAL LIMITATION

This form of understanding involves a personal limitation that prevents one from solving a problem. 18

PHYSICAL FITNESS

Your body's ability to function well at work and at home. 186

PROTEIN

Protein is the building block of body tissues and bone structure and makes up body enzymes, hormones, antibodies, and neurotransmitters. 143

R

REASONS FOR SOCIAL STRESS

This refers to the five main reasons that underlie stressful social interactions. 56

RELAXATION RESPONSE, BY HERBERT BENSON

This is a mental and physical state of low arousal brought about by various relaxation techniques, involving breathing, muscle tone, meditation, hypnosis, and biofeedback training. 112

RELAXED BREATH RATE
Your breathing rate is 5 to 8 breaths per minute with relaxed activities. 120

REPETITION
A repetition is one lift. 205

RESISTANCE
The amount of weight lifted determines the manner and speed with which the body will adapt to the stress. 205

S

SATURATED FAT
This is a straight-bodied trans fatty acid that melts at 110 degrees farenheit. 147

SET
A set is a group of repetitions of an exercise followed by a short rest period. 205

SIMPLE CARBOHYDRATE
The simple sugars called glucose, fructose, and galactose are sugars that appear in fruit, vegetables, and manufactured carbohydrates. 145

SITUATIONAL RECONSTRUCTION
This HardiCoping technique helps people to find perspective and understanding when resolving stressful situations. 19

STRAIN
This is your mental, physical, and behavioral response to the stresses in your life. 98

STRESS RESISTANCE RESOURCES
These resources refer to HardiAttitudes and skills that help people to maintain their performance, leadership, morale, conduct, and health. 8

STRESS, A NEGATIVE EVENT
The death of someone close to you, taxes, or physical illness in you or others in your life. 98

STRESS, A POSITIVE EVENT
The birth of a new baby, a promotion at work, or graduating from school. 98

T

TARGET HEART RATE
This is the heart rate at which you exercise to get cardiorespiratory benefits. 201

THORACIC BREATHING
This type of breathing uses the rib cage and its muscles to expand your lungs during inhalation. 118

THREE SOURCES OF FEEDBACK
These sources of feedback arise from people carrying out their action plans and help in strengthening their HardiAttitudes. 44

TIME PERSPECTIVE
This form of perspective regards stressful situations as time-limited. 18

TRACHEA
Oxygen taken in through the nose or mouth descends through this windpipe. 117

U

UNPREDICTABILITY PERSPECTIVE
This form of perspective views the outcome of stressful situations as unpredictable. 18

UNSATURATED FAT
This Cis fatty acid has more double molecular bonds than saturated fats do, which makes it melt at 55 degrees farenheit. 147

V

VARIABLE RESISTANCE EXERCISE
An isotonic technique that changes the weight load to maintain maximum load throughout the range of motion. 204
In this isotonic exercise, you change the weight to maintain maximum load throughout the range of motion. 204

VICTIMIZATION
In this form of understanding, others falsely blame a person for the stressfulness of a situation. 19

VIGOROUS BREATH RATE
Your breathing rate is 15 to 18 breaths per

minute in vigorous activity. 120

W

WAIST-HIP RATIO

This is the best available index for determining disease risk associated with fat distribution. 192

WEIGHT TRAINING

Muscular strength and endurance is most directly increased through weight training. 203

WORK OR SCHOOL FRIENDSHIP

This is friendship that forms out of work- or school task. 56

Z

ZONE NUTRITION APPROACH

This approach concerns itself more with food nutrient percentages per meal than overall daily food nutrient percentages, as in the American Dietetic Standard. 164

Copyright© 1999-2008, The Hardiness Institute, Inc.

Made in the USA
Lexington, KY
13 October 2012